# Competitiveness and Knowledge



In the twenty-first century technology has become global, and firms compete using knowledge and capital. The 'traditional firm' has a need for innovation and depends on efficient knowledge management to improve productivity.

This book examines five firms that produce the same commodity, white chicken meat, in different parts of the world and under very different conditions. It brings to bear the expertise and international perspectives of the author team, utilizing theoretical discussions and case studies to address the question: How do local firms use knowledge to compete in an increasingly globalized world?

This book will be of interest to any postgraduate student, researcher or policymaker hoping to achieve a firmer grasp of innovation and knowledge management: a recurring and highly pertinent theme in contemporary economics.

**Knut Ingar Westeren** has been a Professor of Economics at Nord University in Norway since 2001. He received his Master in Economics from the University of Oslo and his PhD in regional science from the University of Minnesota/NTNU (Trondheim). He teaches knowledge management, knowledge and competitiveness and public economics at Nord University and he also teaches philosophy of science at EDAMBA (European Doctoral Programmes Association in Management and Business Administration). He is professor at UNIOESTE in Paraná, Brazil, and a visiting professor at the University of Wisconsin. He has numerous books and publications dealing with several aspects of the public sector, regional development and the knowledge economy.

**Hanas Cader** is Associate Professor of Economics at American University of Kuwait, where he has been a faculty member since 2008. He received his Master of Business Administration from University of Peradeniya, Sri Lanka, and Master and PhD in Agricultural Economics from Kansas State University. He teaches economics, economic development, knowledge economy and labor economics. He has published many journal articles and book chapters related to regional economic development, entrepreneurship, knowledge economy and e-learning.

**Maria de Fátima Sales** has been a Professor of Economics at the State University of Londrina (UEL), Brazil, since 1995, where she is working with the Graduate and Postgraduate Program in Regional Economics. She has her PhD in Economics from the Federal University of Pernambuco (UFPE), Recife, Brazil. She teaches international trade and international finance. Her primary fields of research are international economics, labor market analysis and regional economics, where she has numerous publications.

**Jan Ole Similä** has been an Associate Professor of Organization Theory at Nord University in Norway since 2009. He received both his Master in Public Administration and PhD in Organization Theory and Management from Copenhagen Business School. He teaches contract economics, contracts management and procurement management at Nord University. He is also a visiting scholar at Kristiania University College in Oslo, Norway. He has several publications dealing with contract management, contract economics, procurement management, and knowledge management.

**Jefferson Staduto** received his PhD in Economics from the University of São Paulo (USP), Brazil. Since 1995 he has been Professor in Economics at State University of the West of Paraná (UNIOESTE), Brazil, where he is working with the Postgraduate Program in Economics and Regional Development and Agribusiness. He is also visiting researcher at the University of Rhein Waal, Germany. He teaches macroeconomics, labor economics and rural development. He has several publications dealing with labor market, regional and rural economics, and gender and development.

## Routledge Advances in Regional Economics, Science and Policy

19 **Applied Spatial Modelling and Planning**
*Edited by John R. Lombard, Eliahu Stern and Graham Clarke*

20 **Smart Development in Smart Communities**
*Edited by Gilberto Antonelli and Giuseppe Cappiello*

21 **Post-Metropolitan Territories and Urban Space**
*Edited by Alessandro Balducci, Valeria Fedeli and Francesco Curci*

22 **Big Data for Regional Science**
*Edited by Laurie A. Schintler and Zhenhua Chen*

23 **The Spatial and Economic Transformation of Mountain Regions**
Landscapes as Commodities
*Manfred Perlik*

24 **Neoliberalism and Urban Development in Latin America**
The Case of Santiago
*Edited by Camillo Boano and Francisco Vergara-Perucich*

25 **Rural Housing and Economic Development**
*Edited by Don E. Albrecht, Scott Loveridge, Stephan Goetz and Rachel Welborn*

26 **Creative Ageing Cities**
Place Design with Older People in Asian Cities
*Edited Keng Hua Chong and Mihye Cho*

27 **Competitiveness and Knowledge**
An International Comparison of Traditional Firms
*Knut Ingar Westeren, Hanas Cader, Maria de Fátima Sales, Jan Ole Similä and Jefferson Staduto*

For a full list of titles in this series, please visit www.routledge.com/series/RAIRESP

# Competitiveness and Knowledge

## An International Comparison of Traditional Firms

**Knut Ingar Westeren, Hanas Cader, Maria de Fátima Sales, Jan Ole Similä and Jefferson Staduto**

Routledge
Taylor & Francis Group
LONDON AND NEW YORK

First published 2018 by Routledge

2 Park Square, Milton Park, Abingdon, Oxfordshire OX14 4RN
52 Vanderbilt Avenue, New York, NY 10017

*Routledge is an imprint of the Taylor & Francis Group, an informa business*

First issued in paperback 2020



*British Library Cataloguing-in-Publication Data*
A catalogue record for this book is available from the British Library

*Library of Congress Cataloging-in-Publication Data*
A catalog record for this book has been requested

ISBN: 978-1-138-65046-6 (hbk)
ISBN: 978-0-367-66704-7 (pbk)

Typeset in Bembo
by Apex CoVantage, LLC

# Contents

# Figures

# Tables

# Preface

This book project started as a scientific discussion among colleagues in 2012. For some years I had been Professor (Ajunta) at UNIOESTE, campus Toledo and my colleague there, Professor Jefferson Staduto, had been working with representatives from the firm LAR (Cooperativa Agroindustrial, Unidade Industrial de Aves e Carnes, Matelândia (PR), Brazil) and discussing with them "What is competitiveness?" This also gave rise to the question: how can LAR meet the challenges of the knowledge economy?

My colleague in Norway, Associate Professor Jan Ole Similä, had been working with vertical integration for some years and when looking at LAR, he understood that the firm is managing the vertical chain in a cost-effective way. My colleague living partly in Kuwait and partly in Sri Lanka, Hanas Cader, had been studying production economics of firms for some time and had been wondering about the sentence "firms start competing based on the prevailing cost structure," what does this really mean and related to this, which role does the wage rate play in an international perspective? After a short time, the five firms, LAR in Brazil, Danpo in Denmark, Ytterøykylling in Norway, Crysbro in Sri Lanka, and KUPCO in Kuwait had agreed to join the project. We understood quickly that this project must have a perspective from international economics because white meat is an important international commodity and Maria de Fátima Sales joined the project to take care of this.

We have been writing together and working together since 2012 and we have been discussing and learning from the firms. The ambition has at all times been to write an integrated book with one coherent story. Of course, this story has several aspects and the responsibilities have been the following:

Knut Ingar Westeren: Chapter 1: Introduction
Hanas Cader: Chapter 2: Cost structure and competitive situation
Jan Ole Similä: Chapter 3: Vertical integration and management of inputs to production
Knut Ingar Westeren and Jefferson Staduto: Chapter 4: Knowledge and competitiveness
Knut Ingar Westeren: Chapter 5: Innovations, knowledge and competitiveness

Maria de Fátima Sales: Chapter 6: Competitiveness in the global chicken market
All authors: Chapter 7: Summary, conclusions, and policy implications

Knut Ingar Westeren has coordinated the project work and the writing of the book.

*Knut Ingar Westeren, Nord University, Steinkjer, Norway*
*Hanas Cader, American University of Kuwait, Safat, Kuwait*
*Maria de Fátima Sales, Universidade Estadual de Londrina, Londrina, Paraná, Brazil*
*Jan Ole Similä, Nord University, Steinkjer, Norway*
*Jefferson Staduto, UNIOESTE, Toledo, Paraná, Brazil*
*September 2017*

# Acknowledgements

We started this project in 2012 and during the period 2012 to 2014, we were granted substantial financial support from Nord-Trøndelag University College (HiNT). Without this understanding and support we would not have been able to conduct the project. This project was more unconventional, riskier, and more costly than the 'normal' research projects at HiNT and the key persons to support this were former Dean Joar Nyborg and former Head of Section Jørgen Grinde at HiNT (in 2017 HiNT merged with and is now part of Nord University). The administrative support from Inger Elsa Kaldahl Einvik is also greatly appreciated.

We also received great encouragement from Steinar Nebb, Rector at HiNT from 2011–2015, who, sadly, died from cancer in early 2016. In 2013 Steinar travelled with us to Brazil to visit LAR so he could see how we did the data collection. He was outstanding in his interest and care for his faculty members.

Our colleague and friend, professor Hans Siggaard Jensen (University of Aarhus/Copenhagen Campus), has followed the project for many years and has given us advice and encouragement all through the process. This project has lasted for some years and we all time have been followed up very nicely with advice from Routledge. For a long time we were assisted by Elanor Best, and in the last months by Anna Cuthbert, your patience and good advice have been highly appreciated.

We are a team of five that have written the manuscript for the book and we are all non-native English speaking persons. Margaret Otto has done a tremendous job of transforming our manuscripts into readable English. Any residual ambiguities are the responsibility of the authors.

We have been cooperating closely with the firms and they have shown an openness that has been admirable. Their friendliness, cooperation and generosity with their time were far more than we could dream about. To the LAR firm, our gratitude goes to Clédio Roberto Marschall and Lérida Fantin de Vargas. We have seen Lérida several times every year since 2012, and view ourselves as a part of the LAR family now.

At Danpo we have been received by Anja Winther Sørensen and she has organized everything for us.

At Ytterøykylling, Kjetil Stavran gave us entry into the firm and later Lasse Kjønstad has organized our visits, we are grateful to them and their colleagues for all assistance.

We are very grateful to Mr. M. Imtiaz, CEO at Crysbro, for his friendly and open discussions and giving us access to all detailed information about the company. He was available for us at every visit to Crysbro.

We had access to all data we wanted from KUPCO. Our sincere appreciation goes to the top management team and their colleagues for their generous support and warm reception we had during our visits.

As project leader, my sincere appreciation goes to the team members, whose ardent dedication has allowed us to tell a coherent story about how firms, in theory and practice, develop competitiveness to enter the knowledge economy.

*Knut Ingar Westeren*

# 1 Introduction

## 1.1 The point of departure

Our understanding is that in the twenty-first century the technology has become global but firms compete with knowledge, their customized technology/capital solutions and innovative initiatives based on prevailing wage structure. With this in mind we want to provide a discussion about new trends and results in the analysis of competitiveness based on the following main questions:

- How do we assess knowledge in individual firms?
- How do we account for knowledge through all stages of the production process?
- How do firms combine knowledge, capital and market information in the managerial process to be innovative?
- How do local firms compete using knowledge in domestic/international markets in an increasingly globalized world?

This book differs from others in its focus on answers for the above questions that combine theoretical discussions with case studies.

The concept of competitiveness has been fundamental since economics became a scientific field; many studies still cite Ricardo (1821) when they start an analysis about competition and trade. The new resurgence of the discussion about competition in the twentieth century came with Porter and his diamond model. Delgado, *et al.* (2012) have now developed the concept further to embrace foundational competitiveness. There have been many warnings about letting competitiveness be the most focused and dominant of all concepts in economics. One of the most important warnings comes from Krugman (1994) in his article 'Competitiveness: a dangerous obsession'.

When we look at the discussion about competitiveness from 1980 up to now two aspects are still fundamental. Competitiveness is a prerequisite for relatively high wages and thereby a high standard of living in a country – this recognition was the leading line of thought for the discussion of competitiveness in the EU starting with the Lisbon agenda. Competitiveness is also what every firm must have in mind to survive. The discussion about competitiveness started with the firm as the organizational unit. In later years this has been broadened to include the majority of organizations in the nation – we now talk about the competitiveness of nursing homes and schools and other institutions. The transformation to more market-oriented societies has been one of the megatrends since the last part of the last part of the twentieth century (see Pedersen, 2011).

## 1.2 A short description of the empirical work of the project

In this book we will shed light on some of the new trends in competition analysis. We will use five firms as examples to illustrate the theoretical analysis. We have studied these five firms in-depth for the period 2012–2016 to analyze their competitive situation. Main characteristics of the firms are shown in Table 1.1.

The main idea that led us to write this book was to compile a selection of case studies of traditional industrial firms producing in the same product category – white meat from chicken. We chose very different firms in different parts of the world facing different production conditions.

*Table 1.1* The firms in the study, data for 2015

| *Firm* | *Danpo (Denmark)* | *LAR (Brazil )* | *KUPCO (Kuwait)* | *Crysbro (Sri Lanka)* | *Ytterøy (Norway)* |
|---|---|---|---|---|---|
| Percentage of total production in the country | 38.7% | 1.8% | 33.0% | 10.1% | 5.1% |
| Daily production of chickens | 184,000 | 340,000 | 50,000 | 25,000 | 17,200 |
| Export share | 50% | 40% | 0–5% | Mostly a producer for the local market. | Mostly a producer for the national market. |
| Domestic competitors on the export market | 1 | 30 | (Two big companies in the country, KUPCO and Naif.) | (Mostly a producer for the local market. 4 big producers in Sri Lanka, including Crysbro.) | (Three bigger companies. Only marginal export) |
| Number of employees | 550 | 4451 | 180 | 120 | 96 |

Source: authors' data collection.

At the start we specifically focused on the study of traditional firms. This means that we wanted to look at firms where:

1 Production was based on reasonably stable routines.
2 Labor cost played an important role.
3 The production technology was available on the world market but the adaptation of the technology in production was unique to the firm.
4 All firms had a need for innovations to improve productivity.
5 All firms were dependent on efficient knowledge management to improve productivity.
6 All firms had to efficiently manage the procurements of inputs.
7 All firms faced market competition in one way or another.

At the start of the project we assumed that we could establish a concept like a 'traditional firm' when the firm, to a reasonable degree, fulfilled the conditions mentioned above. After having done the study we think this is still possible but we also see more clearly the importance of the uniqueness of firms. When we look at the discussions about how to delineate the 'high-tech' firm from 'traditional firms' we find the main differences in the factors 1, 2 and 3 in the list above. Our understanding of the traditional firm is in line with what the *The Oxford handbook of innovations* calls 'Low and Medium Tech Firms' (see von Tunzelmann and Acha 2005).

We started out with a belief that the resource-based theory of the firm would be the most relevant and applicable fundament. After finishing the project, we are reinforced in the belief that this is correct – and the argument that the uniqueness of firms which is central in this book – is an important building block in the resource-based firm theory.

To make the analysis as comparable as possible we chose firms producing the same product category: white meat from chicken. But we soon found that the diversification hypothesis in the theory of competition also was fulfilled for these firms. All firms had what we can call a brand strategy. The Norwegian firm was a typical niche producer where the marketing was focused on the origin of the product – the meat was produced under very secure hygienic conditions, and the firm tried to link several other positive characteristics to the location of production. On the other end we had the Brazilian producer, a more bulk-oriented, high-volume producer but where brand also played a role. For all firms the halal rules for slaughtering played an important part.

We built our empirical analysis on an in-depth study of five firms during five years. During this time, we have done data collection the following way.

1 We have been to all firms a minimum of four times (some firms five and six times) and then we collected data using a formal questionnaire. The production of white meat was organized in departments and each department had a department leader, whom we called the supervisor or the group leader. The biggest firm in the study, LAR in Brazil, had about twenty supervisors while the smallest, Ytterøy in Norway, had ten.

This questionnaire filled in by the supervisors had about forty questions with the following headlines: formalities; production capacity; communication and competence; technology; production stops; changes in routines; quality control; cultural background (cultural background we have identified by using Hofstede's indicator set, Hofstede, *et al.* (1991). This questionnaire has been translated to Portuguese (for Brazil), Scandinavian languages for Norway and Denmark, Arabic (for Kuwait) and English for use in Sri Lanka and by English speaking persons in the firms.

2 We have interviewed the CEO or CEO Deputy about innovation in the firm. Here we used the same semi-structured interview guide in all firms.
3 We also interviewed the CEO or market manager about markets and export strategies using a semi-structured interview guide in all firms.

From this we have information that sheds light on the competitive situation for firms during a five-year period.

## 1.3 Linking theory and empirical studies together in a search to find trends – changes in old, the emergence of new – in competitiveness

We know very well we cannot statistically generalize from a sample of five firms. But this study provides insight that challenges other theoretical and empirical studies about competition. As an introduction, we analyze trends of competitiveness in the light of the more general megatrends of the twenty-first century. The first megatrend is the development in the direction of the knowledge-based economy and the information society. Here we find clear links to changes in trends in competitiveness which we will discuss in Chapter 4. A second megatrend is globalization and this will enter into the discussion in several of the chapters, especially Chapter 6. A third megatrend we believe will get more attention and increase in importance is culture as a driver of processes in the society – like production. We find results indicating that culture already plays a role and this is important for the analysis of competitiveness, see Chapter 4.

The book will be divided into the following chapters:

| | |
|---|---|
| Chapter 2 | Cost structure and competitive situation |
| Chapter 3 | Vertical integration and management of inputs to production |
| Chapter 4 | Knowledge and competitiveness |
| Chapter 5 | Innovations, knowledge and competitiveness |
| Chapter 6 | Competitiveness in the global chicken market |
| Chapter 7 | Summary, conclusions, and policy implications |

Chapter 2 on cost structure and competitive situation shows that discussions about labor productivity and how this is related to the other cost components is a necessary chapter as a start of a book about competitiveness in the twenty-first century. One important message from the book is how labor cost can be related to other central variables and then this determines the competitiveness of the firm. Briefly, this can be illustrated with the following story from a Norwegian firm (Aker/Kvaerner) producing steel equipment for off-shore petroleum production. This firm's main competing firm is situated in Spain (Dragados) and the Spanish firm has a labor cost level 50% lower than the Norwegian firm. When the Norwegian firm won an international contract of about 267 million USD the CEO said (translated from Norwegian, see www.upstreamonline.com/live/1108074/aker 2014): 'This is easy to explain – we buy cheap, we have efficient knowledge utilization and management, we look for improvements (innovations) every day and we use cost-efficient front edge technology, and the market believes in us.'

In our interviews with the CEOs of the meat producing firms they express views in very similar ways, although meat production differs greatly compared to steel equipment production. The white meat-producing CEO's say that the labor cost is the starting point (Chapter 2), then they have to manage the inputs in an efficient way (Chapter 3). All firms say they focus on taking advantage of entering the knowledge economy, developing competitiveness based on knowledge creation and dissemination (Chapter 4). The more general arguments about technology/innovations (Chapter 5) and market/internationalization (Chapter 6) are also astonishingly parallel whether we look at huge steel structures or white meat production.

## 1.4 The knowledge economy

In this chapter we will not take up all discussions about all aspects concerning the knowledge economy but concentrate on what is most relevant for the focus of the book. Our main concern in this chapter is to shed light on the question of how 'the knowledge economy' can be an understandable concept at the same time for the business manager and the economic scientist. We have a large literature that gives both conceptual and operational discussions of the knowledge economy in the direction of competitiveness, some more recent examples are Rodrigues (2002), Nijkamp and Siedschlag (2011), Westeren (2012), Karlsson, *et al.* (2013) and Park (2015). These books extend the knowledge economy discussions in the direction of innovations, entrepreneurship and regional/national/international perspectives. These books also present an understanding regarding what to put into the concepts of the knowledge economy.

### *1.4.1 The big picture from the influential organizations*

In this book, we have firms from different parts of the world and all emphasized that they had to change into more knowledge-based production to improve competitiveness. But how can we talk about a knowledge economy from both a societal and a firm perspective? Production has in one way or the other always been based on knowledge, from the construction of the pyramids to the iPhone. After the Second World War, many other economists linked knowledge to the analysis of production, but it was first in the late 1980s that the concept of the knowledge economy was developed. In 1998 Joseph Stiglitz, chief economist of the World Bank, said: 'Today the World Bank has shifted much of its emphasis to the intangibles of knowledge, institutions, and culture in an attempt to forge a more comprehensive New Development Framework for our work.' (Stiglitz, 1999: 2)

In March 2000 the European Union had their meetings in Lisbon and the Presidency Conclusion from this meeting was the following:

> The Union has today set itself **a new strategic goal** for the next decade: to become the most competitive and dynamic knowledge-based economy in the world capable of sustainable economic growth with more and better jobs and greater social cohesion.
>
> European Council (2000: 2)

This emphasis of change for the EU into knowledge-based production had (at least) three main justifications.

1 The most important was the combination of economic growth and that the countries in EU should be able to have a relatively high and growing wage level and thereby increase wealth for the inhabitants.
2 Knowledge also contributes to a higher level of satisfaction and prosperity for the individual person and society more in general.
3 Knowledge was also looked at as an advantageous factor for EU countries meeting the globalization trends we had seen reinforced during the latter part of the 1990s.

There have been many studies and evaluations about how successful the Lisbon strategy for the European Union has been and a more general conclusion is that it only partly matched the goals that were originally formulated (see e.g. Lundvall and Lorenz, 2012 and Borrás and Radaelli, 2011).

In 2010 European Commission launched the Europe 2020 strategy:

> The development of the European Union by 2020 should be significantly influenced by the strategy Europe 2020. Europe 2020 puts forward three mutually reinforcing priorities:
>
> - Smart growth: developing an economy based on knowledge and innovations.
> - Sustainable growth: promoting a more resource efficient, greener and more competitive economy.
> - Inclusive growth: fostering a high-employment economy delivering social and territorial cohesion.
>
> European Commission (2010: 3)

We can take the statements from The World Bank as an indicator about what is happening in developing economies and the EU policies representing developed economies and we see that the main international organizations have a 'knowledge strategy'. So, no doubt there are strong signals and billions of euros and dollars used to strengthen the knowledge economy as a competitive base for firms in nearly every country. But how this is reflected varies widely in national strategies and in the way international, national and regional policy-making influences the functioning of the economy. This provides a framework for knowledge competitiveness and serves as a primary focus throughout this book.

### *1.4.2 Understanding of the knowledge economy*

There have been many discussions and suggestions about how to formulate and give content to the concept of the knowledge economy but there have also been many warnings from famous economists like Lundvall:

> There is little agreement on questions such as: What is the meaning of knowledge and knowledge production? What separations and distinctions between different kinds of knowledge are most useful for understanding the interaction between learning, knowledge and economic development?
>
> Lundvall (2003: 2)

Often we look at knowledge as a part of the knowledge economy from three points of view:

1. Knowledge as a commodity that can be sold within the framework of a market economy and how it can appear as a public good.
2. How knowledge is created and exchanged within the producing institution, between producing institutions and other institutions of the society. Some authors use the formulation of 'producing institution' instead of the word 'firm' or 'company'. This is looked upon as a good idea because then we can include e.g. hospitals, schools, recreational parks and other institutions that we normally do not speak about as firms.
3. We look at knowledge and how it develops in relation to information and communication technologies (ICT) and the significance it has for speed, focus and content in the knowledge exchange.

When we look at the literature we can find a large number of definitions of the knowledge economy concept, Foray (2004) and Carlaw, *et al.* (2006) are often cited sources. Many articles and books start with the following definition of the knowledge economy from the OECD: 'Economies which are directly based on production, distribution and use of knowledge and information', OECD (1996: 7).

This definition is widely used yet highly criticized. The criticism is that this definition is not operational. In the definition, it is claimed that production must be directly based on knowledge. This raises the question of how production is delineated based on direct or indirect knowledge. The other two keywords in the definition are about distribution and use of knowledge and here one can say that almost all production has been based on distribution and use of knowledge to some extent. The most interesting aspect of this definition by OECD is that it focuses on the importance of knowledge.

Here we will give only a few examples of definitions of the knowledge economy of which many include the following:

- Knowledge as an attribute of labor as a factor of production.
- Knowledge as a prerequisite for effective use of capital and ICT.
- Knowledge as a creator of innovativeness.

Capello, *et al.* (2014) have the following definition of The knowledge economy:

> Basic idea: *knowledge-based economy does not have a unique interpretative paradigm.*
>
> Different approaches are necessary:
>
> ***A1. Sectorial approach*** (presence in the region of science-based, high-technology sectors).
>
> ***A2. Functional approach*** (presence in the region of functions like R&D, ICT, patents, human capital).
>
> ***A3. Relation-based approach*** (presence in the region of interactive and collective learning processes).
>
> Capello, *et al.* (2014: 5)

The first approach Capello talks about is that knowledge must be present in the region of science-based and high-technology sectors. This is of course correct but this point also raises the question about high-tech and low-tech production. If for example, we look at the food processing sector this is normally considered to be medium- or low-tech production. But in the later years we have seen developments in production processes in this sector that use high-tech capital equipment. On the other hand, we also can look at some sectors that are classified as high-tech – for example production of electronic equipment. Some parts of the production here are routinized and do not demand advanced capital equipment or high-skilled human knowledge. So, when Capello emphasizes the sector approach we must be aware of the fact that firms in sectors classified as low-tech may have very different levels of technology and use of knowledge. A more thorough discussion of this can be found in the *Oxford Handbook of Innovation*, Fagerberg, *et al.* (2005).

The second criteria from Capello is that knowledge must have a functional approach and she mentions functions like research and development (R&D),

ICT, patents and human capital development. We found one of the meat producing firms had an advanced quality control meat analysis unit with front-end technology and doctoral-level employees.

In the third approach Capello talks about interactive and collective learning processes. In the project analyzed in this book as well as many others, learning is a key factor but also the process of disseminating knowledge in the firm and out to other firms and institutions is important. In summary, we see that the definitions of the knowledge economy have developed considerably from the OECD definition from 1996 to the recent definition by Capello. The understanding in this book clearly supports Capello's view that the knowledge-based economy does not have a unique interpretative paradigm. We find her paradigms relevant and fruitful and from the results presented in this book will also argue that a fourth culture-based approach can be appropriate, a discussion that will be taken up in Chapter 4. Some discussions have also occurred regarding if it is necessary to use different definitions and understanding for 'the knowledge economy' and 'knowledge-based production' (see Cooke and Leydesdorff 2006). We will not take up this discussion here; our main objective is to present an understanding that has both a conceptual value and can be understood in an operational sense and to do this we use the formulation of the knowledge economy.

### *1.4.3 Indicators for the knowledge economy*

The definitions we previously cited can be looked at as difficult to use in actual analysis. Contributions to the research literature with reasonable criteria that can be used in practice can be found in in Raspe and Van Oort (2008). They use eight indicators to analyze the emergence of the knowledge economy for regions (municipalities) in the Netherlands.

1 Knowledge level
The population (the working force) is divided into groups by level of education.
2 Share of employees in 'creative sectors'
Sectors seen as creative are (e.g.) design, business services, etc.
3 ICT density
This is measured by looking at sectors that have a relatively high occurrence of PCs and terminals per employee in the industry.
4 Communicative skills
Several occupations where communicative knowledge is particularly important are examined.
5 Research and development (R&D)
Here they look at sectors that have high R&D costs relative to employment and production.
6 Proportion of companies with high and medium technological level
Companies are ranked according to production methods.

7 Technical innovation
High technical innovation is defined as the frequent occurrence of new products and/or processes as defined in the EU innovation survey.
8 Non-technical innovation development
Sectors where there are large organization and/or management changes are observed.

These eight factors can be described statistically, but of course, not all the definitions and estimations compare equally well. Raspe and Van Oort (2008) say that we have a knowledge economy in a region when the region has high values of the indicators that are set up. To make this more manageable the eight factors are compressed into three.

*Main factor A: Many knowledge workers*
This means we have high values on: knowledge level, employees in 'creative sectors', ICT density and communicative skills.
*Main factor B: Large innovation activity*
That means we have high values on: technical innovation and non-technical innovation.
*Main factor C: Large occurrence of research and development*
That means we have high values on: research and development and companies with high technological level.

Controlling for the firm's age, size and industry, Raspe and Van Oort find indications that firms experience higher growth rates when located in a region with:

- A higher intensity of successful innovative firms
- With a high intensity of research and development activities

Splitting the analysis into separate models for manufacturing and business services gives the insight that whereas employing knowledge workers has no significant impact on firm growth in general, for business services it does foster growth.

As the factor 'knowledge workers' is spatially related to cities and agglomerations rather than rural and peripheral regions, this strengthens the hypothesis that the growth of business service firms is enhanced by urban knowledge contexts. It also may be the case that regions with strong clusters grow faster than regions that generally score high on the criteria of the knowledge economy. In the analysis of our firms producing white meat we see the same tendencies (see Chapter 4) that the knowledge workers are the most important for competitiveness based on knowledge, but this factor is the most difficult to isolate in statistical analysis. Many of the discussions about the knowledge economy and the consequences for the individual countries and firms look at the Knowledge Economy Index (KEI) from the World Bank (2012) and material from the World Economic Forum (2016). This, we discuss as an introduction to business climate when we address knowledge transfer and competitiveness in Chapter 4.

### 1.4.4 *Knowledge – the product or embedded in the product and the explicit/tacit split*

It was the emergence of the resource-based theory of the firm that started the discussion of the knowledge base of products (Penrose 1959, Teece 1980 and Nelson and Winter 1982, a summary of this discussion can be found in Ozman 2010).

When we look at the output of product it is interesting to see if knowledge can be looked at as a separate product or embedded in the product. One end of the scale is the research institute that produces a report for development of a new production process for a product. Here we can say that the knowledge factor is the fundamental part of the production process of the institute. Then the firm also asks the institute to instruct them how to integrate a new technology in the production process together with the firm that produces the hardware for the new technology. The firm normally asks for a description of new routines and the new technology standards, this requires explicit instructions. This also often includes new programming software that also is explicit information.

But when the firm initially begins using this new technology, people from the research institute and the hardware producing firm are there to explain how the firm can use the technology and give advice. When processes like this take place, the knowledge transferred also has a tacit knowledge component.

The transfer of tacit knowledge is also very important for the success the firm has using the new technology and developing competitiveness. There are many studies that separate the functions of explicit and tacit knowledge intending to show how this contributes to improved competitiveness (see e.g. Anand, Ward and Tatikonda 2010). The early belief was that tacit knowledge was most important for high-tech firms, the empirical part of this book shows that this is equally true for medium- and low-tech firms. We will return to some aspects about tacit knowledge when we deal with innovation. The fundamental theory about tacit knowledge came with Polanyi (1962/2012). The more general introduction of this theme in the business world was done by Nonaka and Takeuchi (1995) in their book about *The knowledge-creating company*. This book has been one of the most influential and cited books in the field (about 35,000 citations) and has been followed up in numerous articles like Lam (2000), Smith (2001) and Nonaka and Von Krogh (2009).

Knowledge can be presented in many ways to firms, but to utilize the knowledge for improving competitiveness the firm needs what has been called absorptive capacity (ACAP). The introduction of this concept came with Cohen and Levinthal (1990) and it has been discussed and developed further by Zahra and George (2002). They write 'We propose a reconceptualization of ACAP as a dynamic capability to pertaining knowledge creation and utilization that enhances a firm's capability to gain and sustain a competitive advantage' (Zahra and George 2002: 185).

The knowledge transfer process has always a sender-receiver situation. For a firm, it is important to offer knowledge at the appropriate level and delivered in such a way that it matches the ACAP of the receiver.

In the empirical part of this project we give an example about how a meat producing firm buys new technology, such as digital quality control of meat, and makes it operational in the firm. In this case the firm had two possibilities when it came to the software, one was to pay a relatively high price and know all source codes of the computer programs. Then the firm would be able to manage and test out all operations themselves. The other option was to pay a lower price but then the firm was not given access to the source codes and had to contract and pay the supplying firm for tests, updates and maintenance. Here we see a link between the cost and absorption capacity argument. It is an advantage for the firm to have full control over the knowledge situation running all ICT equipment, but if this requires a very high technology level with high cost for the ICT solution the firms must decide where to invest money to build the core competencies of the firm.

Generally, it is normal that companies which sell capital equipment with a specific knowledge component often use a two-price system. One price is specifically for the knowledge component which is the part of the product that no one can imitate and one price for the actual capital equipment that can be developed and/or bought on the world market with no big problems.

### *1.4.5 Knowledge – a private or a public good*

Knowledge is a phenomenon that is directly linked to the human mind. Knowledge is also linked to human behavior and the feeling of well-being for individuals more in general. When we analyze knowledge as a public good we normally do that in relation to two criteria, non-rivalry and non-exclusiveness. What most textbooks say is that when knowledge is discovered and made public, there are no or low marginal costs to adding more users and it is costly to exclude additional users. A commonly used example here is that in earlier times along the coasts of most countries there were lighthouses that sent out signals boats could use to navigate.

Now we are in the digital era and it is possible for correctly equipped boats to receive signals. The technology has developed in a way such that unique identification is possible. Signals are sent but only the people that pay for fees and equipment can make use of the signals. The conclusion is that when knowledge fulfils the two criteria of being a public good then the public sector must cover costs for knowledge production. Under these circumstances, the market will not produce this knowledge. This also has the effect of public sector prioritization; policy signals for public goods are initiated to efficiently provide the type of knowledge beneficial to society. We have seen a trend towards very low costs for the dissemination of knowledge. For example, the internet has reduced information costs from open sources.

There have been many discussions about under which circumstances private persons, firms, organizations and the public sector shall be able to protect knowledge. We will not go into the discussions about the need to keep knowledge protected but just refer to the tendency for more open knowledge transfers. One indicator for this is the move towards 'open innovations' which attempts to keep all channels open – before and after the innovations take place. We also see a tendency towards more open knowledge exchange even when firms develop new production processes based on unique knowledge (see Haeussler 2006). The conclusion is that since knowledge is anthropocentric and part of societal life it must be treated with more care and require diversified types of analysis as compared to a normal physical good.

## References


Anand, G., Ward, P. T., & Tatikonda, M. V. (2010). Role of explicit and tacit knowledge in six sigma projects: An empirical examination of differential project success. *Journal of Operations Management, 28*(4), 303–315.

Borrás, S., & Radaelli, C. M. (2011). The politics of governance architectures: Creation, change and effects of the EU Lisbon strategy. *Journal of European Public Policy, 18*(4), 463–484.

Capello, R., Camagni, R., Lenzi, C., & Caragliu, A. (2014). *Knowledge, innovation and territory.* Presentation at: 'ESPON and your Needs', 21 May 2014, Roma.

Carlaw, K., Oxley, L., Walker, P., Thorns, D., & Nuth, M. (2006). Beyond the hype: Intellectual property and the knowledge society/knowledge economy. *Journal of Economic Surveys, 20*(4), 633–690.

Cohen, W. M., & Levinthal, D. A. (1990). Absorptive capacity: A new perspective on learning and innovation. *Administrative Science Quarterly*, 128–152.

Cooke, P., & Leydesdorff, L. (2006). Regional development in the knowledge-based economy: The construction of advantage. *The Journal of Technology Transfer, 31*(1), 5–15.

Delgado, M., Ketels, C., Porter, M. E., & Stern, S. (2012). *The determinants of national competitiveness* (No. w18249). Cambridge, MA: National Bureau of Economic Research.

European Commission. (2010). *Communication from the Commission. Europe 2020: A strategy for smart, sustainable and inclusive growth.* Brussels: COM (2010) 2020 final.

European Council. (2000). *Presidency note on employment, economic reforms and social cohesion: Towards a Europe based on innovation and knowledge.* Brussels: European Council 5256/00 + ADD1 COR 1 (en).

Fagerberg, J., Mowery, D. C., & Nelson, R. R. (Eds.). (2005). *The Oxford handbook of innovation.* Oxford: Oxford University Press.

Foray, D. (2004). *Economics of knowledge.* Cambridge, MA: MIT Press.

Haeussler, C. (2006). *'Take and give' versus 'knowledge catching' – Empirical analysis of the management of knowledge flows.* Munich: Ludwig-Maximilian University of Munich.

Hofstede, G., Hofstede, G. J., & Minkov, M. (1991). *Cultures and organizations: Software of the mind* (Vol. 2). London: McGraw-Hill. Retrieved from www.upstreamonline.com/live/1108074/aker (2014).

Karlsson, C., Johansson, B., & Stough, R. (Eds.). (2013). *Innovation, technology and knowledge.* London: Routledge.

Krugman, P. (1994). Competitiveness: A dangerous obsession. *Foreign Affairs, 73*(2), 28–44.

Lam, A. (2000). Tacit knowledge, organizational learning and societal institutions: An integrated framework. *Organization Studies, 21*(3), 487–513.

Lundvall, B. Å. (2003). *The economics of knowledge and learning*. Aalborg: Department of Business Studies, Aalborg University.

Lundvall, B. Å., & Lorenz, E. (2012). From the Lisbon strategy to Europe 2020. In N. Morel, B. Palier, & J. Palme (Eds.), *Towards a social investment welfare state?: Ideas, policies and challenges* (pp. 333–352). Bristol: Policy Press.

Nelson, R. R., & Winter, S. G. (1982). *An evolutionary theory of economic change*. Cambridge, MA: Harvard University Press.

Nijkamp, P., & Siedschlag, I. (Eds.). (2011). *Innovation, growth and competitiveness: Dynamic regions in the knowledge-based world economy*. Berlin and Heidelberg: Springer-Verlag.

Nonaka, I., & Takeuchi, H. (1995). *The knowledge-creating company: How Japanese companies create the dynamics of innovation*. Oxford: Oxford University Press.

Nonaka, I., & Von Krogh, G. (2009). Perspective-tacit knowledge and knowledge conversion: Controversy and advancement in organizational knowledge creation theory. *Organization Science, 20*(3), 635–652.

OECD. (1996). *The knowledge-based economy*. Paris: OECD.

Ozman, M. (2010). The knowledge base of products: Implications for organizational structures. *Organization Studies, 31*(8), 1129–1154.

Park, S. O. (2015). *Dynamics of economic spaces in the global knowledge-based economy: Theory and East Asian cases*. London and New York: Routledge.

Pedersen, O. K. (2011). *Konkurrencestaten*. Copenhagen: Hans Reitzel.

Penrose, E. (1959). *The theory of the growth of the firm*. New York: John Wiley.

Polanyi, M. (1962/2012). *Personal knowledge*. London: Routledge.

Raspe, O., & Van Oort, F. G. (2008). Firm growth and localized knowledge externalities. *Journal of Regional Analysis and Policy, 38*(2), 100–116.

Ricardo, D. (1821). *Principles of political economy and taxation* (3rd ed.). London: John Murray.

Rodrigues, M. J. (Ed.). (2002). *The new knowledge economy in Europe: A strategy for international competitiveness and social cohesion*. Cheltenham and Northampton, MA: Edward Elgar.

Smith, E. A. (2001). The role of tacit and explicit knowledge in the workplace. *Journal of Knowledge Management, 5*(4), 311–321.

Stiglitz, J. (1999). *Public policy for a knowledge economy*. Remarks at the Department for Trade and Industry and Center for Economic Policy Research London, U.K. January 27, 1999.

Teece, D. (1980). Economies of scope and the scope of the enterprise. *Journal of Economic Behavior and Organization, 1*(3), 223–247.

von Tunzelmann, N., & Acha, V. (2005). Innovation in 'low-tech' industries. In J. Fagerberg, D. C. Mowery, & R. R. Nelson (Eds.), *The Oxford handbook of innovation* (pp. 407–432). Oxford: Oxford University Press.

Westeren, K. I. (Ed.). (2012). *Foundations of the knowledge economy: Innovation, learning and clusters*. Cheltenham and Northampton, MA: Edward Elgar.

World Bank. (2012). *Knowledge Economy Index (KEI) 2012 Rankings*. Retrieved from http://siteresources.worldbank.org/INTUNIKAM/Resources/2012.pdf.

World Economic Forum. (2016). *The global competitiveness report 2015–2016*. Geneva.

Zahra, S. A., & George, G. (2002). Absorptive capacity: A review, reconceptualization, and extension. *Academy of Management Review, 27*(2), 185–203.

# 2 Cost structure and competitive situation

## 2.1 Competitive analysis of firms in global white meat industry

The twenty-first century's globalized world offers unique opportunities and challenges for firms that are operating in a global industry. In a broader strategic perspective, the organizational environment plays an important role in the firm's structure, orientation and strategic choices. Within the same global industrial environment, international firms operating in competing international markets may differ substantially. On the other hand, within a country, domestic firms' different strategies are mainly based on internal capabilities and regional and national relationships. Research on the former and latter is very well documented and comparable to manufactured goods. But the research on comparison of several domestic firms' strategic choices in different countries in the global industry that deals with live products input is not very well documented. The meat industry of many countries has evolved based on domestic preferences and life habits and, after some time has expanded to become a part of the global food industry. Thus, in a globalized meat industry one can observe very high variations in technology and utilization of labor representing domestic industry preferences. In this context, examining the competition and survival of domestic meat industry firms in the global meat industry is a very complex exercise. Consequently, there is a need for more micro-analytic analysis of selected firms in different countries. In this chapter, the focus is aimed at five white meat-producing firms that operate in five different countries to examine their competitiveness, as stated in Chapter 1. The analysis in this chapter is focused on the cost structure of the individual firms. Specifically, we have looked at the sources of competitiveness and the firm's ability to achieve market power.

Firm-level productivity is an important factor in determining competitive advantage. Technological advancements and organizational learning are the key sources for improving this. Use of technology in improving productivity is very well researched and documented. The complementary nature of technological advancements and organizational learning signify that both sources are important. In this context, Sterman's (2000) inventory-workforce model recognizes two main sources of productivity: (1) knowledgeable labor and (2) the application of technology in the production process. Sterman (2000) also contended that productivity positively impacted production output and relatively decreased the volume of the workforce.

However, surprisingly the poultry industry in the US witnessed exactly the opposite. Hetrick (1994) reported that between 1980 and 1992 poultry employment grew by about 64%, while during the same period poultry industry productivity increased at an annual rate of 3.1%. Demand for poultry products increased in general, but at a higher than average rate for unprocessed chicken parts and labor-intensive processed chicken parts, Hetrick (1994). This is only possible based on conventional labor economics theory that states that increased marginal product shifts the marginal revenue product curve to right (see Figure 4 in Grant, *et al.*, 2003: 86). Either a constant wage or a relatively small increase in wage compared to improvement in productivity is likely to result in more employment. Further, Hetrick (1994) found that the employment and productivity gain in the poultry industry was very much in contrast to the red meat industry where we saw an annual loss of 4% employment compared to 0.5% gain in productivity. Here, a relatively higher increase in wages decreased employment despite improvement in productivity.

The intuitive implication of productivity on employment is very simple as fewer workers are required to produce the same level of output with increased labor productivity. However, labor economic theory suggests that increased productivity results in higher demand for labor when the wage remains the same or with a modest proportional wage increase. Poultry productivity and employment require an in-depth analysis on what is really taking place in poultry processing facilities and in national and international markets. What are the underlying factors that are propelling productivity in poultry processing? A study in 2011 by the Australian Chicken Meat Federation (ACMF) claimed that industry efficiency and productivity was achieved in Australia by embracing the best new technology from all over the world and adapting it for the local circumstances (ACMF 2011:9). As reported from Australia, the technical know-how and adaptation of the knowledge in processing was the key determinant to improving productivity. The findings in Australia's poultry processing industry are very much in line with Drucker's (1974) general argument on productivity, where he claims that knowledge work is the key area where the workers can improve productivity.

A significant portion of the global poultry meat production comes from large-scale specialized poultry producers (see da Silva 2013). In poultry processing we see different types of technology, from low-tech labor-intensive to high-tech capital-intensive technologies. In our selection of firms, KUPCO, LAR and Crysbro are relatively labor-intensive while the Norwegian firm, Ytterøykylling, is moderately capital-intensive and the Danish firm, Danpo, is highly capital-intensive with high-tech equipment. A new poultry processing firm may start operations as labor-intensive and gradually transform into a capital intensive one. Commonly, the large-scale processing factories are primarily using capital-intensive technology in Europe and the US. Capital intensive technology can offer substantial cost saving through automation of the processing. Henry and

Rothwell (1995) found that in both developed and developing countries poultry processing was moving towards vertical integration to benefit from economies of scale, lowering cost and controlling technical inputs and to maintain biosecurity and quality control. Different types of solutions, from hierarchical to market-based will be discussed in Chapter 3.

In today's globalized world, poultry processing technology is readily available worldwide without limitations and in general all countries have improved their productivity by acquiring the new technology (Narrod, Pray and Tiongco, 2008). In the 1980's and 1990's we saw research pointing at the ability of developing countries to take advantage of new technologies to improve their competitiveness relative to developed countries (Henry and Rothwell, 1995). Recently, we have also seen substantial technological improvements in developed countries, setting new standards for a best industry practice. Even if processing technology is universally available, best practices may vary from region to region, nations to nations and culture to culture. These best practices can have an immense impact on productivity as technology adaptation and innovation take place in different regions in the world. Micro-level data enable us to examine whether firms in developing countries can compete with the firms in developed countries. This is one of the fundamental discussions we want to take up in this book.

The global poultry industry has grown significantly over the years. Developing countries are expected to increase production by about 27% while developed countries will increase production by 20% between 2012–14 and 2024 (Rushton, *et al.* 2014). International trade aspects will be discussed more in detail in Chapter 6. Globalized transfer of technology (including better bird strains) and processing technology has become easier to access but requires more knowledge resources to successfully operate. Given the universality of technology, information and capital movement, the global market dynamism and competition causes constant changes in production patterns.

## 2.2 Production and properties of the firms

Central properties of the firms' and country production information are reported in Table 2.1. Firms' annual production (2015) ranges from 4,700 metric tons (MT) to 23,700 MT. Production ranges show a high degree of variability in different countries. The firm in Norway is the smallest in size while the Brazilian firm is the largest among the selected firms. National annual poultry production data show the lowest annual production per capita in Sri Lanka and Kuwait while Brazil's annual production is the highest among all five nations both in total and per capita.

National firm-level share of production data show that LAR's share of national production is the lowest (1.82% of Brazil), while Danpo is the largest (38.74% of Denmark). KUPCO also produces a significant share (33.00% of Kuwait) of national production. Higher market share (30% or more) by a single firm is considered to be market strength, indicating greater opportunities for profit. The

*Table 2.1* National production of chicken, production by firm and other cost/price characteristics (2015 data unless otherwise stated)

| *Country* | *Kuwait* | *Sri Lanka* | *Norway* | *Denmark* | *Brazil* |
|---|---|---|---|---|---|
| *Firm* | *KUPCO* | *Crysbro* | *Ytterøy* | *Danpo* | *LAR* |
| Firm production in MT | 16,500 | 14,196 | 4,706 | 73,992 | 239,700 |
| Country poultry production in MT (*) | 50,000 | 140,000 | 92,532 | 191,000 | 13,146,000 |
| Per capita production in KG in the country (*) | 1.27 | 0.67 | 1.78 | 3.36 | 6.38 |
| Firm's share of national production in% | 33.00 | 10.14 | 5.09 | 38.74 | 1.82 |
| Cost of live chicken (USD)/KG | 1.833 | 1.178 | 1.995 | 0.970 | 0.667 |
| Price (USD)/KG | 3.191 | 2.282 | 3.722 | 2.299 | 1.441 |
| Number of employees | 180 | 120 | 96 | 550 | 4451 |
| Firm production in MT/employee | 91.67 | 118.30 | 49.02 | 134.53 | 53.85 |

Source: authors' data collection.

(*) and Index Mundi (www. indexmundi.com/, accessed May 2017).

advantage of having a higher market share can be translated to market power. As the firm increases its market share the firm has the potential to increase the price and profit.

A firm's comparative advantage and competitiveness can be examined from at least four perspectives. A Ricardian point of view is based on opportunity cost. Heckscher-Ohlin theory is based on using intensely abundant factors. Then we have Porter's approach and knowledge-based approaches as presented in Chapter 4. The North American Meat Institute (NAMI) considers the poultry industry to be relatively labor-intensive (NAMI 2016). Our data collection show that relatively fewer workers are employed in Denmark, which indicates poultry production in this country appears to be relatively capital intensive.

All the managers from the five firms indicated that workforce was the most important source for developing productivity. In this project, we have looked at the use of labor compared to other factors of production from two points of view. In Table 2.1 we have calculated firm production in metric tons per employee to get a more technical picture of the firms' use of labor. This measure shows LAR and Ytterøy as labor-intensive producers, but because of different circumstances. Labor is much cheaper in Brazil compared to Norway so even if LAR does large-scale production they have a relatively high number of employees because capital is relatively expensive. Crysbro and KUPCO are in the middle range while Danpo from the more technical point of view is using high-tech capital intensive equipment with labor saving technologies.

We also use labor cost as a share of total cost to evaluate labor/capital intensity of production.

We have collected information about cost structure for all firms. To get comparable numbers for total cost we looked at the (yearly average) price of processed chicken sold (at the factory door) multiplied by quantity. We collected direct information about total labor cost and how this was split into total production labor cost and total administrative labor cost. We also got the firms direct estimation of the cost of live chicken. For capital costs we collected the interest rate and book value of (total) production facilities (machinery + buildings) and from this made an estimation of capital cost. For the Scandinavian firms we had more complete accounting data and found that our estimations match reasonably well. To protect the firm's integrity and confidentiality we avoided collecting all detailed cost components from the firms.

We calculated cost shares for live chicken cost, production labor cost, administrative labor cost and capital cost share.

$$\text{Share of Live Chicken Cost} = (\text{Live Chicken Cost/Total cost}) \star 100 \quad (1)$$

$$\text{Production Labor Cost Share} = (\text{Production Labor Cost/Total cost}) \star 100 \quad (2)$$

$$\text{Administrative Labor Cost Share} = (\text{Administrative Labor Cost/Total cost}) \star 100 \quad (3)$$

$$\text{Capital cost Share} = (\text{Capital Cost/Total cost}) \star 100 \quad (4)$$

The cost shares for the five firms are presented in Table 2.2.

*Table 2.2* Cost share for different inputs (2015 data)

| *Country* | *Kuwait* | *Sri Lanka* | *Norway* | *Denmark* | *Brazil* |
|---|---|---|---|---|---|
| *Firm* | *KUPCO* | *Crysbro* | *Ytterøy* | *Danpo* | *LAR* |
| Cost share of live chicken | 57.45 | 51.61 | 53.61 | 42.21 | 46.25 |
| Total labor cost share | 4.23 | 7.69 | 24.93 | 19.40 | 10.60 |
| Capital cost share | 0.89 | 3.24 | 2.14 | 3.97 | 3.39 |
| Other cost share | 37.43 | 37.46 | 19.32 | 34.42 | 39.76 |
| Total | 100.00 | 100.00 | 100.00 | 100.00 | 100.00 |
| Labor in direct production cost share | 4.00(★) | 5.45 | 19.97 | 15.38 | 9.50 |
| Labor in administrative jobs cost share | 0.23 | 2.24 | 4.96 | 4.02 | 1.10 |
| Cost of borrowing capital (interest rate) | 4% | 10% | 5% | 5% | 10% |

Source: authors' data collection.

(★) Estimated, see text for explanation.

Live chicken is the main and most important input in poultry processing. Any gain in reducing the live chicken cost share would be an added advantage for the firms. A significant variation was found among different cost share components. The different values of cost share must be examined with caution as they are not absolute values but relative. Significant differences in prices and cost exist because the level of income and wages are very different in the respective countries. Among the five firms, the Danish firm has the lowest live chicken cost share. This may result from economies of scale for producing the live chicken combined with securing a relatively high price for the processed chicken. Since live chicken is the primary input, this contributes to a stronger comparative advantage for the Danish firm.

The Brazilian firm also has a similar comparative advantage. The Brazilian firm's production volume is higher compared to other firms. The lower live chicken cost share for the Danish firm is remarkable. The other three firms' live chicken cost share is more than 50%, indicating a relatively higher live chicken cost. The Norwegian firm's live chicken cost share is about 53%, reflecting both a high sales price and high cost of inputs. This makes the firm less competitive in the international trade market. The Kuwaiti firm's live chicken cost share is about 57% and this figure is also relatively high. One factor to explain this is that the environmental conditions of the desert are not very conducive to producing poultry and they must rely on imports to produce live chickens domestically. Surprisingly, the Sri Lankan firm's relatively higher live chicken cost share indicates a combination of a growing demand for chicken in Sri Lanka and that live chicken producing farms have diseconomies of scale. The latter argument is most conducive since a part of the live chicken supply comes from contract growers and those farms are relatively small family operated farms.

Production labor cost share is highest for the Norwegian firm with about 20% of total cost. Gale and Arnade (2015) reported that broiler production labor cost share often varied between 11% and 15%. Higher wages compared to the price of chicken could be related to either the scarcity of labor or the skill level of the workers. In Chapter 4 we see that the skill level of the Norwegian firm is higher than the others. The Danish firm, Danpo, has a labor cost share of about 15% of the price. This is within industry normal/upper range. For the Danish firm, we find a high capital intensity of production compared to a relatively high wage level. The Brazilian, Kuwaiti and Sri Lankan firms have a lower labor cost share to total cost as their shares are less than 11%.

The Kuwaiti firm, KUPCO, has the lowest direct labor cost share of 4%. In Kuwait, chicken prices are relatively high and domestic firms enjoy a premium price for their fresh chicken. Unlike other firms, at KUPCO almost all the workers are foreigners and they work and live near the production processing plant. The labor laws in Kuwait require a sponsor for foreign workers and workers cannot change their jobs without the legal consent of the employer. Lack of freedom for labor movement prevents the labor market from reaching a market wage and most often the workers are underpaid (Human Rights Watch 2010). The Kuwaiti firm also pays several services to the employees that are deducted from their wage. Our understanding after visits was that these costs were little less than the actual paid wages. So, what we can call a 'total employee direct production-related cost' that is comparable with the other firms equals 4% of total cost. This is 2.2% actually paid (this is the number we got from the firm) plus the 1.8% which is our estimated cost for firm services to production employees deducted from their wages. This number is still very low but comparable to the 5.45% at Crysbro. The conclusion is that it is the combination of high chicken prices and low total labor costs that result in this very low labor cost share for the Kuwaiti firm.

The labor cost share in direct production of the Sri Lankan firm, Crysbro, is about 5.45% of the total cost. This figure too is much below the expected range. Sri Lanka is a developing country with a population over 21 million. According to Sri Lanka's annual Labor Force Survey 2015 report (Sri Lanka Labour Force Survey Annual Report 2015) the Kandy district where the firm is located has a labor force participation of 49.6% (male 72.1%, female 32.1%). A considerable number of men and women are available as potential suppliers to the labor market and this gives a downward pressure on the wages. Sri Lankan domestic consumption is mainly met by domestic production (Department of Animal Production and Health (DAPH) 2015). The domestic price of chicken is relatively high without competition from international trade. The Sri Lankan firm, Crysbro, has a higher domestic price for chicken and low wages which together has resulted in a low labor cost share.

The Brazilian firm, LAR, has a close to average labor cost share compared with other countries in the transitional and service oriented countries. The fact that LAR is one of the world's leading exporters of chicken results in a low domestic price. Looking at the national averages, Brazil has an excess supply of labor which may result in a downward pressure for lower wages for workers. Citing Maloney and Núñez (2001), it was reported in the Inter-American Development Bank (2001) annual report that Brazil has a high ratio of wages close to the minimum wage. There are large regional differences in Brazil's labor market. LAR is situated in Paraná which is one state with average wage and income levels. Compared to the Danish firm, LAR utilizes a large number of people years compared to production in volume, but from a cost point the average wage level is low. Combining low chicken prices and low wage costs results in a fair labor cost ratio for the Brazilian firm.

Administrative labor cost share measures how much each firm is spending on their administrative staff and facilities compared to the total cost of the firm. The Scandinavian firms have an administration cost share of about 4–5%. There are no standard international numbers or ratios to compare for white meat production but the numbers indicate relatively high administrative cost shares in Scandinavia. This gives the firms a disadvantage in their efforts to be competitive. Wages and salaries of administrative staffs are likely to be higher in those two countries because of a high wage level and the structure of the firms. The Danish firm has high-tech capital equipment that needs frequent follow up. The Norwegian firm is a niche producer and requires frequent and resource consuming contact with the market. The Kuwaiti and Sri Lankan firms have low administrative cost shares that reflect the low labor cost.

Capital costs are measured by multiplying the total capital value of the firms (the value of buildings, machinery etc. as reported in the firm's bookkeeping/accounting) by the interest rate. This is the best approximation we could do because direct estimates of e.g. profits were not available for several of the firms. Also, some of the firms did not have comparable numbers. In Sri Lanka and Brazil, the interest rates are higher (10%) while in Kuwait, Norway and Denmark the interest rates are lower (4%–5%). At the time of the survey the Kuwaiti firm, KUPCO, had capital equipment (machines) that were old. Their capital value was therefore less when compared to other firms which resulted in a lower capital cost ratio. The countries with lower interest rates are likely to use more capital compared to labor. The Danish firm was equipped with more modern capital equipment than the others. However, its share of capital cost is similar to Sri Lanka and Brazil. This is primarily attributed to the fact that the interest rate in Denmark is half of Sri Lankan and Brazilian interest rates.

In the 'other cost share' group we found items like water, electricity, other items used in production like packaging, and selected fees and capital transfers. Because of different definitions and data availability it was not possible to make further analysis here.

Comparative advantage alone is not sufficient for the firm to be able to maximize profits. The firms also need to have market power (White 2013). Economic theory recognizes the existence of market power but there are only a few models that exist to estimate real market power. For example, the Lerner Index (1934) is commonly used to measure the degree of monopoly power. This rent or supernormal profit represents a firm's ability to sustain competitive advantage over its rivals (Bowman 1974; Rumelt 1984; Rumelt 1987; Barney 1986; Liebeskin 1996). There are many theories put forward to explain the sources of the rents. Penrose (1959) and Winter (1988) have argued that the resource-based theory of the firm is the most applicable, including taking the knowledge aspects into consideration as we have argued in Chapter 4. The aspects of commercialization of knowledge assets are built into the Lerner Index measure indicating that a greater monopoly power contributes to a higher profit for the firm. The Lerner Index measure alone may not be sufficient. Bain (1941) suggested that there is no single measure of monopoly power and monopoly power may vary in different situations.

$$\text{Lerner Index} = \frac{P - MC}{P}$$

Where P: price and MC: marginal cost.

In a perfectly competitive market the Lerner Index value is assumed to be zero (as P = MC) indicating no monopoly power while a greater divergence between P and MC would lead to greater monopoly power. Pindyck (1985) identified the Lerner Index measure as a static behavior that failed to reflect the beneficial effect of technological change and innovation. Since our study focused on a cross sectional study of five firms, it is possible to estimate the Lerner Index to compare the degree of monopoly power. To estimate the Lerner Index, it is necessary to know the marginal cost of each firm. All the firms buy live chicken for processing. Because of the way the firms do their processing, we can assume that costs in the short run are fixed and only live chicken price is variable. Based on this assumption we modified the Lerner Index equation to be the following:

$$\text{Modified Lerner Index} = \frac{\text{Price of produced chicken} - \text{Live Chicken Cost}}{\text{Price of produced chicken}}$$

The Learner index value can range from 0 to 1. A zero value would indicate no market power at all (competitive market) and a value of one would indicate full market power (Lerner 1934). The original Lerner Index estimated values reflected monopoly market power. For example, in 1995, the US Department of Justice (DOJ) initiated a case against Eastman Kodak for having too much market power. The DOJ experts estimated the Lerner Index value to be 0.5 and argued that Kodak had too much monopoly power. When the case came to court it rejected the DOJ experts' evaluations and concluded that Kodak did not have market power to secure monopoly profit (Klein 1999).

We have defined a modified Lerner Index to show the firm's ability to sell the products either at a premium price or be able to buy live chicken at a cheaper price. We call this combined effect market strength power. In our case, this represents more a potential for market strength than the traditional definition of monopoly. We have presented the estimated modified Lerner Index values in Table 2.3.

The Danpo firm's market strength power stems from its ability to purchase live chicken at a relatively lower price compared to other firms. The Brazilian firm's market power is less but very close to Danpo. It is very interesting to note that LAR has the lowest market share among all the firms. LAR enjoys the lowest live chicken cost and can sell the fresh and frozen chicken at a reasonably high price compared to the live chicken cost. Conventional economic theory suggests that market share is important. However, our modified Lerner Index estimate results show that smaller market share firms can have a greater market strength power if the firm can achieve a cost advantage over the other firms. The Norwegian firm, Ytterøy, has moderately high market strength power and a low market share. Ytterøy receives the highest price among all five firms and the firm also pays a relatively higher price for its live chicken. This confirms Ytterøy as a niche producer in a market with relatively high income for the customers.

*Table 2.3* The Lerner Index and total cost shares of price for the firms

| *Country*<br>*Firm* | *Kuwait*<br>*KUPCO* | *Sri Lanka*<br>*Crysbro* | *Norway*<br>*Ytterøy* | *Denmark*<br>*Danpo* | *Brazil*<br>*LAR* |
|---|---|---|---|---|---|
| Modified Lerner Index, Degree of market strength | 0.426 | 0.484 | 0.464 | 0.578 | 0.537 |

Source: authors' data collection.

## 2.3 Conclusions

As we see in Table 2.1 the firms differ substantially in size, internal organization, market condition and the structure and development conditions of the society surrounding the firms. We expected to find differences in labor cost and labor utilization but some of the differences are large. We did not get data for wage per hour for production workers for the firms in Brazil, Kuwait and Sri Lanka. An estimate we made from unofficial sources indicates that the average wage rate for production workers in US dollars is five times higher in Norway/Denmark compared to Brazil. When we look at the more technical term 'Firm production in metric tons per employee' we find that LAR utilizes about 2.5 times more employees per produced ton white meat than Danpo. Ytterøy and LAR using this metric operate on close to the same level. The Norwegian result here is understandable but the result from LAR shows a high use of manpower. We expected large differences between LAR and Danpo. An important part of the explanation is the labor cost relative to capital. When labor is so low priced compared to capital it is profitable for LAR to use a high share of person-hours in production. In Chapter 4 we have analyzed the structure and content of knowledge transfers necessary to operate high-tech capital equipment. The differences tell us that LAR also must do a substantial knowledge upgrade to enter the level of Danpo.

The labor cost shares differed more than expected. The situation in Kuwait and Sri Lanka show labor cost far below the international average. The wage level differences explain some of the difference between Brazil and Norway/Denmark. Ytterøy was expected to be labor cost intensive, the Danpo numbers are higher than expected.

Key figures for competitiveness include both the unit price of total production and the cost of live chicken in an absolute sense. They also reflect the relative sense when numbers are used to calculate the Lerner Index. As we will see in Chapter 6, LAR is the only firm that is competitive on the international market in general. They have a very optimized vertical chain with a low wage level combined with low prices on important components of the feed, like soya. They also have good control of animal health and stability of deliverances. We knew that Brazil was a world leader in white meat production and this is in line with the numbers in Table 2.1. Danpo is competitive inside the EU rules and the Danish national market. Throughout the book we see Danpo as successful in utilization of high end technology, knowledge management and innovativeness. It is interesting to see how low Danpo can get the cost of live chicken with little direct control over the supply chain. This is similar to Brazil which has a very competitive value chain organization in international terms.

## References

Australian Chicken Meat Federation. (2011). *The Australian chicken meat industry: An industry in profile*. Retrieved from www.chicken.org.au/industryprofile/downloads/The_Australian_Chicken_Meat_Industry_An_Industry_in_Profile.pdf.

Bain, J. S. (1941). The profit rate as a measure of monopoly power. *Quarterly Journal of Economics*, *55*, 271–293.

Barney, J. (1986). Strategic factor markets: Expectations, luck, and business strategy. *Management Science, 32*, 1231–1241.

Bowman, E. H. (1974). Epistemology, corporate strategy, and academe. *Sloan Management Review, 15*, 35–50.

da Silva, M. V. (2013). Poultry and poultry products – Risks for Human Health. *Poultry Development Review*, Food and Agriculture Organization (FAO), Rome. Retrieved from www.fao.org/docrep/019/i3531e/i3531e.pdf.

Department of Animal Production and Health (DAPH). (2015). *Livestock statistical bulletin.* Retrieved from www.daph.gov.lk/web/images/content_image/publications/other_publications/stat_bulletin_2015.PDF.

Drucker, P. F. (1974). *Management: Tasks, responsibilities, practices.* Oxford: Butterworth Heinemann.

Gale, L., & Arnade, C. (2015). Effects of rising feed and labor costs on China's chicken price. *International Food and Agribusiness Management Review, 18*(A), 137–150.

Grant, S., Vidler, C., & Smith, C. (2003). *Heinemann economics A2 for AQA.* London: Heinemann Educational.

Henry, R., & Rothwell, G. (1995). *The world poultry industry.* International Finance Corporation Global Agribusiness Series. Washington, DC: World Bank.

Hetrick, R. L. (1994). Why did employment expand in poultry processing plants? *Monthly Labor Review, 117*(6), 31–34.

Human Rights Watch. (2010). *Walls at every turn: Abuse of migrant domestic workers through Kuwait's sponsorship system.* Retrieved from www.hrw.org/report/2010/10/06/walls-every-turn/abuse-migrant-domestic-workers-through-kuwaits-sponsorship-system.

Inter-American Development Bank (IDB). (2001). *Competitiveness: The business of growth.* 2001 Report Economic and Social Progress in Latin America. Washington, DC: IDB.

Klein, B. (1999). Market power in franchise cases in the wake of Kodak: Applying post-contract hold-up analysis to vertical relationships, *Antitrust Law Journal, 70*, 283–362.

Lerner, A. P. (1934). The concept of monopoly and the measurement of monopoly. *Review of Economic Studies, 1*, 157–175.

Liebeskind, J. P. (1996). Knowledge, strategy, and the theory of the firm. *Strategic Management Journal, 17*, 93–107, Special Issue: Knowledge and the Firm.

Maloney, W., & Núñez, J. (2001). *Minimum wages in Latin America.* Washington, DC: World Bank.

Narrod, A. C., Pray, E. C., & Tiongco, M. (2008). *Technology transfer, policies, and the role of the private sector in the global poultry revolution.* IFPRI Discussion Paper 00841 December 2008. Retrieved from www.ifpri.org/publication/technology-transfer-policies-and-role-private-sector-global-poultry-revolution.

North American Meat Institute (NAMI). (2016). *Worker safety in the meat and poultry industry.* Retrieved from www.meatinstitute.org/index.php?ht=a/GetDocumentAction/i/128394.

Penrose, E. (1959). *The theory of the growth of the firm.* New York: Wiley.

Pindyck, R. S. (1985). The measurement of monopoly power in dynamic markets. *Journal of Law & Economics, 28*, 193–221.

Rumelt, R. P. (1984). Towards a strategic theory of the firm. In R. B. Lamb (Ed.), *Competitive strategic management* (pp. 132–145). Englewood Cliffs, NJ: Prentice Hall.

Rumelt, R. P. (1987). Theory, strategy, and entrepreneurship. In D. Teece (Ed.), *The Competitive challenge* (pp. 556–570). Ballinger, Cambridge, MA,

Rushton, J., Ferreira, J. P., & Stärk, K. D. (2014). *Antimicrobial resistance: The use of antimicrobials in the livestock sector.* OECD Food, Agriculture and Fisheries Papers, No. 68, OECD Publishing. Retrieved from http://dx.doi.org/10.1787/5jxvl3dwk3f0-en.

Sri Lanka Labour Force Survey Annual Report. (2015). *Department of census and statistics Sri Lanka.* Retrieved from www.statistics.gov.lk/.

Sterman, J. D. (2000). *Business dynamics: Systems thinking and modeling for a complex world.* New York: McGraw-Hill/Irwin.

White, L. J. (2013). Market power: How does it arise? How is it measured? In C. Thomas & W. F. Shugart (Eds.), *The Oxford handbook of managerial economics* (pp. 389–408). Oxford: Oxford University Press.

Winter, S. (1988). Knowledge and competence as strategic assets. In D. Teece (Ed.), *The competitive challenge: Strategies for industrial innovation and renewal* (pp. 165–187). Cambridge, MA: Ballinger.

# 3 Vertical integration and management of inputs to production

## 3.1 Introduction

Knowledge about the functioning of the organization is important when we try to understand and develop the competitiveness of the firm. When Michael Porter (1985) forwarded his analysis of competitiveness, he introduced the concept of the value chain. This included all primary activities related to inbound logistics, operations, outbound operations and marketing, sales, and supporting activities like procurement, technology development and human resource management. The main idea behind this type of analysis was to discover how the total value creation of the firm could be identified by the different stages and activities.

A related discussion must include how a firm from a managerial point of departure approaches the total value chain, from ultra-raw materials to ultimate consumers. This is the discussion about vertical integration: an assessment of whether to use the market or the hierarchy as a starting point in the development of the firm. Choosing one or the other, hierarchy or market, or a hybrid, gives rise to a series of different challenges about how to uphold the firm's control over the end products that are being presented to the market. A hierarchical solution means that the firm has ownership of the means of production, and thus has the power to make decisions about investment, employment, production and distribution. A market solution means that the firm is operating on the spot market. Control is gained through contracts. One reason a firm considers the question of vertical integration may be that it is '*a way of increasing a firm's value-added margins for a particular chain of processing from ultra-raw materials to ultimate consumers*' (Harrigan, 1985: 396). Another reason might be to gain better control of the production, regarding both production stability and the quality of the products offered to the market.

In our research, we have been focusing on traditional firms in a business where the benchmark is the vertically integrated or vertically controlled firm (normally controlled by the slaughtering and further processing firm) that produces white meat (c.f. Henry and Rothwell, 1995; MacDonald, 2008; Hennessy, 1996). The value chain is the same all over the world, and can be illustrated by Figure 3.1.

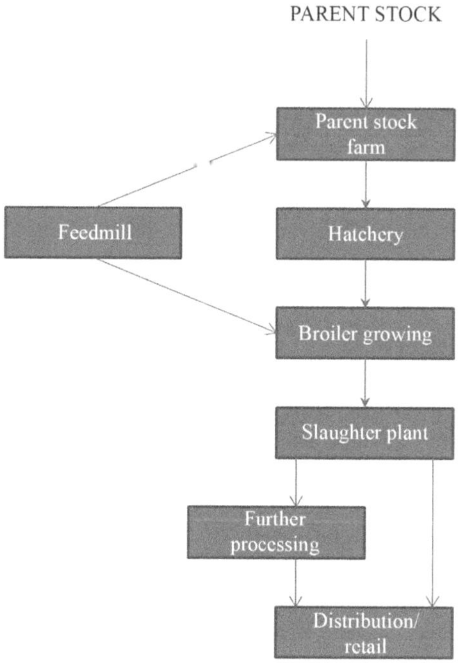


*Figure 3.1* Value chain of chicken production

As the figure illustrates, there are different stages in the production of white meat, from the parent stock farm until the meat is ready for the market. The feed mill is included in the value chain, as the quality and cost of the feed, and eventually the feed conversion rate, give you a good indication of the efficiency of the production of white meat. Each step of the process can be organized as single firms, or they can all be included in an integrated firm.

When vertical integration is being discussed, the basic question has to do with how you organize the value chain, and how many levels of production will be organized within one independent single firm. When each production process is organized within different firms, then we can talk about a market solution. If two or more production processes are organized within one single firm, the term vertical integration can be used. What we found in our research was evidence of different types of governance structures, ranging from market solutions (formally a hybrid with a contract) on one end and hierarchical solutions (ones that include all production levels) on the other. This is a somewhat surprising finding considering that the production process is generic and that the best practice promotes vertical integration or at least strong vertical control.

An interesting part of the discussion on vertical integration is that the level of vertical integration has consequences relating to the types of managerial challenges the firm must deal with. Seeking efficient coordination of the vertical value chain is important if the firm intends to gain effects from their selected choice of vertical integration. Our focus will be a discussion on the more central managerial parameters related to the kind of governance structure the firm has chosen, limiting it to elements like incentive intensity, administrative control, contract law and adaptability described by Williamson (1991; 2002).

Stepping back for a moment: If we want to understand why a discussion on vertical integration is of importance to the competitiveness of the firm, it is well worth reading the analysis made by Coase (1937) in his seminal paper on 'The Nature of the Firm'. The simple question as to why firms exist is still an intriguing question, because it deals with the existence, the size, and the competitiveness of the firm. The relatively simple relation that was developed, consisting of the elements market price, transaction cost, and production cost, is still at the heart of the discussion. The main challenge is to find the equilibrium where market price plus transaction costs equals the in-house production cost, as both the existence, size and the competitiveness of the firm is dependent on where this tipping point is. The argument goes like this: if the marginal cost of in-house production is lower than market price plus transaction costs, the firm is competitive and can continue to grow. Then, when the in-house productions cost is higher than the market price plus transaction costs, the firm is not competitive. This is a very neat abstraction but a challenging equation.

On an abstract level, it is rather easy to conceptualize the equation, as it consists of three well-known concepts: production cost, transaction cost, and market price. The challenging part is when we go deeper into the different parts of the equation, as they represent different theoretical strands to economic organizations. We are approaching economic organization through the choice of vertical integration type. We follow the transaction cost here, in Chapter 2 we discuss market price in relation to production cost structure for the firms in the project. An important reason for this choice is that we are studying traditional firms producing white meat where vertical integration and vertical control is high on the agenda, (see e.g. Henry and Rothwell, 1995; MacDonald, 2008; Hennessy, 1996). A support for our choice of approach is that 'transaction cost theory has become the predominant theoretical framework for explaining organizational boundary decisions' (Geyskens, *et al.*, 2006: 519).

We recognize however, that transaction cost theory does have limitations, especially as production costs are treated as a constant. Technology is being held as a constant across alternative modes of organization when the question on the boundaries of the firm is explored (Williamson, 1985: 88). This comparative static approach is the way that transaction cost theory works, even though it is logical to think that technologies would vary with different modes of governance – market, hybrid or hierarchy. Milgrom and Roberts (1992: 33–34) point their fingers at theoretical problems you can face when you try to separate production and mode of governance and their corresponding costs: production cost and transaction cost are dependent 'both on the organization and on technology, which makes the conceptual separation between production and transaction costs troublesome' (p. 34).

Another limitation is that transaction cost theory sets aside societal culture, such as norms, customs, traditions and so on, which are found in the regions where the economic organizations are located (Williamson, 1998). Societal culture is treated as an informal constraint. Also, institutions that 'are the product of politics and provide the rules of the game within which economic activity is organized' (p. 27) are only treated as shift parameters, even though they are recognized as 'vitally important to the economic productivity of an economy' (p. 27).

The production cost side of the equation is analyzed more in-depth in Chapter 2 where we approach the production costs from a more mainstream economic point of view, analyzing part of the production function. From the perspective of capabilities and knowledge (as it is called by Langlois and Foss, 1999), we look in Chapter 4 at how organizations are dealing with the production processes.

In our empirical study of the traditional firms we have been collecting data to understand more about the choice of vertical integration in different firms, how internal processes can influence the production process, and if and how the societal culture might affect choices on vertical integration and production processes. This means we will examine elements that are not included in the transaction cost analysis, but are included in the original and classic equation developed from Coase.

## 3.2 Theory on vertical integration

The theoretical foundation for a discussion on vertical integration was launched by Ronald Coase's article 'The Nature of the Firm' in 1937. The explication of market costs (known as transaction costs) was introduced as a key to understanding the growth of firms. Even though focusing solely on transaction costs as the key element in a discussion on the choice of governance structure is a simplification, it has been of tremendous importance to help us get more insight into the challenges related to vertical integration. Oliver Williamson has been a driving force in this area since the 1970s and for this he received the Nobel Prize in economic sciences in 2009.

What then are we to understand by the term vertical integration? This has been discussed in the literature (see e.g. Williamson, 1971, 1975; Grossman and Hart, 1986; Balakrishnan and Wernerfelt, 1986; Perry, 1989; Joskow, 1985, 2005). The predominant view is that vertical integration represents one extreme of an organizational continuum, ranging from vertical integration to the spot market: 'inherent in the notion of vertical integration is the elimination of contractual or market exchanges' (Perry, 1989: 185). The elimination of contractual and market exchanges means that the firm has ownership to the means of production, and thus has the power to make decisions about investment, employment, production and distribution. Grossman and Hart (1986) do not distinguish between ownership and control in their definitions of the firm, and this can cause some challenges. Ownership is a simple concept, own or do not own, whereas control is a much more complex concept, where you need to understand what causes control. Just to mention a couple; the cause of control can be through a contract, it can be through political regulation, or through traditions within specific sectors (e.g. cooperatives). The contractual approach to control is covered by transaction cost theory, whereas the political and cultural approach is not.

In reality, it might be that what is described as a vertically integrated chain of production, combines ownership and control – see Perry (1989) who writes that: 'a firm can be described as vertically integrated if it encompasses two single-out-put production processes' (p. 185). If we are talking about a value chain that encompasses more than two levels, and there is a mix of ownership and contractual control, it is labelled a hybrid in the transaction cost literature. If the control 'mechanism' cannot be identified as contractual (or ownership), we are dealing with a market solution. When we consider the managerial challenges that follow from the different choices of governance structures, we will see that it is necessary to be precise in our definition of vertical integration, as managerial challenges differ between ownership, contractual control, and market approaches.

In an assessment of whether to use the market or the hierarchy, Williamson (1971) states that vertical integration will provide access to special incentives, control instruments and structural advantages. In the hierarchy, you will have access to incentives that make it easier to deal with potential opportunism. In a vertically integrated structure, you will also have access to constitutional authority, easy access to decision data and easier access to dispute resolution mechanisms. As for information or knowledge exchange, it is not obvious that being within a vertically integrated structure is better than the market solution. We found education, technology level and cultural factors like power distance to be more important than organizational structure for efficient knowledge transfer (see Chapters 4 and 5).

Williamson (1979) suggests we have a closer look into the level of transaction-specific investments, transaction frequency and uncertainty when we are making considerations about which governance structure is the best for our firm. Transaction-specific investments are understood as 'durable investments that are undertaken in support of particular transactions' (Williamson, 1985: 55). Transaction frequency is of course related to the number of transactions within a given time. Uncertainty is linked to various factors such as technological development, consumer behavior, and incidents. Furthermore, it is linked to behavioral uncertainty (Williamson, 1975). The behavioral assumption including the concepts of both bounded rationality and opportunism (Williamson, 1981) is of course important when you are making considerations about the choice of governance structure. On the other hand, Das (2004) comments that we should not be too anxious about opportunistic behavior, as the market in the end will eliminate actors who are known to act opportunistically. The asset specificity is 'the most important dimension for describing transactions' (Williamson, 1981: 555). Asset specificity can arise from site-specific investments, physical asset specificity, and human asset specificity. What makes the asset specificity the most important dimension is (according to Williamson) 'once an investment has been made, buyer and seller are effectively operating in a bilateral (or at least quasi-bilateral) exchange relation for a considerable period thereafter' (p. 555). Where the investment will be locked into 'the transaction to a significant degree' (p. 555). Even though we are encouraged to keep a close eye on asset specificity, we will have to take into consideration the combination of transaction frequency, transaction-specific investments and uncertainty, when making a decision on whether to seek vertical integration or not.

When we look at the poultry industry, it is a processing industry with an extremely high degree of dependency between different stages of the production process. Avoiding unnecessary disruption in the production process is considered important (Gilson, *et al.* 2009; Martinez, 2002), as a disruption on one level will have a massive impact on the whole chain of production. In addition to the interdependency, this is also an industry where product pricing, and hence production cost, are key competitive elements in the industry. Biosecurity, quality, and optimization of capital resources are also important factors (Henry and Rothwell, 1995; Martinez, 2002). Another thing we can see from the literature is that the constructions of specialized production facilities represent a significant investment for growers. The broiler houses are expanding, and technological solutions are becoming ever more sophisticated, and in the end, these investments have limited alternative applications (MacDonald, 2008). Another factor that can be added is the need for a relatively large geographical proximity between growers and slaughter plants, which helps strengthen the dependency. A relocation of the slaughter plant, which we have seen in Norway, can cause huge problems for farmers that have invested in breeding facilities.

From the section above, we can see that we are dealing with an industry with relatively high and stable transaction frequencies. Then, we can also observe that there are transaction-specific investments regarding site-specific investments and physical specific investments. At this point, it is possible to understand why 'the poultry industry is characterized in most countries by a high level of vertical coordination' (Henry and Rothwell, 1995: 1). From the literature, we see that 'integrators usually own hatcheries, feed mills, slaughter plants, and processing plants – that is, they may be vertically integrated into all stages except for broiler production, where they rely on networks of growers assembled through production contracts '(MacDonald (2008: 3).

What about the uncertainty element in transaction cost theory? We can focus on the production process, where the broiler growing process normally is kept outside the integrated firm, and look at how this is dealt with. In the literature, we can see that the relationship between integrator and breeders seems to be relatively long-lasting and stable, with an average of 13 years. The contracts vary though, from contracts per flock to long-term contracts up to 15 years (MacDonald, 2008). Breeders with the most up to date technology tend to have the longest contracts while breeders with older production facilities have contracts of shorter duration. The predominant type of contract used in the industry, at least if we look at the US, is a production contract (Martinez, 2002), where breeders receive a payment for services rendered (MacDonald, *et al.*, 2004; MacDonald,

2008). One of the things they try to control through the contract is the room for opportunistic behavior. We can see from articles related to the poultry industry, where Tsoulouhas (1999) is having a discussion about the two-sided moral hazard problem, Dubois and Vukina (2009) are discussing the optimal incentive opportunity for opportunism, and Leegomonchai and Vukina (2005) discuss the dynamic incentives and the possibility of discrimination by agents. It is pointed out that both principal and agent can exercise opportunistic behavior.

## 3.3 The managerial challenges within the different governance structures

### *3.3.1 Introduction*

What kind of managerial challenges you face depends on the choice of governance structure: market, hybrid or hierarchy. Williamson (1991; 2002; 2009) defines four different attributes that the managers need to look at: incentive intensity, administrative command and control, contract law regime and adaptability. Choosing a market structure will imply that managers have to develop incentive strategies, and at the same time have the awareness that different firms will make autonomous decisions regarding market changes in order to maximize individual utility. Looking at the other extreme, the hierarchy, managers will have stronger administrative control, which can be used to exercise coordinated changes and adaptations throughout the value chain, and to settle disputes between different stages of production. In a market solution disputes between successive stages may be settled by court order.

When considering the different governance structures, it will be the hybrid model that brings most challenges to the managers (see Table 3.1), as the

*Table 3.1* Distinguishing attributes of market, hybrid, and hierarchy governance structures

| *Distinguishing attributes of market, hybrid, and hierarchy governance structures★* | | | |
|---|---|---|---|
| *Attributes* | *Governance structure* | | |
| | *Market* | *Hybrid* | *Hierarchy* |
| Instruments: | | | |
| Incentive intensity | ++ | + | 0 |
| Administrative controls | 0 | + | ++ |
| Performance attributes: | | | |
| Adaptation (A) | ++ | + | 0 |
| Adaptation (C) | 0 | + | ++ |
| Contract law | ++ | + | 0 |

Source: Williamson, 1991: 281.

★ ++ = strong; + = semi-strong; 0 = weak

organization must be able to balance incentives and obtain administrative control. Some parts of the value chain will respond to hierarchical command, while you must operate appropriate incentives in other parts of the value chain. Second, there should be a balance in adapting the whole supply chain to changes. For instance, in the market you not only need to think about coordinated adaptations for the total chain of production but also about adaptations that will be advantageous for those parts within the hierarchy. Third, there is a need to be able to deal with business challenges through legal channels and through the chain of command within the hierarchy.

### 3.3.2 Incentive intensity

Balancing the incentives facing managers in traditional firms can be a challenging thing to do. In the balancing process, the integrators must deal with issues like: risk assessment, moral hazard, preventing situations where breeders can end up in bankruptcy and level of performance-based payment. The overall goal is to secure high-quality products, stable deliverance, and a healthy economy. From the literature, especially the US-based literature, we can see that they use tournament contracts, and according to Zheng and Vukina (2007), 'virtually all modern broiler contracts are settled using a two-part cardinal-tournament scheme' (p. 846). These are contracts with a fixed base payment and a variable performance-based payment, where they compete on variables like feed conversion rate, mortality, and kilograms of live birds (Vukina and Zheng, 2007). According to Vukina (2001) the performance element of the contract constitutes between 50% and 100% of the payment to the breeder. In this type of contract winners take it all and losers will in the end be forced out of business, unless they can turn things around. It is no surprise that 'growers and policy-makers often refer to tournaments as an 'unfair practice' and have sought to make them illegal' (Wu, 2006: 505).

Other types of contracts used over the years since the 1950s are open account contracts, open account no-loss contracts, guaranteed-price contracts, flat-fee contracts, share contracts (flat-fee contracts with some incentives) and basic feed conversion contracts (Vukina, 2001). What we can see is that the incentives have become stronger and stronger over the years, ending with the tournament contracts.

### 3.3.3 Administrative command and control

We are looking at a process industry where there is little room for disruption when the process is under way. There is also great focus on production costs, biosecurity, and quality in the business. If a firm wants to sell their products to e.g. McDonald's, they must implement quality management systems, like ISO 9001, ISO 22000, and GFSI standards, which means they need to be able to trace the food all the way from the farms, via slaughtering and processing, and ultimately to the restaurants. All these elements require development of a coordination and control mechanism throughout the value chain.

Coordination and dispute resolution will be central elements within such a system. In a process industry like poultry production it is a necessity to be able to coordinate all levels of production to secure a stable output at the end of the production chain. Coordination can be obtained through a traditional hierarchy, through contracts, and even the traditional market mechanism. Dispute resolution can be sought in different ways, but for our purpose, we think of dispute resolution either through instruments within the hierarchy or through instruments built into contracts, which in the end may be dealt with through the legal system.

### *3.3.4 Adaptability*

There is obviously a need to make adaptations to market changes in the poultry industry. If we look at statistics from FAOSTAT (United Nations, FAOSTAT, 2017) there has been a constant growth of the world poultry production since the early 1960s, with a 5% average growth rate per year, but with variations between 2% and 10% (see Chapter 6 for a more detailed presentation). As a commodity on the world market, there has been an 8% average growth in export per year since the early 1960s, with variations between +25% to -6%. The growth rates indicate that this is a business where the single firm must be prepared to deal with both growth and shocks, e.g. because of the bird flu where production will suffer. From the literature, we can observe that integrators try to transfer some of the risks regarding market fluctuations to the chicken breeders, where the fee can be adjusted according to the market price. In addition, contracts can include seasonal fee adjustments in relation to energy costs (MacDonald and Corb, 2011).

### *3.3.5 Contract law regime*

'Contract production has been controversial in the livestock, meat, and poultry sectors, with many farm activists alleging that the market power held by large processors combined with the use of contracts can be exploitive of growers' (Wu and MacDonald, 2015: 1). James Jr., *et al.* (2013) highlight the dependency between integrator and chicken farmers in the US poultry industry, where 'there is a significant dependency disadvantage of growers relative to integrators' (p. 114). The asymmetrical power relationship will exist whether you have a contractual or a hierarchical governance structure, if there is a clear principal or a situation where one part has a stronger dependency towards the other. From a cynical perspective, there might be ethical issues regarding contractual relationships, but from a legal perspective, there is no problem provided the contract is within the law. When there is a small farmer breeding chickens for a relatively big integrator, the strength of the parties is from the outset uneven.

### 3.3.6 Summing up the theoretical discussion

From a theoretical point of view, we learn that the general focus on the study of governance 'is concerned with the identification, explication, and mitigation of all forms of contractual hazards' (Williamson, 1996: 5). From a transaction cost perspective, which provides a more explicit approach, the choice of governance structure is related to providing cost-effective relief against maladaptation hazards. From a managerial perspective, it will be important to balance the incentive intensity, administrative control, different types of adaptation and regulatory mechanisms to avoid maladaptation and gain cost-effectiveness.

No matter how interesting theory and theoretical discussions are, real world solutions are always more interesting, because there you are confronted with real world complexity. In the following, we will consider traditional firms within the poultry industry and from different countries on different continents to see how they have dealt with issues regarding vertical integration.

Based on the introduction and the theoretical discussion, combined with experiences from the US poultry industry reported in many articles and reports, there seems to be the general conclusion so far that the best way to arrange this industry is through vertically integrating the different levels of production. Transactions of input from one level to the next need to be stable. Quality of production on one level will be reflected in the quality of the next level, and in the production costs. There is a need to make transaction-specific investments and site-specific physical investments, which create a lock-in situation. Technological developments create some sort of insecurity especially for breeders who need some sort of security before investing. What seems to be a strong anticipation in the business (this will happen more in some countries than in others depending on cultural factors and negative feedback mechanisms), is that actors will behave opportunistic if the possibility arises, and thus the strong focus on developing strong performance-based production contracts.

Benchmark firms experience administrative challenges due to vertical integration. With the exception of chicken breeding processes, which are typically contracted, challenges are due to the hybrid governance structure. The extreme type of performance incentives used in the production contracts seem to tip in the direction of a market type of governance structure, whereas the asymmetrical power relationship tips in the direction of a hierarchical structure, where decisions can be made by the integrator. Adaptations clearly seem to be governed from the integrator, where they can use the contract with the breeders to require investment in new technology.

## 3.4 Case study

### 3.4.1 Contextual knowledge

In Chapter 1 we presented the five different firms used in our study, LAR in Brazil, KUPCO in Kuwait, Crysbro in Sri Lanka, Danpo in Denmark, and Ytterøy in Norway. These organizations are part of different cultural clusters, as they are defined by the Hofstede (1980, 2001) and in the GLOBE study (House, *et al.*, 2004). In the GLOBE study, social culture is defined as '*shared motives, values, beliefs, identities, and interpretation of meanings of significant events that result from common experiences of members of collectives and are transmitted across age generations*' (House, *et al.*, 2002: 5). In our study we build on an extended version of the cultural indicators presented by Hofstede, see Hofstede (1980; 2001). The indicators and the actual questions used in the study are the following:

1 Uncertainty avoidance – question used: Do you try to avoid uncertainty?
2 Power distance – question used: Do you expect and agree that power should be unequally shared?
3 Collectivism – question used: Do you encourage and reward collective distribution of resources and collective action?
4 Expressed opinions – question used: Do you express pride and loyalty in the firm where you work?
5 Gender egalitarianism – question used: Do you try to minimize roles between men and women?
6 Assertiveness – question used: Are you conferential in relationships with other people in the firm?
7 Future orientation – question used: Do you engage in future oriented behaviors such as planning and investing in the future?
8 Human orientation – question used: Do you encourage and reward individuals for being fair, generous, caring and kind to others?

The data we collected (see detailed table in Chapter 4) from the different companies is largely comparable with cultural descriptions made by others.

In the Brazilian company, we found medium to low power distance, a wish to avoid uncertainty, a strong focus on the collective, and a relatively strong future orientation. Dorfman, *et al.* (2004) describe the Latin American culture, which Brazil is part of, as a culture characterized by high power distance and low performance orientation, uncertainty avoidance, future orientation, and institutional collectivism.

In the Kuwaiti company, we found a medium to low effort to avoid uncertainty, a high power distance, a low score on equality between men and women, a medium focus on the collective, but a high focus on the future. Kabasakal and Bodur (2002) describe the Arab culture, which Kuwait is part of as a culture characterized by a high focus on in-group collectivism and high power distance. It is also a culture with a low score on future orientation and gender equality.

The cultural characteristics we found in the Sri Lankan company, was a culture with medium uncertainty avoidance, medium power distance, medium gender equality, and highly focused on the future, and on collectivism. The general description of the Southern Asian culture where we find Sri Lanka is that it is a culture characterized by high group collectivism, high power distance, humane orientation and low on gender egalitarianism (Gupta, *et al.*, 2002).

In our data from the Danish and the Norwegian company, there are great similarities between them; we find in both companies a strong focus on uncertainty avoidance, gender equality, future orientation and collectivism, and a small power distance. The Nordic culture described by Dorfman, *et al.* (2004) is a culture characterized by a moderate to strong practice in relation to uncertainty avoidance, future orientation, and gender equality. Practice is weaker compared to the collectivism, performance orientation, assertiveness and power distance.

The benchmark we use for our discussion on vertical integration is drawn from the US literature on poultry production. Looking at the Anglican culture we find that, 'overall, the Anglo cluster emphasizes performance' (Ashkanasy, *etal.*: 35). It is also a very individualistic culture.

Chapter 4 has a table where we can see the results of the cultural indicators from the firms in our study.

### *3.4.2 Empirical introduction*

The empirical results presented in this chapter are mainly collected through interviews with representatives from the different firms. Some of the data comes from firm documents, and some from production surveys we conducted in each firm. We have focused our efforts on how the firm did integrate the slaughter plant (including further processing) in the value chain. The main purpose of the interviews was a best possible understanding of the organization of the production process from the fertile egg to the market. We had three main groups of questions covering:

- Ownership of the means of production throughout the whole value chain
- The design of production contracts (contract with broiler breeders)
- The contract process (with the broiler breeders)

We interviewed in each firm several people in different managerial positions to get the overview and the in-depth information we needed and we repeated some of the questions when coming back one to two years later. The interview was semi-structured. The interview subjects were informed what the main purpose of the interview and the project was about. In our research team, we had people with local knowledge regarding societal and business culture for all firms. Together with their knowledge of the firms and with direct access to central people in the organizations, it was easier to build the necessary trust for the data collection. Gaining trust is important when you are going to ask questions about issues that firms consider as business secrets. In Norway, for instance the financial statements of firms are openly accessible, whereas in Kuwait and Sri Lanka, they are not, and they will normally be reluctant to provide this kind of private information to outsiders. Some sort of cultural sensitivity is therefore vital.

*Table 3.2* Summary of empirical data on vertical integration

| *Company* | *Bencmark (USA)* | *Danpo (Denmark)* | *LAR (Brazil )* | *KUPCO (Kuwait)* | *Crysbro (Sri Lanka)* | *Ytterøy (Norway)* |
|---|---|---|---|---|---|---|
| Vertical integration | *Most parts are vertically integrated, except broiler growing which is contract based.* | No integration. Everything is market and/or contract based. | Most parts are integrated, except broiler growing which is 100% based on contracts. | Total vertical integration. | From parent stock to distribution, except feed mill and 40% of the broiler growing (60% in-house). Plans for building their own feed mill. | No integration. Everything is market and/or contract based. |
| Vertical control | *Medium/strong*<br>*Breeders will be dependent on having a contract to finance investments. Few integrators and many breeders increase the control.* | Low/medium<br>Cultural attribute in the agribusiness to be part of a cooperative, so loyalty is normally strong | Medium/strong | Strong<br>Ownership<br>Cultural attribute towards keeping business within the 'family' | Strong<br>Collateral in farmer's property | Low/medium<br>Cultural attribute in the agribusiness to be part of a cooperative, so loyalty is normally strong |
| Domestic competitors on the export market | | 1 | 30 | (2 big firms, KUPCO and Naif.) | Mostly a producer for the local market. 4 big producers in Sri Lanka, including Crysbro. | (3 bigger firms in Norway. Only marginal export) |
| Percentage of total production | | 38,7% | 1,8% | 33% | 10,1% | 5,1% |
| Daily production of chickens | | 184.000 | 340.000 | 50.000 | 25.000 | 17.200 |
| Export | *USA is the world's largest producer and second largest exporter of chicken (about 18% of production)* | 50% | 40% | 0–5%.<br>Mostly a producer for the local market | Mostly a producer for the local market. | Mostly a producer for the national market. |

*(Continued)*

*Table 3.2* (Continued)

| *Company* | *Bencmark (USA)* | *Danpo (Denmark)* | *LAR (Brazil )* | *KUPCO (Kuwait)* | *Crysbro (Sri Lanka)* | *Ytterøy (Norway)* |
|---|---|---|---|---|---|---|
| Breeders (approx.) | | 80 | 400 | In-house | 300 | 22 |
| Competition for breeders | | Strong | Strong | No | Strong | Strong |
| Input | *Integrator provides birds, feed and medical assistance* | Breeder buying birds, feed and medical assistance | Integrator provides birds, feed and medical assistance | Integrator provides birds, feed and medical assistance | Integrator provides birds, feed and medical assistance | Breeder buying birds, feed and medical assistance |
| Risk – integrator | *All input* | Guaranteed-price | All input | All input and facilities | All input | Guaranteed-price |
| Risk – breeder | *Breeding facility* | All input and breeding facility | Breeding facility | | Breeding facility | All input and breeding facility |
| Production contracts | *Tournament contracts.*<br>*On average 13 years, but vary from flock to flock contracts, to long-term contracts.* | Guaranteed-price/ flat-fee<br>3–5 years (standard contracts) | Feed conversion contract<br>Ongoing (standard contracts) | In-house production | Guaranteed-price<br>Ongoing (standard contracts) | Guaranteed-price/ flat-fee<br>Ongoing (standard contracts) |
| Performance indicator/s | *Productivity formula:*<br>*Weight*<br>*Mortality*<br>*Feed conversion*<br>*Days of breeding* | Number of birds<br>(at target weight)<br>Also measuring:<br>Ammonia combustion<br>Broken wings and legs<br>Size of breast fillets | Productivity formula:<br>Weight<br>Mortality<br>Feed conversion<br>Days of breeding<br>Categorizing breeders in three productivity levels, which also determines level of payment | | Number of birds (at target weight)<br>Also measuring:<br>Feed conversion<br>Mortality | Number of birds (at target weight – two weight levels) |

| | | | | | | |
|---|---|---|---|---|---|---|
| Competition | *Tournaments.*<br>*Two-part cardinal-tournament contracts.* | No direct competition between breeders | No direct competition between breeders. But they are categorized. | | No direct competition between breeders. But they are categorized | No direct competition between breeders |
| Dialog | *Breeders separately* | With breeders and breeders' association | With breeders and breeders 'association' | Hierarchical | With breeders | With breeders and breeders 'association' |
| General contractual approach/relation | *Low trust*<br>*Debate on possible federal regulation on the contracts.* | Collective, trust based, developmental, helpful, but also controlling | Collective, trust based, developmental, helpful, but also controlling | | Collective, trust based, developmental, helpful, but also strongly controlling | Collective, trust based, developmental, helpful |
| Certifications | | BRC-standard<br>HACCP-system<br>Halal certification | ISO 9001<br>GlobalGAP CFM, GSFS, Mc Donald's certification<br>Halal certification | | ISO 9000, ISO 14001, ISO 22000, BRC-standard, HACCP-system<br>Halal certification | (BRC-standard)<br>HACCP-system<br>Halal certification |

Source: authors' data collection.

### *3.4.3 Vertical integration in the poultry industry*

Referring to Harrigan (1985), vertical integration is seen as a way to increase a firm's value-added margins. According to transaction cost theory, you should seek vertical integration if transaction-specific investments are made when there is high transaction frequency and when there is great uncertainty (e.g. regarding technological development or opportunistic behavior). We have seen that the poultry industry is a candidate for vertical integration. Our data displays variation in degree of vertical integration. The benchmark, drawn from the US-based research literature indicates vertical integration of the whole value chain except for the broiler growing which is contracted. The variations in our cases range from the fully integrated firm in Kuwait to a close to market-based structure in the Nordic countries, Norway and Denmark. The Brazilian firm matches the benchmark, whereas the Sri Lankan firm is close to becoming a totally integrated firm.

Here we will discuss two interesting elements from our cases regarding the governance structure:

- Contracting of the broiler growing
- The Nordic deviation from the main structure in the business

*The contractual issue*

Every partial element in the value chain is dependent on each other, and it becomes more and more critical for the business to make a profit in the long run as the production gets closer to the market and the consumers. Why then this risk of contracting the broiler growers? From the Kuwaiti and partially the Sri Lankan case we can observe that broiler growing is being done in-house, meaning the firm has its own broiler growing facilities. This hierarchical solution provides what Williamson (1971) states, a structural advantage and probably an easier access to control instruments, as this is a type of production where you need to be in control of the quality of the feed used, housing conditions, and medication of the chickens. If we look at Klein, *et al.* (1978), they claim that long-term contracts can be an alternative to vertical integration, especially if you are interested in curbing opportunism. Looking at the firms that prefer production contracts to in-house production, we find that the Brazilian, the Norwegian, and the Sri Lankan firm offer ongoing contracts, whereas the Danish firm offers three- to five-year contracts. Taking into account how both the Sri Lankan and the Brazilian firms follow-up on their contract growers with regular inspections, they seem to be in control as if production was in-house. In Sri Lanka the integrator has a collateral in the farmers' property, while in Brazil the integrator follows up closely on their farmers. The Norwegian case is somewhat special, since some of the farmers own shares in the integrating firm, thus they have a common interest in having a good and productive relationship. What also, in some way, forces the Norwegian firm and the breeders to have a close relationship, is that neither of them have alternative partners in close proximity. Another factor to consider in Norway is a strong regulation of production quotas, so a single breeder cannot have a bigger yearly production than 280,000 chickens (until January 2015 the quota was only 140,000 chickens). The strong regulation of chicken production makes it impossible to establish a system with in-house production, and thus the integrator is dependent on contract production. The Danish case is then the case that seemingly is more difficult to explain. But if we take a closer look at the Danish market, the explanations can be found in the market structure. Two integrators, Danpo and Rose, sharing the market approximately fifty-fifty, dominate the poultry market in Denmark. Even if there is strong competition between the integrators to secure a stable delivery of slaughter chickens, the breeders are also dependent on delivering chickens in order to pay off their investments on breeding facilities, so being opportunistic does not represent a healthy strategy for either of the parties. The length of the contract does not seem to be the important issue in the Danish case. For the integrators it is about securing a stable input, whereas for the farmers it is a question of being in the industry or not. Heavy investments in transaction-specific assets will force the farmers to be in the business and avoid opportunistic behavior.

### *A closer look at the Nordic cases*

In the Nordic cases we do not find much that imply vertical integration, instead we find close to market-based solutions. In the Norwegian case we find ongoing contracts between what is normally considered the integrator and the broiler breeding farmers, and in the Danish case they operate with three- to five-year contracts. Formally this kind of structure is called a hybrid structure since there is a contract between a principal and several agents, but we choose to use the term 'close to market-based', as from the outset there is 'apparently limited coordination between processing and primary producers' (Andersen, *et al.*, 2008: 115). What we experience is that there is some sort of trust in the traditional cooperative within agricultural production found in both Denmark and Norway. Our explanation of the relative stability of the production throughout the value chain is the strong cooperative mindset in the agribusiness in these countries (Chloupkova, *et al.* 2003; Gripsrud, *et al.*, 2001). It is suggested that identification, with for instance an agricultural cooperation, can generate trust and hence commitment (Puusa and Tolvanen, 2006). Karantininis (2007) elaborates on the cooperative system in Denmark, where we can find a cooperative network between farms, and then strong coordination or even a federated structure between different levels of the value chain. This way of organizing the business can to a certain extent substitute vertical integration. It is not a hierarchy, but the behavior and mental attitude seem to be hierarchical. Even if the mindset might be 'hierarchical' there are some important deviations; Ownership, profit and risk. First, in the cooperative network, you can of course find a bottom-up ownership, where farmers own a small share of different cooperative firms, but you will not find an integrated structure where e.g. the slaughter plant owns many chicken breeding farms. There is no ownership of the means of production called for in vertically integrated structures. Second, in the vertically integrated firm, you can aggregate the profit that in a market like system is spread among several firms. Third, in the market like system, risk is dispersed on many actors instead of accumulated in one single firm.

What we find in our cases, are factual, path dependent, differences regarding the question on vertical integration, but from a practical point of view, seen from the Nordic cases, it might not be considered a big difference. Implementing the Nordic model in e.g. Brazil, Kuwait or Sri Lanka, would probably not be an option. This would be impractical in Brazil because poultry production is a huge industry, with many integrators, in Kuwait and Sri Lanka, because of elements in the societal culture.

### *3.4.4 Incentive intensity and administrative command and control*

From the theory, we have seen that we can use different instruments to coordinate the production. In the market-based solution, you are expected to use economic incentives. In the hierarchical solution you have access to institutional and hierarchical authority.

In our cases, the Kuwait case is vertically integrated in such a way that they can govern the value chain from a common manager (we did several interviews with this manager), as displayed by Williamson (2009). What we experienced regarding the administrative command and control, was a total respect for decisions made at a higher level in the firm. The other actors interviewed were also balancing what kind of information could be revealed, and what could not. On higher levels, more information could be revealed than on lower levels, which indicates a strong loyalty to the firm and a great power distance. We saw this trend more clearly in Kuwait and Sri Lanka than in the other countries, which also is reflected in the data about firm culture. This can be explained by societal culture, but also from organizational behavior, where top executives often are freer to share information than employees on lower levels can.

The Sri Lankan case is close to being vertically integrated, as 60% of the chicken breeding is done as a part of the processing plant operations and only 40% contracted. The contracts are organized so that the integrator has collateral in the farmers' land, and where they withhold some of the payment to the farmers as some sort of security. Combined, all this is an expression of an extensive control regime with the farmers. The whole setup of the contract regime indicates a system very close to hierarchy. The arguments for the Sri Lankan regime is that the farmers that are contracted are poor, and the temptation to sell feed or chickens on the free market to get quick money is considered likely. In both the Kuwaiti and Sri Lankan case, there is no doubt that there is one common manager controlling all stages of the production. The hierarchy is very clear, and the impression we get from the interviews is that potential disputes will be solved by decisions from the common manager.

In the Brazilian case, the integrator provides chickens, feed and medical input to the breeders, and they have a detailed and complete system for measuring productivity where they focus on feed conversion, weight, mortality and days of breeding. They rank the breeders, where the best breeders get more payment because of the control system calculations, but they do not run any form of competition, as described in the US poultry production. Like the Sri Lankan case, the integrator has a structure where they follow-up on the broiler breeders very closely both with inspections on the production and providing guidance on how to improve. While not harsh, the regime (from the perspective of the US literature) can be described as necessary for contract follow-up on the integrators' assets (feed and chickens). The profit of the breeders is very much up to the breeder himself and the effort they put into the production. If they want a little better payment, they need to put in some extra effort to improve the feed conversion rate and reduce mortality.

In the Nordic cases, the farmers themselves provide chickens, feed and medical assistance, unlike the Sri Lankan and Brazilian cases. The production contracts are flat-fee contracts, where the total payment is based on how many kilos of chicken are being delivered. The incentives are different, as questions on efficiency are left with the breeders. The integrator will of course want to have the agreed upon size of the broiler chickens, but how the weight measures are reached is not included in any incentive scheme. If the breeders perform well, it is good for them, and if they perform poorly, it is their problem.

In none of our cases do we find production contracts that are remotely close to the tournament schemes we read about in the US literature. Especially in the Brazilian and the Nordic cases the contractual relation is treated more like a trustful partnership than a risky business contract. In Demark and Brazil, the scale of the poultry business makes it possible to set up contracts with stronger incentives. In a niche producer situation like Norway, a tournament scheme would not seem suitable. Establishing a system with stronger incentives would incur a stronger control regime in order for the integrator to follow-up on each farmer's performance. Danpo has made investments in a fully automatic system for calculating weight, classification and grading of chickens in the slaughtering process (see Chapter 5). For them, it would be easy to establish contracts with stronger incentives. The Brazilian firm is already grading their farmers, but has not introduced competition between the breeders. The question that must be answered before strengthening the incentives is what can be gained or lost by such a decision. Introducing strong incentives and competition in the Nordic cooperative production system will probably be a game-changer, where the risk-balance will be set in motion. Today broiler breeders take a huge economic risk, as they must finance the production facilities, chickens, the feed, the breeding process, and medical assistance. Some of this economic risk will need to be transferred to the integrator if the business is to be competitive, because it will probably not be sustainable for the integrator to pay the farmers to take all this risk. Having a system with weaker incentives, and a dialogue between integrator and breeders that is close to a hierarchical governance system, seems to be the better choice in all the cases we have been looking at.

### *3.4.5 Adaptability*

Cost-effectiveness and quality are important parameters in the poultry industry. We also know that different markets have different preferences regarding the chickens, e.g. preferred size of the chickens. There is also a focus both from consumers and authorities on the use of medicines, living conditions in the breeding process and how the industry is dealing with the slaughtering process. In vertically integrated systems, like in Kuwait and Sri Lanka, there is no doubt that the integrator should be responsible for developing all sides of the firm, all the processes.

In Sri Lanka the government operates with a price ceiling, where you as a producer can sell chicken at a price below the ceiling but not above. This is of course an incentive to make improvements throughout the value chain, including making improvements on the feed, so the production can become more cost effective. Sri Lanka does not in normal situations import chicken, but they have a limited export. Overall, it will be the competition between the different producers and the price ceiling that are the main incentives for improvement of the production process. Development of the firm was high on the agenda for the CEO, as he wanted to secure the quality of the end product by gaining better control of the quality of the feed they used. To gain necessary control, the firm will build their own feed mill, and seek to establish contracts with farmers producing input to the feed production.

Kuwait has a system where both consumers and the industry are being subsidized by the government. The poultry producers are subsidized when purchasing ingredients for chicken feed on the world market. We know that Kuwait is dependent on the import of chicken meat, so there is an exposure to world market prices. We also know that Kuwaiti poultry producers export a small part of their production. What kind of effect the government subsidy has is difficult to know, except from the direct effect on the consumers. For the producers, there might be the effect that the subsidy conceals an inefficient production, or it might be that it increases the profit for the owners. Which way is difficult to discern, this discussion is also taken up in Chapter 2. The Kuwaiti producer has an additional challenge that we do not find in the other cases, and that is the demand for live chicken on the Kuwait market. About 20% of the production is sold as live chicken in various market places in and around Kuwait City.

Brazilian firms have a structure similar to what is described in the US literature as bulk producers. To be able to deal with approximately 340,000 chickens a day everything needs to be streamlined. The contract and the contractual dialogue between the integrator and the breeders make it possible for the integrator to act almost like a 'common boss' when dealing with different kinds of challenges. For a business that exports about 40%, (the export share will probably increase) of their production to the world market there is of course a challenge to be competitive. Even if we consider our case firm as a big operation, it only has about 2% of the Brazilian production of chicken, and competes with about thirty Brazilian firms on the export market and many more on the domestic market. This means they must be in control of the whole value chain, and cannot tolerate major disruptions.

Looking at the Nordic cases, they are similar regarding the vertical structure, but they differ when we start looking at the level of production and international orientation. The smaller Norwegian firm is a niche producer focused on the domestic market, while the bigger Danish firms are exporting about 50% of their production to countries inside the European Union. Both firms must be competitive to survive. The Danish firm needs to be competitive in the national market and inside the EU market system regulations while the Norwegian firm upholds a position as a niche producer on the Norwegian market. For both firms, having a governance structure close to a market-based solution means there is no 'common boss', and firms at each level of production will be looking at themselves. Being in a cooperative or federated system with strong coordination might substitute for control. It is probable that adaptation processes will be slower because of the separate decision-making processes of different firms and because there might be some game playing between the actors about who should make the first move and who should incur the most costs in the adaptation process.

### 3.4.6 Contract law

Transaction cost theory urges us to look at differences that come from the choice of governance structure. If we look at e.g. dispute resolution, there will be differences in a vertically integrated firm compared to a contract based solution. In our research, we are making comparisons not only on the choice of vertical integration, but also between firms in different countries. We could of course compare legal systems, but our interest has been business practice. How do firms handle their contracts and contract partners? From the US literature, we have seen that integrators would not hesitate to implement rather harsh contracts onto their suppliers of chickens. Discussions about the tournament contracts in the poultry industry in US imply that the integrators are operating on the edge of what is acceptable, perhaps not legally but morally.

We have stated that the Kuwait firm in our case study is vertically integrated, and thus they can deal with disputes between successive stages by private ordering. In all other cases, contracts are involved. We have already dealt with the incentive part of the contracts, so we will not go into that.

From the case summary, we can see that the contractual relations are described as collective, trust based, developmental, helpful, and to a various degree controlling. If we look at differences in the four cases using production contracts, there seems to be greater trust between the parties in the Brazilian, Danish and Norwegian context, than in the Sri Lankan context. In Sri Lanka, the integrator conducts very serious investigation before offering a breeding contract to a farmer, which includes interviewing neighbors. Then, when the contract is offered the integrator also take collateral. After such a process, the integrator can claim there is a trustful relationship. Doing a thorough survey of a contractual partner should be the norm. Claiming collateral could also be looked at as part of business where big money is at stake. In our case, we are talking about relatively small money for the integrator, but from their point of view this is a necessity. We can interpret this as the normal contractual climate.

Both in Norway and Denmark financial collateral is a legal instrument that can be used. What we can see from our cases is more the opposite, where integrators offer a guarantee to their breeders, otherwise the farmers would hesitate to take the level of risk this type of production involves. Even if the contract law regime might allow the integration firms in the Nordic countries to take the same measures as in Sri Lanka, there is a different type of contractual climate in this business now. From a dispute resolution point of view, potential disputes most probably will be solved outside the court. In our Brazilian case, we can see that the contracts have a clause saying that disputes are to be solved within the regional court system. What we learn through our interviews is that differences are solved through dialogue.

### *3.4.7 Contextualizing cultural features*

When you have the chance to do research on firms in different parts of the world, it is of course interesting to include cultural features in the process. Particularly it is of interest to include culture when we are dealing with new institutional economic theory like transaction cost theory where cultural features are filtered out of the theory. In this study, we wanted to see if and how societal culture affects processes within the organizations. In a competitive environment, like the poultry industry, we instinctively thought that several of the cultural features would have an impact on the ways things are being carried out in the different organizations, e.g. the communication processes, choice of performance incentives, and organizational choices. We do not have direct measures for all the things the analysis found that could merit a closer look (e.g. organizational choice or degree of vertical integration) but we do have some measures that can help give us an indication of cultural influences.

In an analysis of vertical integration, which is the focus in this chapter, we know that parameters like transaction frequency, level of transaction-specific investments, and uncertainty should be reflected upon. In the previous discussion, we have seen that asset specificity is the most important dimension. Specific investments generate long-term bilateral exchange relations, where a lock-in situation, based on the relative power of the contracting partners, can be an outcome. If the theory of vertical integration was within the domain of neoclassical economics, we could just solve the equation to find the optimal solution. Since we do not operate within the domain of instrumental rationality, but within institutional theory, we need to take into consideration the complexity of human behavior. In particular, North (1990) urges us to consider human motivation and how we interpret our environment: It might not be that we always seek maximum utility, but behave altruistically. Then, existing mental models help shape our understanding of our environment. This brings norms, values and belief systems, close to the equation. The challenge though is that internalized norms and values, and institutionalized behavior, might not be visible to us, in the same way as e.g. asset specificity.

Based on the previous argument, it is of great interest to have a closer look at cultural variables, when we are discussing decision situations like vertical integration. In our data, power distance stands out as a significant variable. Power distance measures the expectancy of unequal distribution of power. This again, gives us an idea about distribution of authority in organizations, and how people respond to both power and authority.

In Table 3.3, we display the cultural differences from the GLOBE study regarding power distance, concerning the cases included in our study.

We can see that the Nordic countries stand out from the other cultural regions with a low power distance, while the rest of the regions are in the mid-score clusters. We included the Anglo cultural cluster, where the USA is one of the countries, as we have been using the USA as a benchmark in the discussion about vertical integration. We should also mention that there are variances within the established cultural clusters, so the table displayed gives a little rougher picture than if we went into detail.

We collected our data from the firm in the value chain that is normally seen as the integrator, the firm making the decision on the degree of vertical integration. We do have data from people at the assembly line and support levels (including middle management), but we do not have the same statistical data for top management. Data that reflects top management levels would be of interest because CEOs or the board of directors most probably makes decisions about vertical integration. Our findings, displayed in Table 3.4, correspond with the findings in the GLOBE study with one exception. In our data, Kuwait is an outlier, as explained below.

Table 3.4 is based on the question asking if the respondent agrees with the statement that power should be unequally shared. The answers are based on a

*Table 3.3* Cultural clusters (adapted from Gupta and Hanges, 2004: 193)

| *Cultural dimension* | *High score clusters* | *Mid-score clusters* | *Low score clusters* |
|---|---|---|---|
| Power distance | | Southern Asia | Nordic Europe |
| | | Latin America | |
| | | Middle East | |
| | | Anglo (including USA) | |

*Table 3.4* Cultural construct

| | *Power unequal* |
|---|---|
| Danpo N = 39 | 1.64 |
| LAR N = 266 | 2.58 |
| Ytterøy N = 30 | 1.67 |
| Crysbro N = 40 | 3.19 |
| KUPCO N = 33 | 4.24 |

Source: authors' data collection.

N: number of observations.

five-point Likert scale where one is completely disagree and five is completely agree. Lower numbers mean a small power distance. We got the expected results that the power distance in Scandinavian countries is very low. Brazil is in the middle range, and Sri Lanka is in the upper part of the middle range. Kuwait is clearly in high score range in our data. The explanations for this we find in Chapters 2 and 4 where it is stated that the workers at the Kuwait firm come mainly from Asian countries (like India and Sri Lanka) and work on time-limited contracts. The work processes are strongly routinized with a lower level of communicative activities than in the other firms.

The question then, is if culture has any effect on decisions about vertical integration. It is of course difficult to have a very clear answer to that question, without having a more direct measure to that particular relation. What we can say is based on our findings on both the survey and the interviews we conducted. There are differences regarding the power distance variable, and the different levels match the different levels of vertical integration. The three firms that are most integrated are actively seeking integration to gain more control over the production to secure their position, whilst the focus in the Nordic cases is on improving productivity at the slaughtering plant, and securing stable deliverance of chickens for slaughter. Further integration does not seem to be on the agenda. If the need to be in control and command of the total production stream exists (and hence the value chain), cultural propensity might be a variable alongside economic variables to be considered when assessing vertical integration.

### *3.4.8 Vertical integration in practice*

Through theory and empirical findings, we have laid the foundation for a discussion of vertical integration and management of input to production. The overall challenge for a firm would normally be long-term survival. To survive means the firm has to be competitive. For all our case firms they have to be competitive on the domestic market. If poultry meat is imported, world market prices will be implemented on the domestic market, unless import barriers or subsidies are used to protect domestic production. If the firm relies heavily on export, they need to be competitive on the world market. A discussion about vertical integration and managerial challenges following the choice of governance structure is not confined by the size of the market, national, regional or world market.

Perry (1989) states that vertical integration can be initiated by technological economies, transactional economies or market imperfections. In the poultry industry the main approach is the transaction cost approach. We can look at this from two points of departure, a cost reduction point of departure, which is the main approach in transaction cost theory, and a marginal value-added point of departure, like Harrigan (1985) does. Which way it is might depend on your position in the value chain. From an integrator's perspective it most probably is both cost reduction and value-add, but if you are at an earlier stage in the production it most probably boils down to cost reduction. In the research literature on the poultry industry, we can see that they want to prevent disruptions in the production, being in control of the quality of the end product, and of course try to be in control of the costs. From a transaction cost point of view, we can argue that disruptions at any level of the production will increase transaction costs, and so will poor quality.

What do we find in our cases when we look at the total value chain? We find that there are big variations concerning the question of vertical integration. We find one firm in Kuwait that is totally integrated, one in Sri Lanka very close to being totally integrated, one in Brazil that matches the benchmark in the business, where every level of production, except broiler growing is integrated, and two firms in the Nordic countries that have a structure close to the market solution described in transaction cost theory. Can we explain this from a transaction cost theory approach? We can of course conduct analysis based on transaction cost theory, but to fully understand the findings we need to have contextual understanding – what kind of path dependency are in motion.

In order to keep business going, there is a constant need for input at every level of the value chain. There can of course be some variation on the volume of input, depending on the market situation. From a general point of view, when we look at statistics (from FAOSTAT, EUROSTAT, or USDA) we are talking about a food production business that has been growing for the last few decades. When the industry is growing, it will create pressure on every level in the value chain, to deliver enough input to the next level, so that market demand in the end can be met. Having stable access to input is crucial. As the market also is demanding high and stable quality, there will be a pressure for stable input of high quality in the value chain. If the industry is in growth, we can make an argument as follows: if you are on the high end of the value chain, dependency on previous stages in the value chain is higher than if you are on the lower end. If you are on the lower end of the value chain, there can be some room to manoeuvre if there is an excess demand. If the market stagnates or declines, the situation between the different levels of the value chain alters. The dependency from the lower end towards the higher end in the value chain will increase. If we look at transaction frequency in the poultry industry, a growing industry, firms on the high end of the value chain should seek vertical integration to secure stability and the possibility to grow. In Kuwait, Sri Lanka, and Brazil we can use the logic we have displayed to say, this is the reason for their choice of governance structure. For the Nordic countries, the logic does not fit, even if the market for poultry meat has been growing together with the income level more in general.

What about asset specificity? Can transaction-specific investments explain the differences in choice of governance structure in our cases? We know from the literature, and from our own research that the chicken breeders have to invest in specialized breeding facilities in order to optimize the breeding process. These investments are done in close geographic proximity with the slaughtering plant. The specificity of these investments creates a dependency towards the poultry business. If there is just one slaughtering plant in close proximity, it also creates dependency towards a specific integrator. The dependency towards the business can of course be tolerable if it is a relatively stable market situation and the income and the length of the contract is at a level where the investment is profitable. The US-based literature pictures contracts between integrator and chicken breeder from about forty days up to fifteen years (MacDonald, 2008). It is obvious that a farmer will need more than forty days to capitalize on an investment in breeding facilities, even fifteen years seems like a short span of time if there is a need to make regular upgrades on the facilities. In our cases, Sri Lanka, Brazil and Norway are operating with ongoing contracts, while in the Danish case three- to five-year contracts are used. Three to five year contracts may provide some stability for the breeders, especially for those who are not on the lower end of the productivity and quality scale.

When we look at the arguments used, we are saying that the asset specific investments are made by the chicken breeder, and this is important. When we are making analysis on vertical integration, we have to be clear on who is doing the asset specific investments, and who is seeking integration. In our cases, the integrator is the slaughtering plant. The chicken breeder might want to be part of an integrated structure to secure their investments, but as long as there is a relatively easy access to breeders, the integrator does not have to initiate an integration. When breeders are making investments that tie them to the business, it creates a situation where the integrator has the upper hand. If the competition on input between different integrators was really tough, they might seek integration. Even if integrators in our research claim that competition is strong between contracting breeders, there is room for tougher competition. In Sri Lanka, the integrator has integrated some of the broiler breeding capacity, so the competition for input (chickens) might be harder there than in Brazil and the Nordic countries. The Kuwait case can be argued to fit the transaction cost model of explanation.

The last element to consider in the discussion on vertical integration is uncertainty. Elements mentioned are incidents, consumer behavior, technological development, and behavior of actors involved in a transaction. We have seen that the poultry business is very much concerned with the quality of the products they bring to the market. Further, there are technological developments regarding production facilities. We have also seen from our cases that there is a concern about the behavior of the breeders, both an anticipated lack of effort (general) and a potentially more direct opportunism (Sri Lanka). To provide good quality products, the integrators need to be in control of the production, which means they also need to establish some control of the behavior of involved actors. We can see that integrators use both incentives and control measures, where some of the incentives and control measures might be considered strong and some weaker. Vertical integration here implies stronger control than a market solution. Except for the Kuwait case, we find that the rest of the integrators use some form of production contracts with their breeders to secure quality inputs to production. In all cases, the incentives are relatively weak compared to the incentives we can read about in the US-based literature, but in both Brazil, and especially in Sri Lanka, we find strong control regimes. In the Nordic cases both incentives and control regimes seem weak. Strong incentives and strong control regimes might imply a lower level of trust in actors, and thus greater uncertainty. Weaker incentives and control regimes would imply higher levels of trust and a lower level of uncertainty. When we can observe that there is a great span in the strength of incentives and control regimes in use, we can speculate on where the tipping point is concerning the discussion on vertical integration. How much uncertainty is tolerable for the integrator, before they seek integration? Transaction cost theory does not provide a clear-cut answer to the question on uncertainty. Theory on societal culture provides some help, as analysis shows that different societal cultures have different levels of tolerance towards uncertainty (Sully de Luque and Javidan, 2004). In our cases, the Nordic countries can tolerate a great deal of uncertainty, while in the Latin American cultures, the Arab cultures, and finally the South Asian cultures there is considerably less tolerance for uncertainty.

### *3.4.9 Managerial challenges in practice*

Transaction cost theory is very specific about attributes derived from different governance structures: incentive intensity, administrative command and control, approach to questions on adaptation and use of contract law to regulate disputes. In our research, we did find situations in the firms operating within all three of the governance structures described by Williamson (1991). The findings give us a good idea on how the value chain is operated. From the literature, the best practice in the poultry industry is to organize in a way that promotes vertical control throughout the value chain. Thus, vertical integration is high on the agenda, including all levels of production except the broiler growing, which is contracted. Production contracts with the breeders, including strong incentives and tournament contracts, are the benchmark. The overall challenge regarding both governance structure and managerial efforts is to promote a competitive firm.

Incentives and administrative control has to do with establishing a system where production is managed in the direction decided by the principal. In three of our cases, Kuwait, Sri Lanka and Brazil, we found integrators with a strong and direct vertical control, while the two Nordic cases seemed to have some kind of vertical control, but a more indirect type of control stemming from the cooperative system of agribusiness in their countries. Then we can ask what kind of system is the best. The best answer might be that it depends on factors like functioning of institutions, market organization, societal culture and level of education.

Hierarchical control might be the most common and most acceptable solution in Kuwait, due to their culture. The very tight control as in the Sri Lankan case might be the only sound solution for them due to the business climate where trust is low. Developing a relationship, as a kind of an in-group relationship, was observed in Brazil. Development of the firm depends on the capability of breeders in addition to pecuniary incentives. As for the two Nordic cases, incentives are rather weak, and the governance of the relationship between the actors in the business seems to be based on a trust in the cooperative way of dealing with agribusiness. Except for the Nordic cases, the integrator is the principal who leads the way for the respective firm. In the Nordic cases, and especially in the Norwegian case, it seemed to be more of a mutual understanding between the actors of the development of the production, than a dominant principal leading the way.

Approaching the analysis from a transaction cost theoretical perspective creates a situation where three of the cases, Kuwait, Sri Lanka, and Brazil, are easily understood, as coordination is done within the firms. It is clear who the principal in the structure is. In the Nordic cases, we can of course say that there is a principal and agents, based on the contractual relationship, but the overall coordination is not in the hand of the principal; it is left with the cooperative as an institutionalized way of doing business in the agricultural sector. We have not been dealing with the cooperative system of agribusiness in our research, but it would be of interest to know how this system affects the development of a single firm, if it promotes or inhibits the chances to develop competitiveness. In the Danish case we have seen that the integrator has installed a system where they measure the quality of every chicken that is being slaughtered. If, or when, the integrator decides to fully implement this system (today they operate a mild version) as a way to rank broiler growers combined with differentiation in payment, they will most probably alter the game. It will both challenge the cooperative as an institution and the cooperation between farmers when terms for breeding broiler chickens are negotiated. Whether such a change will have a positive or negative effect on the business is difficult to speculate about, and that might be the reason why the integrator has not yet decided to take full advantage of the system they have installed.

Norwegian agribusiness is protected small-scale production. Protected by import barriers and kept small through a politically decided quota-system. You most probably will need a radical political shift before we can see a development in how the game is played. It is difficult to have a clear opinion on the effect a more liberal agricultural policy will have on the way the poultry industry is run in Norway. If it leads to increased competition, it will have an effect on how the managerial challenges are dealt with. The integrator will have to become more visible as a principal. Perhaps the measures used to develop the strategic position for the firm will have to become stronger than are currently.

What about the managerial challenges in relation to adaptation processes? In the cases where the integrator stands out as the principal, they are the ones initiating and driving the developmental process in the firm, including the contracted broiler breeders. From the US literature, we could see the integrators using the contracts with the breeders to 'force' through adaptations to new technology. In the hierarchy, the manager will make decisions about developing the value chain, as we could see in Kuwait where a new up-to-date slaughtering plant was planned in order to increase the production capacity and improve competitiveness. The same thing occurred in Sri Lanka, where a new feed mill was planned.

In Brazil the integrator worked together with the breeders to increase their capabilities in order to increase both efficiency and quality. In Denmark the quality of the input (broiler chickens) could be observed by the integrator, thus they knew which farmers were doing well and not so well. Taking the next step, making use of this knowledge to help develop the capabilities of the breeders, was under debate. Our reflection is that the cooperative as an institution is a mental barrier in the developmental process. In the Norwegian case the integrator does not have the same technological system to help them in monitoring the quality of the incoming broiler chickens, but the operation is much smaller than the Danish one, so they can make use of ordinary human (visual) inspections. When it comes to the question of driving the developmental process, the integrator will face the same challenges as in Denmark. Each actor is a sovereign decision maker. With a market-like governance structure, this is also how it should work according to theory, but the contract between integrators and broiler breeders opens a discussion between the contractual partners on future development.

The last of the attributes that distinguishes different governance structures is contract law. Legislation can help with structure in relation to how conflicts between different parties can be resolved, while it also can set limits on what can be allowed in a relationship. In a contractual relationship the contract partners often agree upon how to resolve disputes, where taking a conflict to court often is the last solution. Introducing lawyers in a dispute may harm the relationship between contractual partners, depending on what kind of traditions there are regarding dispute resolution. In the poultry industry, and more specifically in our cases we are talking about relationships between integrators and breeders that are supposed to be long-term. What we learned was that potential conflicts in contractual relationships were resolved in the same way that disagreements would be resolved within a hierarchy. The approach to dispute resolution will in many ways reflect the true relationship between different levels of the value chain. In a long-term relationship where there is a mutual dependency combined with a power imbalance in favor of the integrator, you most probably will find a hierarchical approach to dispute resolution. When theory indicates that contract law is strong in a market-based governance structure, semi-strong in a hybrid structure, our experience is that you will have to look at the real structure of the relationship: dependency, duration and power balance. In the poultry industry as it has been displayed through our cases, the interdependency between different levels of the value chain is high. Asset specific investments made by broiler growers will strengthen their dependency on staying in the industry, and sticking with 'their' integrator, due to geography. In an industry, that experiences growth in demand, and competition on input, long-lasting relationships are sought. Finally, there will be a power imbalance in favor of the integrators as the access to financial and human resources will be in their favor.

### *3.4.10 The cultural influence*

From the analysis of the cultural variables, we found that power distance is a cultural feature we should be particularly aware of, as it affects several of the production variables in our study (more about this in Chapter 4). In a discussion about vertical integration, which we are dealing with in this chapter, we would argue that power distance, as an indicator of the hierarchical relation between people, would have an influence on decisions about vertical integration, alongside the economic variables. We would argue that high power distance, as a cultural value, will support a choice for a more rigid hierarchical structure, and low power distance will support a more flexible approach to the question on structure. Our arguments are not by any means new. Institutional theorists support our claim that societal culture will be reflected in organizations. In more general terms, Scott (2014) writes that 'organizations are deeply embedded in institutional contexts. A given organization is supported and constrained by institutional forces' (p. 104). Meyer and Rowan (1977) are more specific when they argue 'the formal structures of many organizations in postindustrial society dramatically reflect the myths of their institutional environments instead of the demands of their work activities' (p. 341). More recently, the GLOBE study argues that 'in general, organizations tend to mirror the culture of power distance practices and values in their society so they can gain legitimacy and also appeal to the people from their host societies' (Carl, *et al.*, 2004: 534). More specifically, findings in the GLOBE study support an argument that 'societal power distance practices have a significant and strong positive relationship with organizational power distance practices' (p. 543). Our findings strengthen the argument that path dependency has to be taken into account when analyzing managerial decisions made in organizations.

## 3.5 Concluding remarks

Our main interest in this chapter has been to shed light on the question of vertical integration and the management of production input in traditional firms. In a business where vertical integration and vertical control are the benchmarks, it has been interesting to experience firms in the same industry making very different choices. We have seen choices of formal governance structures stretching from hierarchy to market-like structures. Explaining the variance through the lenses of transaction cost theory is not straightforward, as you need to have an understanding of some of the parameters that are left out of the theoretical model, e.g. parameters found within the societal culture and different institutional set ups. You can of course say that 'yes, the Kuwaiti way of organizing poultry production fits both anticipations within transaction cost theory and best practice in this particular business,' and leave it there. The same goes with both the Brazilian and Sri Lankan cases, but the two Nordic cases do not fit best practice or the theoretical model too well. All of our cases seem to be situations with a stable production and do not have to worry too much about the logistics of input.

Lessons learned from this study is that transaction cost theory is a tool that will help you to focus on specific elements when you prepare for fieldwork, like asset specificity, uncertainty, frequency and managerial challenges in connection to different modes of governance. When analyzing data in order to reach an understanding about what is really going on, transaction cost theory (TCT) will of course be helpful, but to reach a greater understanding you will need to expand your toolbox to include some of the elements deliberately left out of TCT. Through the lenses of TCT it is easy to start looking for signs of formal governance structures, which can of course be found. When things are going well despite what seems to be explainable from your basic theoretical model, you can treat some cases as abnormalities, or you can search for an explanation. When cultural theory was brought in as a way to contextualize our study, we could see that societal culture might explain what we thought of as abnormalities. Culture might help create something we can call informal hierarchies, which works almost the same way as the formal hierarchical governance structure.

Best practice might not be universal. The US way of organizing poultry production is said to be the best way; vertical integration and especially the use of harsh tournament schemes in the production contracts might lead you into an understanding of an almost inhumane business. Our findings indicate variance on both the question of integration and the layout of production contracts. In hindsight, a thorough analysis of the benchmark would have been appropriate. Through our analysis of our specific cases, where we are certain that societal culture is of importance when explaining the choice of governance structure, and also what we call 'best practice' is embedded in a specific culture that needs to be explicitly explained.

## References


Andersen, R. K., Skinnarland, S., & Tveterås, R. (2008). *Fra bonde til butikk: En studie av verdikjeder i kjøttbransjen*. Fafo-rapport 2008:19. Oslo: Fafo.

Ashkanasy, N. M., Trevor-Roberts, E., & Earnshaw, L. (2002). The Anglo cluster. Legacy of the British empire. *Journal of World Business, 37*, 28–39.

Balakrishnan, S., & Wernerfelt, B. (1986). Technical change, competition and vertical integration. *Strategic Management Journal*, 7(4), 347–359.

Carl, D., Gupta, V., & Javidan, M. (2004). Power distance. In R. House et al. (Eds.), *Culture, leadership, and organizations* (pp. 513–563). London: SAGE Publications.

Chloupkova, J., Svendsen, H. L. H., & Svendsen, G. T. (2003). Building and destroying social capital: The case of cooperative movements in Denmark and Poland. *Agriculture and Human Values, 20*, 241–252.

Coase, R. H. (1937). The nature of the firm. *Economica, New Series, 4*(16), 386–405.

Das, T. K. (2004). Time-span and risk of partner opportunism in strategic alliances. *Journal of Managerial Psychology, 19*(8), 744–759.

Dorfman, P. W., Hanges, P. J., & Brodbeck, F. C. (2004). The identification of culturally endorsed leadership profiles. In R. House et al. (Eds.), *Culture, leadership, and organizations* (pp. 669–719). London: SAGE Publications.

Dubois, P., & Vukina, T. (2009). Optimal incentives under moral hazard and heterogeneous agents: Evidence from production contracts data. *International Journal of Industrial Organization, 27*, 489–500.

Geyskens, I., Steenkamp, J.-B. E. M., & Kumar, N. (2006). Make, buy, or ally: A transaction cost theory meta-analysis. *Academy of Management Journal, 49*(3), 519–543.

Gilson, R. J., Sabel, C. F., & Scott, R. E. (2009). Contracting for innovation: Vertical disintegration and interfirm collaboration. *Columbia Law Review, 109*(3), 431–502.

Gripsrud, G., Lenvik, G. H., & Olsen, N. V. (2001). Influence activities in agricultural cooperatives: The impact of heterogeneity. In S. O. Borgen (Ed.), *The food sector in transition – Nordic research.* NILF report 2001:2. Oslo: Norwegian Agricultural Economics Research Institute.

Grossman, S. J., & Hart, O. D. (1986). The cost and benefits of ownership: A theory of vertical and lateral integration. *Journal of Political Economy, 94*(4), 691–719.

Gupta, V., & Hanges, P. J. (2004). Regional and climate clustering of societal cultures. In R. House et al. (Eds.), *Culture, leadership, and organization* (pp. 178–218). London: SAGE Publications.

Gupta, V., Surie, G., Javidan, M., & Chhokar, J. (2002). Southern Asia cluster: Where the old meets the new? *Journal of World Business, 37*, 16–27.

Harrigan, K. R. (1985). Vertical integration and corporate strategy. *Academy of Management Journal, 28*(2), 397–425.

Hennessy, D. A. (1996). Information asymmetry as a reason for food industry vertical integration. *American Journal of Agricultural Economy, 78*(4), 1034–1043.

Henry, R., & Rothwell, G. (1995). *The world poultry industry.* IFC Global agribusiness series, Washington, DC: World Bank.

Hofstede, G. H. (1980). Culture and organizations. *International Studies of Management & Organization, 10*(4), 15–41.

Hofstede, G. H., & Hofstede, G. (2001). *Culture's consequences: Comparing values, behaviors, institutions and organizations across nations.* Boston, MA: SAGE Publications.

House, R. J., Hanges, P. J., Javidan, M., Dorfman, P. W., & Gupta, V. (Eds.). (2004). *Culture, leadership and organizations: The GLOBE study of 62 societies.* London: SAGE Publications.

House, R. J., Mansour, J., Hanges, P., & Dorfman, P. (2002). Understanding cultures and implicit leadership theories across the globe: An introduction to project GLOBE. *Journal of World Business, 37*(1), 3–10.

James Jr., H. S., Hendrickson, M. K., & Howard, P. H. (2013). Networks, power and dependency in the agrifood industry. In J. Harvey (Ed.), *The ethics and economics of agrifood competition* (pp. 99–126). Dordrecht: Springer.

Joskow, P. L. (1985). Vertical integration and long-term contracts: The case of coal-burning electric generating plants. *Journal of Law, Economics & Organization, 1*(1), 33–80.

Joskow, P. L. (2005). Vertical integration. In C. Menard & M. M. Shirley (Eds.), *Handbook of new institutional economics* (pp. 319–348). Dordrecht: Springer.

Kabasakal, H., & Bodur, M. (2002). Arabic cluster: A bridge between East and West. *Journal of World Business, 37*(1), 40–54.

Karantininis, K. (2007). The network form of cooperative organizations. In K. Karantininis & J. Nilsson (Eds.), *Vertical markets and cooperative hierarchies: The role of cooperatives in the Agri-food industry* (pp. 19–34). Dordrecht: Springer.

Klein, B., Crawford, R. G., & Alchian, A. A. (1978). Vertical integration, appropriable rents, and the competitive contracting process. *Journal of Law and Economics, 21*(2), 297–326.

Langlois, R. N., & Foss, N. J. (1999). Capabilities and governance the rebirth of production in the theory of economic organization. *Kyklos, 52*(2), 201–218.

Leegomonchai, P., & Vukina, T. (2005). Dynamic incentives and agent discrimination in broiler production tournaments. *Journal of Economics & Management Strategy, 14*(4), 849–877.

MacDonald, J. M. (2008). *The economic organization of U.S. broiler production.* USDA, Economic Information Bulletin, No. 38.

MacDonald, J. M., & Corb, P. (2011). *Agricultural contracting update: Contracts in 2008*. U.S. Department of Agriculture, Economic Research Service. Economic Information Bulletin No. 72. February.

MacDonald, J. M., Perry, J., Ahearn, M., Banker, D., Chambers, W., Dimitri, C., Key, N., Nelson, K., & Southard, L. (2004). *Contracts, markets, and prices: Organizing the production and use of agricultural commodities*. United States Department of Agriculture (USDA), Agricultural Economic Report Number 837.

Martinez, S. W. (2002). *Vertical coordination of marketing systems: Lessons from the poultry, egg, and pork industries*. USDA, Agricultural Economic Report No. 807.

Meyer, J. W., & Rowan, B. (1977). Institutionalized organizations: Formal structure as myth and ceremony. *American Journal of Sociology*, *83*(2), 340–363.

Milgrom, P., & Roberts, J. (1992). *Economics, organization and management*. Englewood Cliffs, NJ: Prentice Hall.

North, D. C. (1990). *Institutions, institutional change and economic performance*. Cambridge: Cambridge University Press.

Perry, M. K. (1989). Vertical integration: Determinants and effects. In R. Schmalensee & R. D. Willig (Eds.), *Handbook of industrial organization* (pp. 183–255). Amsterdam: North-Holland.

Porter, M. E. (1985). *Competitive advantage: Creating and sustaining superior performance*. New York: Free Press.

Puusa, A., & Tolvanen, U. (2006). Organizational identity and trust. *Electronic Journal of Business Ethics and Organization Studies*, *11*(2), 29–33.

Scott, W. R. (2014). *Institutions and organizations: Ideas, interests, and identities*. London: SAGE Publications.

Sully de Luque, M., & Javidan, M. (2004). Uncertainty avoidance. In House et al. (Eds.), *Culture, leadership, and organizations* (pp. 602–653). London: SAGE Publications.

Tsoulouhas, T. (1999). Do tournaments solve two-sided moral hazard problems? *Journal of Economic Behavior & Organization*, *40*, 275–294.

United Nations Food and Agriculture Organization (FAO). FAOSTAT. (2017). Retrieved from www.fao.org/faostat/en/

Vukina, T. (2001). Vertical integration and contracting in the U.S. poultry sector. *Journal of Food Distribution Research*, *32*(2), 29–38.

Vukina, T. and Zheng, X. (2007). Structural estimation of rank-order tournament games with private information. *American Journal of Agricultural Economics*, *89*, 651–664.

Williamson, O. E. (1971). The vertical integration of production: Market failure considerations. *The American Economic Review*, *61*(2), 112–123.

Williamson, O. E. (1975). *Markets and hierarchies: Analysis and antitrust implications*. New York: The Free Press.

Williamson, O. E. (1979). Transaction-cost economics: The governance of contractual relations. *Journal of Law and Economics*, *22*(2), 233–261.

Williamson, O. E. (1981). The economics of organization: The transaction cost approach. *The American Journal of Sociology*, *87*(3), 548–577.

Williamson, O. E. (1985). *The economic institutions of capitalism*. New York: The Free Press.

Williamson, O. E. (1991). Comparative economic organization: The analysis of discrete structural alternatives. *Administrative Science Quarterly*, *36*(2), 269–296.

Williamson, O. E. (1996). *The mechanisms of governance*. Oxford: Oxford University Press.

Williamson, O. E. (1998). Transaction cost economics: How it works; where it is headed. *De Economist*, *146*(1), 23–58.

Williamson, O. E. (2002). The theory of the firm as a governance structure: From choice to contract. *The Journal of Economic Perspectives*, *16*(3), 171–195.

Williamson, O. E. (2009). *Transaction cost economics: The natural progression.* Nobel Price Lecture. Retrieved from www.nobelprize.org/nobel_prizes/economic-sciences/laureates/2009/williamson-lecture.html (23rd of June 2016).

Wu, S. Y. (2006). Contract theory and agricultural policy analysis: A discussion and survey of recent developments. *The Australian Journal of Agricultural and Resource Economics, 50*, 490–509.

Wu, S. Y., & MacDonald, J. (2015). Economics of agricultural contract grower protection legislation. *Choices: The Magazine of Food, Farm, and Resource Issues, 30*(3), 1–6.

Zheng, X., & Vukina, T. (2007). Efficiency gains from organizational innovation: Comparing ordinal and cardinal tournament games in broiler contracts. *International Journal of Industrial Organization, 25*, 843–859.

# 4 Knowledge and competitiveness

## 4.1 Different perspectives of knowledge capital

There have been many discussions and arguments on the question about a link between knowledge and competitiveness. Walter (2005) is more skeptical and says 'there are still a lot of questions and fields of analysis that have to be studied to better to understand the link between knowledge and competitiveness' Walter (2005: 6). Signorini (2008) is more certain 'The link between knowledge and competitiveness is undisputed' Signorini (2008: 259).

And it does not come as a surprise when Hickie (2006) finds that knowledge has played a role in the development of competitiveness in the aerospace industry while the U-Know project from the EU ('Understanding the Relationship between Knowledge and Competitiveness in the Enlarging European Union', Stephan, 2009), has more varied results.

Huggins and Izushi (2007) in their book *Competing for knowledge: creating, connecting and growing* give an in-depth discussion about the link between knowledge and competitiveness. They argue more generally that this question needs to be looked at from different scientific standpoints like sociology, organizational science, human geography and economics, and taking into consideration different contexts and cultures.

One of the first more comprehensive attempts to make more direct measurements of the relationship between knowledge and competitiveness for firms came with the MERITUM project (Measuring intangibles to understand and improve innovation management), MERITUM (2002) and Cañibano, *et al.* (2002).

The logic of the MERITUM project was that when a firm produces its products we can divide the input resources that the firm uses into groups:

- Labor, capital and raw materials.
- Semi-finished products and services.
- Intangible production factors.

One important characteristic we saw emerging during the second half of the twentieth century was that the market value of several firms was much higher than the value of the total book assets. We saw this often for knowledge-based productions like software and consultant firms. One factor to explain this divergence was that the market evaluated the future profits of the firm higher than the actual value of real and financial assets.

The first part of the MERITUM project was to achieve a set of guidelines for measuring the intangible assets to be used for the accounting procedures for the firm. This was important because firms needed fixed guidelines to identify and measure intangibles so the market could readily make correct evaluations of the firm. It is also important that we had similar rules to compare one firm to the other.

The second achievement of the MERITUM project was to serve as a tool for research for the firms that were involved in the project. To do this the firms needed to identify, measure and control the knowledge factors and how knowledge influenced the firms' efficiency and competitiveness.

In the MERITUM project intangibles where defined in the following way:

> Intangibles are non-monetary sources of probable future economic profit lacking physical substance, controlled (or at least influenced) by a firm as a result of previous events and transactions and may or may not be sold separately from other corporative assets.
>
> MERITUM (2002: 9)

This definition allows for knowledge as a separate product produced for example as a consultant service or a computer program, but it also allows for knowledge embodied into and as a part of another product.

After year 2000 the terms 'intangibles' and 'intellectual capital' were developed further and they had some common features. Both were used for non-physical recourses. In general, the concept of intangibles has been more related to accounting and formal analysis of firms while the term intellectual capital appears more in research and socio-economic contexts. The analysis of intellectual capital as a scientific field started in the later part of the 1990s with, among others Leif Edvinsson. The most famous book from the start was Edvinsson and Malone (1997) followed by Bounfour and Edvinsson (2012).

Building on the MERITUM project, which again was inspired by the work of Edvinsson and others, three factors are used to determine the value of intangible assets and knowledge capital.

**Identification:** Here we need to look at knowledge in relation to the processes that are fundamental and decisive for value creation of the firm – often called core competences.

**Measurement:** Here we need to find a useful set of indicators to measure the knowledge capital.

**Management:** Here we must develop a managerial system for the firm where we can consider the effects of knowledge capital to achieve corporate goals, which in the normal case are profit maximization.

This list of three factors shown above is not a table just for illustration of analytical possibilities but has been used by many firms in actual situations, see Sonnier (2008), Bañegil and Sanguino (2007) and Westeren (2012; 2013).

The identification process is crucial because all firms have knowledge about many aspects that are relevant for production. On the other hand, very few firms have resources to develop knowledge and expertise for all purposes that may be relevant. Therefore, they must choose the most fundamental processes, which are often called core competencies. This process must be integrated in the firms' long/medium term profit maximization procedures. Already in 1991 Gary Hamel (Hamel, 1991) wrote a much-cited article about the core competencies of the corporations and he underlined the importance of the process of identifying the core competencies for improving competitiveness. Since then the discussion about core competencies has developed in the business sector but also emerged in sectors like health care and communication.

The discussion about measurement to determine value of knowledge capital is fundamental for how firms can develop competitiveness. The central question is how the firm can find useful indicators to measure the knowledge components. The indicators must fulfil two criteria; the first and most important is that the indicators must reflect the specific knowledge that is needed. The second is that the indicator must be operational so the firm in the production situation can determine if, and to what degree, the knowledge is present or not. Another aspect is that the firm must be able to do this without excessive costs or interruptions in production.

Without integrating the knowledge capital into the managerial system, it is problematic for a firm to develop competitiveness based on knowledge. One problem discussed by firms in the competitive world and in research articles, is that knowledge, as we have stated earlier, is not a physical good. Knowledge often has more insecurities than other goods used for production because knowledge may change in the interaction between people and therefore is not easy to put into managerial optimization processes.

For the firm, it is important to distinguish between the stock and flow of knowledge capital. Knowledge as a stock means that the firm needs to know how much knowledge there is at a point in time. Knowledge as a stock, conceptually, has its challenges because we can only identify and store explicit knowledge. Even if we just look at the explicit knowledge, we have questions about how accessible the stock is, how well it is documented and what kind of resources we need to utilize the knowledge. Knowledge as a stock can have a market value, for example a firm can sell the description of a routine.

Conceptually we must ask the question whether knowledge as a stock can be defined and understood without also thinking about knowledge as a flow. There have been discussions about whether knowledge as a flow can be measured at all and what kind of concept it is. A firm can buy knowledge as a flow for example by hiring consultants to follow-up an innovation process. Then what is bought is a communication process. This process also has a market value and is often combined with a knowledge stock concept such as a description of or a report about what this process resulted in. The conclusion is that both in scientific work and in practice people often say that first we must decide and distinguish between the stock and flow of knowledge capital. But when we go into more detail both from the conceptual side and from the practical point of view, it is not so straight forward. We will go into more detailed discussion when we analyze this in our companies, here we refer to foundational work on this by Argote and Ingram (2000) and Alavi and Leidner (2001).

The next step is to go from intangible assets to knowledge capital. On the operational level, firms can make the following categorization, also used in the MERITUM project.

**Human capital:** The knowledge that employees take with them when they leave the firm. This is, for example, the employees' expertise, education etc.

**Structural capital:** The collection of knowledge that stays in the firm, such as formal rights to knowledge, patents, corporate practices, databases, description of routines etc.

**Relational capital:** All human capital and structural capital associated with the network of all external relationships of the firm such as contacts with subcontractors, external marketing firms etc.

By definition (building on the MERITUM project) then the firm's knowledge capital is equal to the sum of human capital, structural capital and the relational capital. Several other writers have discussed this and presented slightly different classifications, such as Kaplan and Norton (2004). The definition of knowledge capital is also dependent of the epistemology platform used, in this book we will relate to the connectionist understanding of knowledge, see Jelavic (2011) and Venzin, *et al.* (1998).

Firms must be aware of how knowledge can increase in value when it is used. Most other capital factors reduce in value when they are used because of depreciation and other forms of reduction in productivity and capital value. Knowledge as an input factor can have the opposite function and because of learning, processes in the firm can increase in value when used. On the other hand, this is not necessarily true because if the firm does not take initiatives to develop and upgrade the knowledge of the employees the knowledge also can be reduced. Obsolete knowledge can be counterproductive and sometimes needs to be 'destroyed' to encourage innovative behavior. There will be more about this in the Chapter 5 on innovations.

Whatever perspective we have about knowledge in production, it is a dynamic input linked to human cognition. It will change when used in a fundamentally different way compared to 'normal' physical capital. Developed in a correct way knowledge may have increasing returns to scale. This must be seen in light of how successful the firm conducts knowledge management. Knowledge is also culturally dependent and later research, like in this book, has shown that this is a more fundamental factor when we compare firms internationally than earlier assumed, see the GLOBE project, House, *et al.* (2002).

Another discussed aspect is the importance of wealth and income of the country to the possibilities for firms to take advantage of knowledge as a factor of production. Countries with lower income levels measured as gross domestic product (GDP) per capita often have more limited resources to use for education and research. But it is not just about resources, also about how institutions like the educational system functions.

Also, when we look at knowledge and competitiveness in an international perspective we often end up with the same three fundamental factors that have been mentioned earlier, namely knowledge workers, ICT/capital and innovation/R&D. Looking at knowledge workers in an international perspective we find arguments that the educational level is critical to develop into a knowledge economy. Following this argument many industrial and commercial organizations use results from schools at all levels to argue that the government should use more money to improve the educational system. In Europe these arguments are often based on results from the PISA tests. Another discussion that will be briefly mentioned here is the so-called 'knowledge brain drain', which means that rich countries attract the most talented workers from poorer countries.

The last factor to mention about knowledge transfer is the division between explicit and tacit knowledge. From one point of view we see that the development and exchange of explicit knowledge is going very fast, especially because of new and effective communication technologies like the internet. On the other hand, we see growing needs and requirements for tacit knowledge to be used in creative processes in firms. The internationalization of exchange of tacit knowledge has stronger barriers than what takes place nationally. The most important international barriers are language and culture. But when we see firms successfully deal with these barriers then the international exchange of tacit knowledge can be very successful and productive and raise the profit level of the firms considerably. There has been much research on this, especially about what takes place in multinational firms, see Fang, *et al.* (2010), Saliola and Zanfei (2009), and Meyer, *et al.* (2011).

Regarding ICT and knowledge, e-based activities will increase in importance. Therefore, access to networking is essential in acquiring and disseminating knowledge and the internet is the main driver and trendsetter. More advanced ICT use requires higher knowledge levels and communication skills. This means that firms that rely on ICT to develop on an international basis for new products based on innovating technologies also must invest in their own capabilities to receive knowledge and have the communication skills needed. This has led to the more general trend that technology is becoming more global and easier to retrieve but the actual use of the international technology in the firm requires more resources than before to be successful.

## 4.2 Knowledge indexes

Several organizations construct indexes for individual countries to say something about the knowledge economy, competitiveness and innovation. In this chapter, we will look at the following:

- The World Bank (2012): Knowledge Economy Index (KEI) 2012.
- World Economic Forum (Mercer) (2015): The Human Capital Report 2015 (Human Capital Index 2015).

- World Economic Forum (2016): The Global Competitiveness Report 2015–2016 (The Global Competitive Index).
- Dutta, Lanvin and Wunsch-Vicent (2015): The Global Innovation Index 2014.

The reason to have a closer look at the indexes relates back to the citation from Stiglitz in Chapter 1. His message to the World Bank emphasized the importance of understanding the context when we look at institutions and culture for the development of knowledge as the basis for competitiveness.

### *4.2.1 The Knowledge Economy Index (KEI) of the World Bank*

The World Bank collects data and constructs indexes that measure how countries perform vis a vis the knowledge economy, KEI, (World Bank 2012). The knowledge economy index is based on the average of four sub-indexes, which represent what the World Bank calls the four pillars of the knowledge economy, a detailed description of how the pillars are built up is found in World Bank (2012). The different pillars are:

*Economic incentive and institutional regime*

Tariff and non-tariff barriers, regulatory quality, rule of law

*Innovation and technological adoption*

Royalty payments and receipts (US$/pop), Technical journal articles/million people, Patents granted by USPTO/million people

*Education and training*

Gross tertiary enrollment rate, Gross secondary enrollment rate, Average years of schooling

*Communications technologies (ICT) infrastructure*

Internet users per 1,000 people, Computers per 1,000 people, Total telephones per 1,000 people

Results for selected countries are shown in Table 4.1. In this chapter we will give data for the countries of special interest in the project and add data for Germany and USA as a reference. Denmark and Norway can be compared to Germany and the USA which are important in the market for white meat (In the following discussion we have defined groups of countries so we do not need to mention the country names all times; Group 1, Denmark, Norway, Germany and USA). Northern European countries score high in total rank for the knowledge economy with Denmark third, Norway fifth, Germany eighth and the United States twelfth in the world. To treat this as a group of homogenous countries compared to other groups is difficult because of the size of the USA with capabilities 'hidden' behind averages when the indexes are constructed.

*Table 4.1* KEI 2012 for selected countries

| | *Knowledge economy* | | *Economic incentive and institutional regime* | | *Innovation and technological adoption* | | *Education and training* | | *Information and communication technologies* | |
|---|---|---|---|---|---|---|---|---|---|---|
| | *Rank* | *Index* | *Rank* | *Index* | *Rank* | *Index* | *Rank* | *Index* | *Rank* | *Index* |
| Denmark | 3 | 9.16 | 3 | 9.63 | 5 | 9.49 | 15 | 8.63 | 13 | 8.88 |
| Norway | 5 | 9.11 | 8 | 9.47 | 17 | 9.01 | 3 | 9.43 | 17 | 8.53 |
| Germany | 8 | 8.90 | 13 | 9.10 | 12 | 9.11 | 23 | 8.20 | 8 | 9.17 |
| USA | 12 | 8.77 | (*) | 8.41 | (*) | 9.40 | (*) | 8.70 | (*) | 8.51 |
| Brazil | 60 | 5.58 | 82 | 4.17 | 51 | 6.31 | 61 | 5.61 | 58 | 6.24 |
| Kuwait | 64 | 5.33 | (*) | 5.86 | (*) | 5.22 | (*) | 3.70 | (*) | 6.53 |
| Sri Lanka | 101 | 3.63 | (*) | 4.04 | (*) | 3.06 | (*) | 4.61 | (*) | 2.80 |

Source: World Bank 2012.

(*): Unable to access data.

We will return to this when we go into more detailed information. International reports like The Global Competitiveness Report 2015–2016 analyze countries by stage of development. All countries mentioned above can be considered as innovation-driven.

In the next group of countries, we have Brazil ranked as number sixty, Kuwait ranked as number sixty-four and Sri Lanka as number 101 (Group 2, Brazil, Kuwait and Sri Lanka). Brazil is seen as a country developing from 'efficiency-driven' to 'innovation-driven'. Kuwait is an Arabic oil-dependent country and one of the wealthiest in the world looking at GDP per capita, but in a development perspective it is in the transition from 'factor driven' to 'efficiency driven'. Sri Lanka is often looked at as a developing country with a low level of income, but is classified as 'efficiency driven' by the World Economic Forum. Here it also can be problematic to look at these as one group of countries, since Brazil has a much more comprehensive economy and the functioning of markets are culturally different.

The information about the firms in the study (Danpo in Denmark, LAR in Brazil, KUPCO in Kuwait, Crysbro in Sri Lanka and Ytterøy in Norway) is found in Table 1.1 (in Chapter 1). To analyze the relationship between knowledge and competitiveness we must consider (see Chapter 2) that the firms in Denmark and Norway have a substantially higher wage rate than the others and must compensate by utilizing knowledge in a more efficient way to be competitive. We see this reflected in Table 4.1 and we have the following more detailed comments about the Knowledge Economy Index.

The data in the pillar on how institutional regimes functions show how countries provide incentives for the efficient use of existing and new knowledge. It also shows the innovation-driven countries in Group 1 with index values and ranks close to each other – as the best in the world. Using regulatory quality as the example, it is obvious that this represents a cost burden for the Group two countries. These are costs that national and regional authorities impose on the firms are counterproductive to innovations. The indicators in this pillar are quite close to the economic realities we find for the firms.

An efficient innovation system for firms, research centres, universities, consultants and other organizations is important for tapping into the growing stock of global knowledge, assimilating and adapting it to local needs, and creating new technology. We find the index values and ranks quite similar for Group 1, but more uneven results for Group 2. From the firm's perspective, this indicator is built on less relevant components, none of them playing an important role in how the companies directly conduct innovation. The components give a more general picture on the national level.

Education and training can be linked directly to successful operations of the firms and here again we see the group structure of the nations. The education level is, in more general terms, a platform for how regions and companies enter the knowledge economy. But, as we will see in the more detailed discussion about education, it is also necessary to look at how the firms are able to utilize knowledge.

The sub-index Information and Communications Technologies (ICT) has the same problems as the innovation sub-index that is based on general components – interesting on the national level but not very operational for firms. The results also reflect the level of income, not just readiness for the ICT era.

In summary, we can say that KEI gives an interesting picture on the national level about the status and readiness for continued development in the knowledge economy. From the firms' point of view, we need more detailed information for more decisive conclusions.

### 4.2.2 Human capital and competitiveness indexes

One main theme in this book is the link between knowledge and competitiveness and there are many indices to choose among. We begin our examination by looking at the numbers in Table 4.2 and a figure where knowledge represented by 'The Human Capital Index' on one axis and 'The Global Competitiveness Index' on the other, (see Figure 4.1, which is adopted from The Human Capital Report 2015, Figure D2). Figure D2 has a regression line showing an increasing trend, higher values of human capital are associated with better competitiveness. The countries in Group 1 (see Table 4.2/Figure 4.1) with innovation-driven economies form a cluster with very high values on both human capital and competitiveness. Brazil and Sri Lanka are quite close; noteworthy are the high values for Sri Lanka on the Human Capital Index. Kuwait as an outlier has a higher value on competitiveness than Sri Lanka and Brazil but lower on human capital. If we look five to ten years into the future what can happen to the countries forming the regression line?

- The regression line just moves outwards in the diagram as all countries improve human capital and competitive components and countries keep their relative position?

- Are countries on the lower part of the line able to get closer to the countries with high values?
- Will countries with high values increase distance to the lower ones?

Our objective is not do a complete analysis of this here, but the hints we have gotten during the research period is that institutions and culture played a more important role for the countries on the lower part of the line to improve their position than we assumed from the start.

*Table 4.2* Human Capital Index and The Global Competitiveness Index for selected countries

| | *Human Capital Index 2015* | | *The Global Competitiveness Index 2014–2015* | |
|---|---|---|---|---|
| | *Index value* | *Rank* | *Index value* | *Rank* |
| Denmark | 82.47 | 7 | 5.29 | 13 |
| Norway | 83.84 | 2 | 5.35 | 11 |
| Germany | 78.55 | 22 | 5.49 | 5 |
| USA | 79.64 | 17 | 5.54 | 3 |
| Brazil | 64.60 | 78 | 4.34 | 57 |
| Kuwait | 59.31 | 93 | 4.51 | 40 |
| Sri Lanka | 68.19 | 60 | 4.19 | 73 |

Source: World Economic Forum (Mercer) (2015) and World Economic Forum (2016).

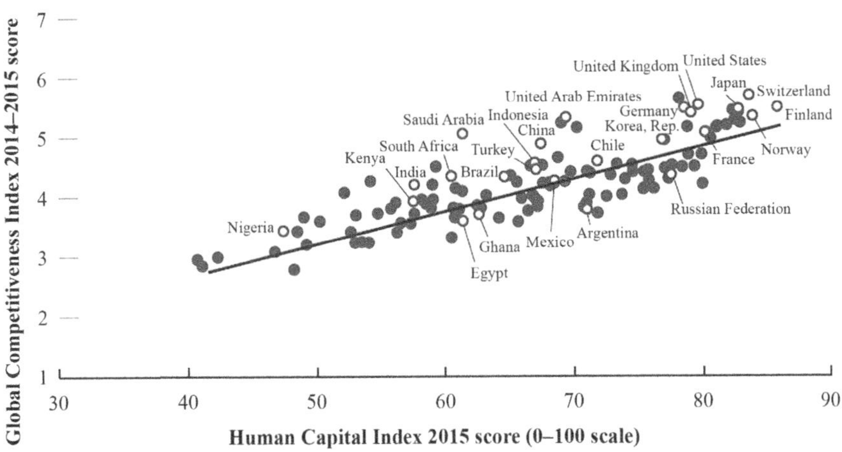


*Figure 4.1* Relationship between the Global Competitiveness Index 2014–2015 and the Human Capital Index 2015

Source: World Economic Forum, 2015: 42.

*Table 4.3* Human Capital Index for selected countries

| *Country* | *Overall Index* | | *Under 15 age group* | | *15–24 age group* | | *25–54 age group* | | *55–64 age group* | | *65 and over age group* | |
|---|---|---|---|---|---|---|---|---|---|---|---|---|
| | *Score* | *Rank* | *Score* | *Rank* | *Score* | *Rank* | *Score* | *Rank* | *Score* | *Rank* | *Score* | *Rank* |
| Norway | 83.84 | 2 | 93.16 | 12 | 83.87 | 3 | 79.48 | 4 | 85.14 | 3 | 74.59 | 2 |
| Denmark | 82.47 | 7 | 91.61 | 25 | 82.31 | 9 | 78.15 | 6 | 83.66 | 7 | 74.12 | 4 |
| United States | 79.64 | 17 | 88.09 | 40 | 82.86 | 7 | 74.64 | 17 | 80.61 | 15 | 70.44 | 16 |
| Germany | 78.55 | 22 | 79.56 | 75 | 79.87 | 12 | 77.55 | 8 | 82.67 | 9 | 73.47 | 5 |
| Sri Lanka | 68.19 | 60 | 87.32 | 43 | 69.63 | 57 | 59.21 | 73 | 68.26 | 64 | 49.34 | 78 |
| Brazil | 64.60 | 78 | 71.86 | 95 | 67.01 | 66 | 61.17 | 66 | 65.72 | 70 | 52.77 | 72 |
| Kuwait | 59.31 | 93 | 85.20 | 51 | 47.83 | 116 | 51.15 | 105 | 57.40 | 91 | 42.62 | 96 |

Source: World Economic Forum, 2015.

The Human Capital Index consists of an overall index and with sub-indexes calculated for defined age groups. In Table 4.3 we also see a split between the Group 1 countries (innovation-driven) and those in Group 2 (mainly efficiency driven) economies. In Group 1 there seems to be a tendency for a two-level structure with the Scandinavian countries on the top level and Germany and USA a little lower. The Scandinavian countries have outstanding scores in all groups except the 'Under 15 age group'. This is confirmed in many other studies that say that e.g. Norway has the highest use of resources for education 6–15 years but the scores in the PISA tests are in the middle range.

The three most resourceful nations in the sample, USA, Brazil and Germany have lower scores than expected in the Under 15 age group, but take back the lost territory when it comes to higher education ages. Sri Lanka and Kuwait do surprisingly well in the youngest age group but Kuwait loses in the higher education ages mainly because of income distribution and cultural factors. When we look at age groups from twenty-five and up we are back to the dualistic pattern with the Group 1 nations on the average ranked substantially higher than the Group 2.

Additional and more detailed numbers about human capital are examined in Table 4.4. The GDP numbers differ substantially with numbers for Kuwait and Norway influenced by the oil economy while Brazil and Sri Lanka form the low-income group. The labor market numbers vary some but not more than expected. Sri Lanka has a larger informal part of the economy than the others. The education attainment rates show low figures for Kuwait because of institutional, cultural and religious factors. One important fact about the Kuwait labor market is that it is partly based on manpower from other countries regulated by contracts for time periods. The attainment rates show Group 1 countries having higher scores in secondary and tertiary education but the differences with respect to Sri Lanka are smaller than expected. While high-skilled employment differs substantially between the innovation and efficiency driven economies, medium-skilled employment showed minimal differences.

*Table 4.4* Selected human capital indicators from Human Capital Report 2015 (*)

| | *Brazil* | *Denmark* | *Germany* | *Kuwait* | *Norway* | *Sri Lanka* | *USA* |
|---|---|---|---|---|---|---|---|
| GDP per capita (const. 2011 US$, PPP) | 15,153 | 44,325 | 44,741 | 70,992 | 65,896 | 10,355 | 54,678 |
| Labor force participation rate (%, 2013) | 69.8 | 62.5 | 59.9 | 68.4 | 64.9 | 55.0 | 62.5 |
| Unemployment rate (%, 2013) | 6.5 | 7.0 | 5.3 | 3.2 | 3.5 | 4.4 | 7.4 |
| Age group 25–54 | | | | | | | |
| Primary education attainment rate (%) | 95.2 | 100.0 | 100.0 | 55.9 | 99.9 | 97.0 | 99.8 |
| Secondary education attainment rate (%) | 63.6 | 99.6 | 96.7 | 26.5 | 99.8 | 77.5 | 94.0 |
| Tertiary education attainment rate (%) | 10.2 | 30.1 | 26.4 | 5.4 | 35.9 | 22.7 | 31.5 |
| High-skilled employment share (%) | 21.3 | 45.8 | 43.1 | 19.3 | 48.8 | 16.1 | 42.2 |
| Medium-skilled employment share (%) | 84.2 | 89.9 | 91.7 | 98.9 | 96.2 | 77.5 | 87.4 |
| Ease of finding skilled employees, index value (1: Low, 7: High) | 3.2 | 4.74 | 4.45 | 3.49 | 4.77 | 4.20 | 4.79 |

Source: The Human Capital Report, 2015.

(*) For more detailed explanation of data and definitions, see source.

Recall the three main components of the knowledge economy:

1 Knowledge workers/human capital
2 ICT/technology/R&D
3 Innovation

To continue the more detailed analysis of contextual factors for the two groups we use selected indexes from the Global Competitiveness Report 2015–2016 (see Table 4.5). The Global Competitiveness Index is composed of 12 pillars (or indicators) and we have selected indicators that are especially relevant for our focus. Table 4.5 shows a densely clustered picture for the Group 1 countries as world leading countries in competitiveness ranking. The pattern is not so apparent for the Group 2 countries where Brazil has a rather low score and Kuwait a high one.

*Table 4.5* Selected indexes from The Global Competitiveness Report 2015–2016

| | *Brazil* | | *Denmark* | | *Germany* | | *Kuwait* | | *Norway* | | *Sri Lanka* | | *USA* | |
|---|---|---|---|---|---|---|---|---|---|---|---|---|---|---|
| | *Value* | *Rank* | *Value* | *Rank* | *Value* | *Rank* | *Value* | *Rank* | *Value* | *Rank* | *Value* | *Rank* | *Value* | *Rank* |
| Global Competitive Index | 4.1 | 75 | 5.3 | 12 | 5.5 | 4 | 4.6 | 34 | 5.4 | 11 | 4.2 | 68 | 5.6 | 3 |
| 1st pillar: Institutions | 3.2 | 121 | 5.5 | 15 | 5.2 | 20 | 4.1 | 56 | 5.8 | 5 | 4.1 | 59 | 4.8 | 28 |
| Some of the detailed indexes: | | | | | | | | | | | | | | |
| 1.09 Burden of government regulation | 1.7 | 139 | 3.3 | 82 | 3.9 | 34 | 2.7 | 125 | 4.1 | 19 | 3.5 | 64 | 3.6 | 51 |
| 2.08 Mobile cell phone subcr./100 pop. | 139.0 | 37 | 126.0 | 50 | 120.4 | 57 | 218.4 | 2 | 116.5 | 62 | 103.2 | 91 | 98.4 | 99 |
| 5.06 Internet access in schools | 3.6 | 97 | 5.9 | 15 | 5.0 | 39 | 4.0 | 81 | 6.3 | 3 | 4.0 | 79 | 5.9 | 17 |
| 6.07 No. of days to start a business | 83.6 | 135 | 5.5 | 24 | 14.5 | 82 | 31.0 | 116 | 5.0 | 18 | 11.0 | 59 | 5.6 | 27 |
| 9.04 Individuals using the internet in% | 57.6 | 58 | 96.0 | 3 | 86.2 | 16 | 78.7 | 29 | 96.3 | 2 | 25.8 | 100 | 87.4 | 13 |
| 9.05 Fixed broadband internet sub./100 pop. | 11.5 | 64 | 41.4 | 2 | 35.8 | 10 | 1.4 | 103 | 38.1 | 6 | 2.6 | 95 | 30.4 | 20 |
| 11.09 Willingness to delegate authority | 4.1 | 39 | 6.1 | 1 | 4.9 | 19 | 4.1 | 38 | 6.0 | 2 | 3.8 | 58 | 5.2 | 9 |
| 12.01 Capacity for innovation | 3.8 | 80 | 5.3 | 11 | 5.6 | 5 | 3.6 | 101 | 5.2 | 18 | 4.5 | 36 | 5.9 | 2 |
| 12.02 Quality of scientific research institutions | 3.6 | 80 | 5.5 | 16 | 5.8 | 9 | 3.3 | 96 | 5.4 | 17 | 4.3 | 59 | 6.1 | 4 |
| 12.03 Company spending on R&D | 3.3 | 60 | 4.9 | 15 | 5.5 | 6 | 2.9 | 102 | 4.7 | 20 | 3.5 | 50 | 5.6 | 3 |
| 12.04 University-industry collaboration in R&D | 3.8 | 54 | 4.9 | 20 | 5.3 | 10 | 3.1 | 107 | 5.0 | 15 | 3.1 | 109 | 5.8 | 2 |
| 12.06 Availability of scientists and engineers | 3.3 | 115 | 4.6 | 35 | 5.0 | 15 | 3.8 | 85 | 5.0 | 12 | 5.0 | [illegible] | 5.4 | 4 |
| 12.07 PCT patents, applications/million pop. | 3.5 | 51 | 215.4 | 8 | 225.2 | 6 | 0.3 | 88 | 138.4 | 12 | 0.6 | 78 | 160.3 | 11 |
| 12th pillar: Innovation | 3.2 | 84 | 5.1 | 10 | 5.5 | 6 | 3.0 | 109 | 5.0 | 13 | 3.6 | 43 | 5.6 | 4 |
| R&D expenditure in% of GDP (§) | 1.2 | | 3.0 | | 2.9 | | 0.3 | | 1.7 | | 0.2 | | 2.8 | |

Source: The Global Competitiveness Report 2015–2016, World Economic Forum, 2015.

Indexes are for 2013; exceptions to this are documented in The Global Competitiveness Report 2015–2016.
All indexes are on a scale from 1–7 where seven is the best, except 2.08, 6.07, 9.04, 9.05 and 12.07 that are actual calculated numbers.
(§): The information about 'R&D expenditure in % of GDP' is from: www.worldbank.org/ (downloaded 02.07.15).

One of the important messages from this book is that the functioning of institutions is crucial. Number of days to start a business is an index for both institutions and business climate. It takes five to six days on average to start a business in Norway, Denmark and USA. Sri Lanka (11.0 days) ranks before Germany with 14.5 days and Kuwait is behind with 31 days. Brazil is close to the bottom of the list with 83.6 days and ranks as 135 out of 140, together with the less developed countries in the world. For Brazil, the results indicate that institutions represent a big disadvantage for competitiveness and the situation in Brazil is far worse than for any of the other countries in the sample.

The more consumption-oriented indexes (use of mobile cell phones and use of the internet) do not show any clear pattern except lower use of the internet in lower income countries. Looking at the internet access in schools indicator, we see the Group 1/Group 2 countries split where the innovation-driven countries pay more attention and use more resources on this than the other countries in the sample. The same can be said about R&D expenditure in % of GDP.

The sub-index 'Willingness to delegate authority' is mainly linked to the cultural side of competitiveness and is fundamental for companies entering the knowledge economy. Jensen (2008) discusses this theme and says that firms must invert the authority pyramid to successfully to enter the knowledge economy. On the other hand some authority is necessary for routines in industrial production (see Westeren, 2015). How this dilemma can be solved is an important discussion in this book.

Firms must handle innovation to develop competitiveness in the knowledge economy. Several sub-indicators for innovations representing the 12th pillar in the Global Competitiveness Index are shown in Table 4.5. The Group 1 innovation-driven economies rank from USA as number 4 to Norway as number 13. The group two countries rank from Sri Lanka as number 43, Brazil 84 and Kuwait 109. The difference between Sri Lanka and Brazil is largely explained by the results for the sub-index 'Availability of scientists and engineers' where Sri Lanka is on the same level as northern European countries while Brazil ranks 115 (out of 140). Our experience and other research (Westeren, 2012) do not support the low score we see for Brazil in the table.

### 4.2.3 Some lessons to be learned from national data about entering the knowledge economy

*Human capital/knowledge workers*

The KEI index and the Human Capital Index both show clear and clustered patterns for Group 1 countries with high rankings globally. Group 2 had significantly lower levels. The different age groups show a more varied picture – in the under 15 age group the Scandinavian countries are losing their top positions. Kuwait and Sri Lanka have close to the same average results as Germany and USA, while Brazil is far behind. In the high education and working age groups we are back to a more dualistic pattern again. A more detailed look at attainment rates and skills show that Sri Lanka and Brazil are lagging mainly because of resource and institutional reasons, Kuwait mainly because of culture.

*ICT and technology*

The general indicators show that all countries are entering the ICT era, countries with lower income levels usually at a lower speed. We can get some indication about the future by looking at internet access in schools. The Group 1 countries still have a lead but the picture is not completely clear. The Group 2 countries are behind because of lower resources (Sri Lanka), a combination of lower resources and institutional reasons (Brazil) and cultural reasons (Kuwait).

*Innovations*

Here again we see a dualistic pattern, but that does not preclude innovative behavior and actual innovations taking place in traditional industries. Indexes, at least to some degree, can be difficult to interpret.

*Institutions and culture*

The indexed ranks and values for institutions provide clear signals. The national statistics shown here conform well with what we find in our case studies as does the cultural information.

## 4.3 Knowledge transfer in firms – theoretical perspectives

### *4.3.1 From the resource-based view to the knowledge-based view of the firm*

The introduction of the resource-based view of the firm often starts with Penrose, where she considers the company as a 'collection of productive resources' (Penrose, 1959:24) and suggests that the unique character of each firm is based on a heterogeneity of productive services available from the firm's own resources.

In the 1990's the resource-based view (RBV) was developed further with a variety of approaches that focused on:

Intangible/invisible assets (Itami, 1987; Sveiby, 2001)
Core competencies (Prahalad and Hamel, 1990)
Dynamic capacity (Teece, Pisano and Shuen, 1997)
Organizational structures (Williamson, 1996)
Knowledge (Grant, 1996)

A much-used definition of resources within the framework of the RBV came from Barney (1991) '*firm resources* include all assets, capabilities, organizational processes, firm attributes, information, knowledge, etc. controlled by a firm that enables the firm to conceive and implement strategies that improve its efficiency and effectiveness' (p. 101, referring to Daft, 1983).

The development of the knowledge society and the growing importance of research focused on knowledge as the most important resource lead to the knowledge-based view (KBV) of the firm during the 1990's (Curado and Bontis, 2006). The KBV was an extension of the RBV (Barney, *et al.*, 2011) and offered a vision of the firm based on the idea that competitiveness is closely linked to the firm's ability to create and utilize knowledge. After the discussion about competitiveness was revitalized around 1980 we have had an ongoing discussion about what constitutes the most important boundaries for firms. The position of the KBV was that the boundaries were determined by the level of efficiency in the coordination of knowledge.

This was the starting point for Grant (1996) since his view was that the firm applies the knowledge created during production 'Hence, firms exist as institutions for producing goods and services because they can create conditions under which multiple individuals can integrate their specialist knowledge' (p. 112).

Grant (1996) draws a distinction between specialized knowledge, related to a particular expertise of individuals in certain areas of knowledge, and common knowledge that reflects the individual knowledge shared within a same organization. Without the benefits of the specialization of knowledge, organizations would not need to integrate multiple individuals. Grant (1996) agrees with Simon (1991) when he says that all learning takes place inside individual human heads. This view is consistent with Polanyi (1958) in his book *Personal knowledge*. There he discusses the fundamentals of the tacit/explicit split of knowledge saying that 'Personal knowledge is always contextual and is always as part of a skill' (p. 24).

After this Polanyi brings in two kinds of awareness – focal awareness and subsidiary awareness – which form the basis for establishing the concept of tacit knowledge, or more precisely, tacit knowing.

There has been a debate since the late 1980's about the definitions of organizational knowledge. Among others, recent articles take up this debate like Tuan (2011). Mahroeian and Forozia (2012) distinguishing two broad traditions:

- A more behavioral related view that sees learning as a systematic change in knowledge assets, standard operating procedures, rules, and routines; and relating to a positivist tradition from the philosophy of science with focus on explicit knowledge.
- A cognitive oriented view that sees learning in relation to shared models and cognitions of organizational members; and relating to hermeneutic and constructivist models from the philosophy of science. This tradition emphasizes both explicit and tacit knowledge and the interplay between them.

### *4.3.2 Knowledge transfers*

In the literature as well as when we get out in the field and interview managers and group leaders in firms, we always get the same answer: transfer of knowledge is fundamental for the existence of the firm. We find at least three quite equal terms describing this – knowledge transfer, knowledge sharing and knowledge flows. There have been discussions about the understanding of this, where Kumar and Ganesh (2009) say:

> It was noted that 'knowledge transfer', 'knowledge sharing' and 'knowledge flow' have a common trait – that of 'an exchange of knowledge' – whereby, knowledge is given by one or more entities and received by others. They are thus essentially similar. For this reason, 'knowledge transfer' has been used in an inclusive sense in this paper, subsuming the connotations of 'knowledge sharing' and 'knowledge flow'.
>
> Kumar and Ganesh (2009: 163)

This is what we will do in this book – say that the concepts are essentially similar and use knowledge transfer in an inclusive sense. This is also in line with Lai, *et al.* (2016) who contend that knowledge transfer is the more general concept which can consist of knowledge inflows and outflows.

One commonly used definition of knowledge transfer came from Argote and Ingram (2000: 151) 'Knowledge transfer in organizations is the process through which one unit (e.g., group, department, or division) is affected by the experience of another.'

This definition emphasizes the dynamic aspects of the transfer of knowledge and links it to organizational learning. Our understanding also takes the individual aspect more clearly into account and the definition by Duan, *et al.* (2010) works better. First they refer to the definition by Argote and Ingram (2000), cited above, then they end up by saying that knowledge transfer is defined as a process by which: 'Knowledge is exchanged between or among individuals, teams, groups, or organizations' (Duan, *et al.* 2010: 359).

The literature on firm knowledge transfers take up many aspects, one important delineation is whether it is a multinational firm or not. To get the theoretical discussion in line with the empirical part we will concentrate on the national level, but for firms in different countries with different cultures and contexts.

Spraggon and Bodolica (2012) suggest that the literature about successes and failures of knowledge transfers can be divided into three groups:

1 The central role to the spiral model of knowledge conversion when examining its relationship with knowledge transfer endeavors
2 Communication/ICT/media richness capacities of various processes that lead to the achievement of effective knowledge transfers
3 Intra-firm knowledge transfer barriers and enablers

The first point about knowledge conversion refers to the SECI model by Nonaka and Takeuchi (1995) and Nonaka, *et al.* (2000). SECI is based on a metaphor where different knowledge processes follow each other and are put on top of each other like a spiral movement. The Nonaka and Takeuchi book has received more than 35,000 citations so there is no need to give an introduction about the story. In relation to the discussions here there is room for two comments. At the heart of the conversion logic the model goes from:

1 Socialization: tacit – tacit knowledge
2 Externalization: tacit – explicit knowledge
3 Combination: explicit – explicit knowledge
4 Internalization: explicit – tacit knowledge

There has been serious criticism about the use of the tacit knowledge concept by Nonaka and Takeuchi, see e.g. Gourlay (2004; 2006) and Tsoukas (2005). Nonaka and Takeuchi (1995) say they build on Polanyi's concept of tacit knowledge (more correctly termed tacit knowing or the tacit component) and add elements from Japanese philosophy to their understanding of Polanyi. This raises the question about how clearly defined and understood is Nonaka's tacit knowledge concept. Most skeptics agree that Nonaka is not completely in line with Polanyi (1958). In the empirical part of this book we will also analyze tacit knowledge as part of the knowledge transfer process and then we will use Polanyi as directly as possible.

The other comment about the SECI model is that it is used in a way so the spiral movement seems to continue without interruptions or barriers. This is normally not the case (see e.g. Westeren 2012).

The concept of and discussion about media richness is now standard in most textbooks in knowledge management like Hislop (2013). This discussion is important for the business sector but has also appeared for institutions like hospitals and nursing homes. Face-to-face communication is looked at as a 'rich' communication mode while digital transmission via computers like SKYPE (or by internal computers in a company) is less 'rich' but is much more effective and cost saving. In our white meat firms, we had many different modes of communication including ICT, but if something really went wrong in production, face-to-face communication was often necessary.

## 4.4 Empirical analysis of knowledge transfers and consequences for competitiveness

### *4.4.1 Introduction*

A discussion about knowledge capital and how this can be used by firms to improve competitiveness was presented in Chapter 4.1. The general message from the MERITUM project and other similar research projects is that firms must be able to identify their core competences, to develop indicators to measure the knowledge capital and to integrate this into the firm's managerial system to take advantage of their knowledge base. In Chapter 4.2 we looked at the construction of different types of knowledge indexes. The more general trend is that countries with high scores on knowledge indexes also do better in competitiveness. In this chapter, we will give a detailed empirical analysis of firms in the project to see how the more general trends can be interpreted on the firm level.

How knowledge transfers in organizations like firms can be defined and understood was discussed in Chapter 4.3. One important assumption is that knowledge transfers can best be interpreted within the concept of the knowledge-based firm. This fits well into the framework we use because all our firms look at themselves as belonging in the knowledge-based group.

The most important characteristics of the firms in the study are shown in Table 1.1 in Chapter 1. The first firm is called Danpo and is localized in Denmark. The firm is large in a Scandinavian setting, but is more medium sized compared to the United States and Brazil. The firm produces 184,000 chickens daily, which is about 50 million a year; this is about 40% of the total production in Denmark, and with an export share of about 50%. Production is based partly on traditional white meat production operations and partly on use of high-technology equipment for enhancing productivity. The speed of the assembly line at Danpo is about 50% faster than the speed at the other firms; the speed of the other firms is about the same. In short, we can say that Danpo is a highly industrialized producer using front edge capital equipment and ICT systems.

The second firm in the study is LAR in Paraná, Brazil with a daily production of 340,000 chickens. Brazil is the biggest exporter of chicken in the world. The export share from LAR is about 40% of the firm's total production, which is about 2% of Brazil 's total. The LAR firm is a modern firm with standard technology solutions, but compared to production volume they have a higher share of employees than Northern Europe.

KUPCO, situated in Kuwait, is one of the two big white meat producers in the country with a daily production of about 50,000 chickens. Their export share is minimal and the firm has traditional capital equipment and an integrated production system.

Crysbro, in Kandy, Sri Lanka, is one of the four big producers in the country. Production capacity is 25,000 chickens per day and the firm is mostly a producer for the local market. The firm has standard capital equipment.

Ytterøy (Ytterøykylling) is a firm in Norway and one of the smallest chicken producers in the country. The firm produces 17,200 chickens a day with a national market share of about 5% and only marginal exports. The firm is a typical niche producer with more specialized products. Capital equipment is updated and the knowledge base is developed to the market situation.

### *4.4.2 The data collection in the project*

Data collection in the project began in 2012 and continued to 2016. Visits and data collections were done at least three times in every firm, based on a questionnaire. Production of white meat is based on a system following stages – from department to department, see Table 4.6.

The number of answers (or observations) in the project are shown in Table 4.6. We have more answers from LAR than the other firms because we did data collection several consecutive days at LAR, while at the other firms we did data collection on the day we visited.

*Table 4.6* Layout of departments and number of answers to the questionnaires from the group leaders in the firms

| | *Number of answers from group leaders* | | | | |
|---|---|---|---|---|---|
| | *Danpo* | *LAR* | *Ytterøy* | *Crysbro* | *KUPCO* |
| Receiving | 6 | 35 | 3 | 6 | 3 |
| Killing | | 50 | | | 3 |
| Defeathering | | | | 6 | 3 |
| Evisceration | | | | 6 | |
| Deboning and partitioning | 6 | 77 | 6 | 6 | 3 |
| Packing | 9 | | 3 | | 3 |
| Assembly line | 21 | 162 | 12 | 24 | 15 |
| Freezing | 3 | 37 | 3 | 6 | 3 |
| Expedition | 3 | 22 | 3 | | 6 |
| Maintenance | 6 | 0 | 6 | 6 | 3 |
| Hygiene and quality control | 3 | 34 | 3 | 6 | 3 |
| Management | 3 | 11 | 3 | 0 | 3 |
| Support functions | 18 | 104 | 18 | 18 | 18 |
| Total: Assembly line + Support functions | 39 | 266 | 30 | 42 | 33 |

Source: authors' data collection.

The first function of white meat production from chicken is receiving. Then the next operations include killing the birds, defeathering, evisceration, deboning and partitioning and packing. The functions from killing to packing are normally called assembly line functions. We also add receiving to assembly line functions because the speed of the assembly line is vital to planning and performing the receiving. The assembly line functions had seven group leaders in Danpo, thirteen at LAR, four at Ytterøy, eight at Crysbro and five at KUPCO.

Freezing, expedition, maintenance, hygiene and quality control and management are labelled as support functions. How the firms perform these functions varies, but they do not directly rely on the speed of the assembly line. The main reason for having a division between assembly line functions and support functions is that we want to analyze transfer of knowledge under different circumstances in and between the firms. The research team visited the firms many times and it was easy to observe that communication, knowledge flows and innovative behavior took place in different ways regarding the assembly line functions compared to the support functions, the analysis of the data explains the characteristics of these differences.

Data collection was done by using a questionnaire. Members of the research team went to the firms for data collection. The group leaders filled in the questionnaire but in conversations on-site, we were able to discern a lot of additional context information.

The questionnaire can be split into separate parts depending on the variables.

Background variables – the variables in this group tell about the structure of the firm and give a background for the analysis:

- Experience – how many years the group leader has worked in the firm and how many years he has had the role as group leader
- Production capacity

*Outcome variables*

- Speed of production
- Number of production stops
- Quality control

*Communication variables*

- Communication from the group leader to the management level
- Communication from the group leader to the group
- Communication (initiatives) from group members to the group leader

*Competence variables*

- Education
- Understanding of technology
- Course participation

*Innovation variables*

- Changes in routines – here we have information about suggestions for changes, when it did happen and what the suggestion was about
- Formal written suggestions
- If the suggestions where acted upon

*Cultural variables*

- Do you try to avoid uncertainty?
- Do you expect and agree that power should be unequally shared?
- Do you encourage and reward collective distribution of resources and collective actions?
- Do you express pride and loyalty in the firm where you work?
- Do you try to minimize the roles between men and women?
- Are you confrontational in relationships with other people in the firm?
- Do you engage in future oriented behaviors such as planning, investing in the future?
- Do you reward and encourage individuals for being fair, generous, caring and kind to others?

We will go more into details about how the variables are defined, operationalized and measured when we do the actual analysis.

### *4.4.3 Work experience*

The work experience of the group leader in the different firms is examined in Table 4.7. It is interesting to see that the average total number of years the group leaders have worked in the firms in most cases are higher in Brazil, Sri Lanka and Kuwait compared to Norway and Denmark. In all firms, except the Norwegian, the number of years of work for the group leader at assembly line functions is relatively high. Group leaders for support functions have less years of experience but also quite different problems needing solutions. The hygiene and quality control personnel had very high levels of skills and experience. The maintenance work was quite different between firms. Danish firms had more advanced ITC systems and other capital equipment. At LAR, which is a much bigger firm than the others, maintenance included many specific jobs like water support and wastewater cleaning. These functions also needed solutions at the other firms, but in different ways depending on the environmental restrictions. Our clear impression is that the support functions demanded higher levels and faster changes in knowledge than the tasks on the assembly line.

*Table 4.7* Years of experience of the group leader at the firm

| | | *Observations* | *Years in the same position* | *Total years in the firm* |
|---|---|---|---|---|
| Danpo | Assembly line | 21 | 9.14 | 9.95 |
| Danpo | Support functions | 18 | 4.33 | 7.17 |
| Danpo | Total | 39 | 6.92 | 8.67 |
| LAR | Assembly line | 162 | 7.34 | 10.57 |
| LAR | Support functions | 104 | 3.37 | 9.45 |
| LAR | Total | 266 | 5.79 | 10.13 |
| Ytterøy | Assembly line | 12 | 3.33 | 5.25 |
| Ytterøy | Support functions | 18 | 4.44 | 7.39 |
| Ytterøy | Total | 30 | 4.00 | 6.53 |
| Crysbro | Assembly line | 24 | 10.29 | 14.58 |
| Crysbro | Support functions | 18 | 5.11 | 5.11 |
| Crysbro | Total | 42 | 8.07 | 10.52 |
| KUPCO | Assembly line | 15 | 8.80 | 14.07 |
| KUPCO | Support functions | 18 | 5.39 | 14.83 |
| KUPCO | Total | 33 | 6.94 | 14.48 |

Source: authors' data collection.

### 4.4.4 Outcome variables

Outcome variables including whether the *speed of production* functioned satisfactorily are shown in Table 4.8. This variable is measured on a five-level scale where the group leaders were asked to evaluate: 'To your knowledge was the speed of production satisfactory today?'

1 A big problem
2 A small problem
3 Neutral
4 Going well
5 Going very well

The results here are based on the individual group leader's understanding of the situation. The perception of what constitutes a problem can vary. During our visits, we got the impression talking to the group leaders that there was a reasonably equal interpretation of this question. One interesting result from this variable is that all firms score higher on supporting functions than assembly line functions. The average for the firms is around four and we will give detailed statistical analysis later, but the general impression was that higher speed of

*Table 4.8* Results of outcome variables of production

| | *Speed of production ok* | *Stops not planned* | *Results from control* |
|---|---|---|---|
| Danpo A, N = 21 | 4.24 | 1.95 | 1.43 |
| Danpo S, N = 18 | 4.50 | 1.44 | 1.56 |
| Danpo T, N = 39 | 4.36 | 1.72 | 1.49 |
| LAR A, N = 162 | 3.85 | 1.91 | 2.93 |
| LAR S, N = 104 | 4.14 | 0.67 | 2.82 |
| LAR T, N = 166 | 3.97 | 1.43 | 2.89 |
| Ytterøy A, N = 12 | 4.00 | 0.33 | 1.75 |
| Ytterøy S, N = 18 | 4.06 | 0.50 | 1.72 |
| Ytterøy T, N = 30 | 4.03 | 0.43 | 1.73 |
| Crysbro A, N = 24 | 3.33 | 0.33 | 2.13 |
| Crysbro S, N = 18 | 4.72 | 0.22 | 1.28 |
| Crysbro T, N = 40 | 3.93 | 0.29 | 1.76 |
| KUPCO A, N = 15 | 3.13 | 0.00 | 1.93 |
| KUPCO S, N = 18 | 3.83 | 0.00 | 1.56 |
| KUPCO T, N = 33 | 3.52 | 0.00 | 1.73 |

Source: authors' data collection.

(In Tables 4.8–4.12 we use the following abbreviations: A: Assembly line functions, S: Support functions, T: Total, N: Number of observations)

production is associated with higher (positive) values on the communication variables.

The next variable examined is the average number of *stops not planned* in productions the day of registration. Danpo has an average of 1.72 stops not planned during in the day and LAR 1.43, while the other firms have very low scores with Ytterøy 0.43, Crysbro 0.29 and KUPCO 0.0. The conclusion is that the most technologically advanced firms and firms with the largest organizational systems are the ones with higher numbers of stops not planned compared to the smaller and more transparent firms. It is not a big problem for Danpo to have some unplanned stops if they have resources and an effective organization to take care of this. We can even find the opposite result that unplanned stops provoke the system to be more innovative.

The third outcome variable is *Results from quality control*. Group leaders were asked to give answers based on the following scale based on the quality control of the day:

1 All in order – no consequences or suggestions for changes
2 All in order – but proposals for changes
3 Found problems – no consequences or suggestions for changes
4 Found problems took actions (did changes)

When we analyze the data, we found that alternative three was not chosen many times because when they found problems they needed to take actions. The results from this analysis show that all firms except LAR average from 1.49 to 1.76 which means that the results are quite close and showing few problems when we use the averages for the firm. The three smallest firms with standard technology have the same result. Danpo has a high-tech advanced computerised quality control system and has the best score. LAR, a big organization with high volume production has a substantially higher score, meaning more problems since many people with different levels of knowledge are involved in production.

### *4.4.5 Communication variables*

In the data collection, we have three communication variables. The first one is based on the question 'how many times did you (the group leader) speak with your leader (responsible manager) today' (interpreted as an 'average' day in the recent past). Related to this we also asked what subjects they talked about such as (1) volume of production, (2) employees, (3) technology and (4) other issues. The results from the communication variables are in Table 4.9 and we saw striking differences between the firms. We have the results from the Norwegian and Danish firms where the group leader took the initiative to speak to their responsible manager about ten times each day when we collected data. LAR is somewhat below this with an average of 7.14 and quite low we find Crysbro

*Table 4.9* Number of communicative initiatives collected

| | *Comm. number up to manager* | *Number speak to own group* | *Group member initiatives to you* |
|---|---|---|---|
| Danpo A, N = 21 | 7.19 | 13.43 | 18.00 |
| Danpo S, N = 18 | 15.22 | 22.94 | 26.17 |
| Danpo T, N = 39 | 10.90 | 17.82 | 21.77 |
| LAR A, N = 162 | 7.63 | 11.70 | 7.13 |
| LAR S, N = 104 | 6.38 | 10.30 | 10.31 |
| LAR T, N = 266 | 7.14 | 11.15 | 8.37 |
| Ytterøy A, N = 12 | 8.83 | 9.58 | 10.08 |
| Ytterøy S, N = 18 | 10.22 | 11.83 | 11.00 |
| Ytterøy T, N = 30 | 9.67 | 10.93 | 10.63 |
| Crysbro A, N = 24 | 3.67 | 3.67 | 3.33 |
| Crysbro S, N = 18 | 8.17 | 7.89 | 7.72 |
| Crysbro T, N = 40 | 5.60 | 5.48 | 5.21 |
| KUPCO A, N = 15 | 3.20 | 3.27 | 2.13 |
| KUPCO S, N = 18 | 3.89 | 3.17 | 3.17 |
| KUPCO T, N = 33 | 3.58 | 3.21 | 2.70 |

Source: authors' data collection (for explanation of abbreviations see Table 4.8).

with 5.60 and KUPCO with 3.58 times on the average. In general, the results from the theory and other investigations are that more communication is better. Combining theory from Baker (2002) and Conrad and Poole (2012) with our impressions from walking around the firms we assumed that a high number of communication occurrences were an indication of a well-functioning system. It showed that the firm was able to find solutions to problems and make the production flow better. The Norwegian and Danish firms had a similar communication structure when dividing into assembly line functions and support functions. Communication in support functions had a higher number compared to assembly lines. Danpo, the firm with the highest speed assembly line and with the most advanced technology and IT systems, has the highest average of contacts between the group leader and the managerial level. Later, we do a more detailed analysis for each firm and analyze why we find a different communicating pattern in the different firms with respect to communication from the group leader and up to the managerial level.

The next communication variable is about how many times in one the day the group leader took the initiative to talk to members of his/her group. The results from this communication variable also show large differences between the firms. Danpo has on the average close to eighteen conversations between group leader and group during the day while LAR and Ytterøy have eleven.

Crysbro has 5.48 and KUPCO has 3.21 which correspond with the results from the first communication variable. When we look at the results from different functions, we see that Danpo has an even stronger divide between assembly line and support functions where the support functions communication pattern is a little less than two times that on the assembly line. For the other firms, except to some degree Crysbro, the communication between assembly line and support function is quite evenly divided.

When we look at communication as initiatives from members of the group to the group leader, the differences between the firms are large. Danpo with an average of 21.77 is more than twice that of the next firm, Ytterøy with 10.63. LAR is somewhat lower with 8.37 while Crysbro and especially KUPCO are very low compared to the other firms. The results from the communications variables show large differences between the firms. We will further investigate the reasons for this in the following sections but suggestions for explanations are educational level and homogeneity of culture.

### *4.4.6 Competence variables*

The next group of variables are competence variables which we find in Table 4.10. Here we have measured education levels of the group members, the group members understanding of technology and group member course participation.

The competence/education variable was measured by having the group leader distribute members of his group into six standard education levels.

1 Did not finish primary school/illiterate
2 Finished primary school – can read and write simple text
3 Finished secondary school – general level (9 years of education)
4 Finished secondary school with special relevant skills for the job
5 Finished high-school (12 years of education)
6 University education

If a group consist of six members with one in each group, then the average score is 3.5. We have calculated *Average educational level* scores in this way for all groups in all firms. The results from Table 4.10 correspond with what we see from the index values in Chapter 4.2 where the Scandinavian countries rank high and the three other countries have quite close averages. The similarity of the Danish and the Norwegian firms was that educational levels of the workers in support functions were high. The difference was that the workers on the assembly line have a substantially higher educational level in the Norwegian firm compared to the Danish. The Danish firm has the traditional split in employees between assembly line and support workers, while this is not the case in the Norwegian firm. The reason for this is that the Norwegian firm is a niche producer where specialized operations at the assembly line demand higher skills than normal.

*Table 4.10* Competence variables

| | *Educational average* | *Technical level* | *Number of group members participated in training last month* |
|---|---|---|---|
| Danpo A, N = 21 | 3.084 | 1.71 | 1.19 |
| Danpo S, N = 18 | 4.262 | 1.33 | 3.78 |
| Danpo T, N = 39 | 3.628 | 1.54 | 2.38 |
| LAR A, N = 162 | 2.771 | 3.09 | 1.19 |
| LAR S, N = 104 | 4.056 | 2.48 | 5.16 |
| LAR T, N = 166 | 3.273 | 2.85 | 2.74 |
| Ytterøy A, N = 12 | 4.243 | 1.42 | 1.83 |
| Ytterøy S, N = 18 | 4.339 | 1.61 | 1.50 |
| Ytterøy T, N = 30 | 4.301 | 1.53 | 1.63 |
| Crysbro A, N = 24 | 2.558 | 2.21 | 0.21 |
| Crysbro S, N = 18 | 4.231 | 1.33 | 1.89 |
| Crysbro T, N = 40 | 3.275 | 1.83 | 0.93 |
| KUPCO A, N = 15 | 2.907 | 1.73 | 0.07 |
| KUPCO S, N = 18 | 3.625 | 1.50 | 0.06 |
| KUPCO T, N = 33 | 3.299 | 1.61 | 0.06 |

Source: authors' data collection (for explanation of abbreviations see Table 4.8).

Another explanation for this is that the educational level in Norway in general is high for all kinds of professions.

The next competence variable is about technology and the understanding of technology by the workers in the group. The question which is raised, is the following:

For the average participant of the group – what is the competence level for understanding technology?

1 Understand immediately without no explanation
2 Understand immediately with short (less than 10 minutes) explanation
3 Must have more than 10 minutes but less than 30 minutes explanation
4 Must have special training and or long (more than 30 minutes) explanation

When we look at the results and our impressions during data collection this variable is reasonably equally understood in the different firms even under different cultural conditions. For this variable, the lower numbers are better and we see quite equal results for all firms except LAR. As expected, we received the lowest numbers from the Scandinavian firms. One part of the explanation for the special number at LAR is high turnover and younger age of the employees, especially on the assembly line.

In the questionnaire, we have the following question:

> Number of group members who have participated in courses/training:
>
> - In the last year, number of times
> - In the last month, number of times

We 'normalized' the results by group size. Results suggest that Scandinavian firms intensively train their employees. LAR had a special internal training program for the support function employees. It is interesting to see that low training activities takes place in Crysbro compared to KUPCO, which matches the knowledge indexes.

### 4.4.7 *Innovative behavior*

We look at innovations from three points of view in this project. The first is substantial change in technology like at Danpo, the second is what we call innovative behavior, and the third is innovation management. To analyze innovative behavior, we first ask the group leaders if anyone in the group has come up with proposals for changes in routines within their area of responsibility.

> Has anyone in the group come up with proposals for changes in routines within your area of responsibility in:
>
> 1 The last week
> 2 The last month
> 3 The last three months
> 4 Any time in the past you can remember
> 5 Never

Then we asked about what kind of proposal it was, if it concerned product, process, organization or logistics. To get a clearer picture about the seriousness of the suggestions we asked about the number of suggestions that had been formalized.

> Have there been formal (written) suggestions from members of your group to change routines? (This question had the same answer categories as the question above)

The lower numbers in Table 4.11 indicate more innovative behavior. The results show a three-level pattern where most innovative activities occur in the Danish firm, with LAR and Ytterøy at about the same level, while Crysbro and KUPCO have less innovative behavior. The results here are what we might expect looking at the indexes with the exception that the Brazilian firm results does better that expected and especially the assembly line functions have an impressive score. These results will be discussed in more detail in Chapter 5 about innovations.

*Table 4.11* Innovative behavior

| | *Suggested changes in routines* | *Formalized suggested changes in routines* |
|---|---|---|
| Danpo A, N = 21 | 1.90 | 2.10 |
| Danpo S, N = 18 | 1.28 | 1.22 |
| Danpo T, N = 39 | 1.62 | 1.69 |
| LAR A, N = 162 | 2.09 | 2.67 |
| LAR S, N = 104 | 1.24 | 1.55 |
| LAR T, N = 166 | 1.75 | 2.21 |
| Ytterøy A, N = 12 | 2.17 | 2.17 |
| Ytterøy S, N = 18 | 1.67 | 2.06 |
| Ytterøy T, N = 30 | 1.87 | 2.10 |
| Crysbro A, N = 24 | 3.69 | 3.89 |
| Crysbro S, N = 18 | 2.17 | 3.00 |
| Crysbro T, N = 40 | 2.98 | 3.45 |
| KUPCO A, N = 15 | 3.20 | 3.40 |
| KUPCO S, N = 18 | 2.78 | 3.01 |
| KUPCO T, N = 33 | 2.94 | 3.18 |

Source: authors' data collection (for explanation of abbreviations see Table 4.8).

### 4.4.8 *Cultural variables*

Cultural variables have gained more and more attention for explaining how and why firms enter the knowledge economy and how they can use knowledge to improve their competitiveness, see Hofstede (1980), Hofstede and Hofstede (2001) and House, *et al.* (2002). In this project, we have used the cultural indicators developed by Hofstede. Hofstede calls the different indicators cultural constructs and the first is about uncertainty avoidance. The question in the questionnaire is the following:

> Do you try to avoid uncertainty?

and the answer alternatives are:

1 Disagree
2 Partly disagree
3 Neutral
4 Partly agree
5 Agree

A traditional Likert scale was used in the original work by Hofstede and in many other projects and investigations about the role of culture in firms. This indicator was based on human behavior where the assumption is that people, like the group leaders in our project, do not want unexpected events. The content of this statement was based on individual reliance on social norms and procedures related to the group and society they live in.

The second cultural construct is about power distance and the question is:

> Do you expect and agree that power should be unequally shared?

We used the same formulation as Hofstede in which the word *unequally* shared indicates that the more you agree with this sentence, (the higher the number filled in) the more unequal distribution of power is assumed. Hofstede wrote that this cultural construct is formulated in this way because employees in firms are, or at least should be, expected to obey their leaders without questioning their decisions. When we look at the results from the firms related to this construct we must realize that one of the fundamental changes from management to knowledge management is the inversion of the authority pyramid (see Jensen 2008). So, this construct should have high scores when production is based on very strict routines that are not supposed to be discussed, and group leaders that do not want to discuss them. If we see innovative behavior as a good idea, then suggestions about changes in routines and changes in production modes are also good ideas. This is what we assume about entering the knowledge economy successfully more in general, that power distance should be low. This indicator is fundamentally related to the main topic in this book about firms entering the knowledge economy and trying to improve competitiveness with more extensive use of knowledge.

The next construct is about collectivism and the question is:

> Do you encourage and reward collective distribution of resources and collective action?

Most production activities are based on collectivism in the way that people work together. This index goes one step further and asks about attitudes that encourage and reward collective action. The higher numbers show a more positive attitude to collectivism.

The next cultural construct is related to behavior and expressed opinions, the question is:

> Do you express pride and loyalty in the firm where you work?

The question is raised in such a way that it means pride and loyalty to your colleagues and other relations in the firm. But this question also addresses pride and loyalty when the person (the group leader) is outside of the firm in social relations like family, friends and participation in social activities.

The next cultural construct is about gender egalitarianism and the question is:

> Do you try to minimize roles between men and women?

This question is understood by group leaders as mainly relating to what takes place inside the firm. Since the firms are in different countries with very different religious attitudes we expected that the results would differ significantly. We must also be aware of how the question is formulated, it is about if the group leaders *try* to minimize the roles, this does not mean they have to think about the results they have achieved.

The next cultural construct is about what is often called assertiveness and the question is:

> Are you confrontational in relationships with other people in the firm?

The content of the answers here is to get an idea if the group leaders are or want to be dominant.

The next cultural construct about future orientation is:

> Do you engage in future oriented behaviors such as planning and investing in the future?

This is a construct where we want to get some idea about the time horizon of the group leader. A high score on this indicator is normally also is interpreted as a more positive attitude about what is going on in the firm.

The last construct has the keyword human orientation and is formulated in the following way:

> Do you encourage and reward individuals for being fair, generous, caring and kind to others?

Being fair, generous and kind are positive attributes in most cultures. But the understanding about what kinds of actions at the firm can be defined in this way may vary.

The interpretation of the results from cultural indicators is not straight forward and there have been many discussions in the literature about this, see e.g. House, *et al.* (2002). The results from the project are found in Table 4.12. When we look at the construct of avoiding uncertainty we have very high values in Denmark and Norway and a slightly lower value at LAR in Brazil. We find medium scores in Sri Lanka and quite low scores at KUPCO in Kuwait. Our understanding of the results from Kuwait is that there is not much uncertainty to avoid; the firm is run in a quite strict but well-organized way and the group leaders know what to do because the routines are quite strongly institutionalized. It is understandable that the Danish firm has high scores because they have the most advanced capital and ICT equipment and highest speed. If they are not able to avoid uncertainty it can be very costly for the firm. In a cultural sense, the Norwegian firm is like one big family where people support each other. It also is a common responsibility to keep production going which means that they do not like uncertainty. The explanation in Brazil is somewhat different because this is a large organization where there would be significant consequences if something went wrong. Therefore, it is a good idea to avoid uncertainty.

*Table 4.12* Cultural constructs

| | *Avoid uncertainty* | *Power unequal* | *Reward collective* | *Pride in firm* | *Equality men/ women* | *Confron-tational in firm* | *Future oriented* | *Generous* |
|---|---|---|---|---|---|---|---|---|
| Danpo A, N = 21 | 4.52 | 1.57 | 3.86 | 4.95 | 4.76 | 2.29 | 4.81 | 4.76 |
| Danpo S, N = 18 | 4.56 | 1.72 | 4.11 | 4.50 | 4.28 | 2.06 | 4.83 | 4.61 |
| Danpo T, N = 39 | 4.54 | 1.64 | 3.97 | 4.74 | 4.54 | 2.18 | 4.82 | 4.69 |
| LAR A, N = 162 | 3.89 | 2.48 | 4.31 | 4.59 | 4.23 | 3.57 | 3.79 | 4.59 |
| LAR S, N = 104 | 4.46 | 2.74 | 4.73 | 4.87 | 4.71 | 4.22 | 4.44 | 4.68 |
| LAR T, N = 166 | 4.11 | 2.58 | 4.47 | 4.70 | 4.42 | 3.82 | 4.05 | 4.62 |
| Ytterøy A, N = 12 | 4.67 | 1.75 | 4.67 | 4.75 | 4.50 | 1.83 | 4.83 | 4.83 |
| Ytterøy S, N = 18 | 4.61 | 1.61 | 4.28 | 4.56 | 4.28 | 1.83 | 4.56 | 4.67 |
| Ytterøy T, N = 30 | 4.63 | 1.67 | 4.43 | 4.63 | 4.37 | 1.83 | 4.67 | 4.73 |
| Crysbro A, N = 24 | 3.04 | 4.00 | 4.33 | 4.71 | 2.58 | 2.21 | 4.50 | 4.75 |
| Crysbro S, N = 18 | 4.17 | 2.11 | 4.17 | 4.78 | 3.28 | 1.39 | 4.89 | 4.78 |
| Crysbro T, N = 40 | 3.52 | 3.19 | 4.26 | 4.74 | 2.88 | 1.86 | 4.67 | 4.76 |
| KUPCO A, N = 15 | 2.20 | 4.60 | 3.60 | 4.13 | 2.20 | 1.07 | 4.33 | 4.53 |
| KUPCO S, N = 18 | 2.78 | 3.94 | 3.89 | 4.39 | 1.06 | 1.06 | 4.78 | 4.78 |
| KUPCO T, N = 33 | 2.52 | 4.24 | 3.76 | 4.27 | 1.58 | 1.06 | 4.58 | 4.67 |

Source: authors' data collection (for explanation of abbreviations see Table 4.8).

Power distance is one of the most interesting and important cultural constructs showing significant differences in the firms. This indicator tells a story about authority. The results here for Scandinavian firms tended towards lower numbers for power distance. Upon closer examination, the problem for Scandinavian firms was not that the group leader lacked worker respect. In Scandinavian firms workers at all levels can take up subjects for discussion and try to find new and better solutions without being looked at as disobedient. This is a very significant result for a positive transformation of traditional industrial production into the knowledge economy and we saw the same result from the knowledge indexes.

The other three firms show different results where LAR is ranked as number three from the point of view that it is a good idea to keep the power distance low. The results reflect that LAR is a bigger organization which normally requires more authority but as a part of a cultural construct, authority is more strictly built into the Brazilian way of organizing production compared to the Scandinavian countries.

While visiting the firms, it was easy to see that Crysbro and KUPCO were based more on discipline and authority in production compared to the other firms. Crysbro has a mix of Tamil and Singhalese culture where authority plays a part but is not so dominating compared to KUPCO which has a traditional Muslim culture. KUPCO was also based on production workers with time limited contracts coming from other countries like Sri Lanka and India.

The next cultural construct is about reward of collective distribution of resources and actions. For this indicator, the results for the three firms LAR, Ytterøy and Crysbro, have high values. The Danish and Kuwaiti firms are both slightly lower. It is understandable that KUPCO has the lowest numbers because of the more disciplined way production takes place, but the result from the Danish firm is a little surprising. The result of the indicator to which degree the group leader expresses pride and loyalty is equal for all firms. The main reason for this is that all firms have a policy that the workers shall have a positive attitude about the firm.

The results regarding the gender construct vary considerably. The results from the Scandinavian countries are as expected, with high and equal scores for Danpo and Ytterøy. The high scores for LAR in Brazil are somewhat surprising because other investigations indicate that Brazilian culture is perceived as more male oriented than Scandinavian culture. The most likely reasons for the high scores at LAR is that about 20% of all group leaders are female and female participation on all levels of the firms is relatively high. The females at LAR are also highly respected for their skills such as in veterinarian and product control operations.

The results from Crysbro and KUPCO show that religion and local cultural aspects have a strong influence. The results from KUPCO show that they do not want to minimize differences in roles between men and women and this is understandable because this is a traditional Muslim society. We also find this point of view in Crysbro in Sri Lanka and it is quite interesting to see that the results differ between assembly line production functions and support functions. In support functions the level of education is much higher than for assembly line workers. This reflects the fact that higher levels of education normally go together with a more positive attitude of egalitarianism between men and women.

The next construct about confrontational relationships was disagreed with at KUPCO. This was mainly because discipline was strong. The numbers for the total results are similar in Crysbro and in Ytterøy but the explanations are quite different. At the Crysbro firm, they are not confrontational because it is a quite disciplined system that actually works. At Ytterøy there is no need to be confrontational because, as earlier stated, the firm works and looks like a big family. The higher results on this indicator at Danpo and LAR are mainly explained by the characteristics of the firm with a high-tech and advanced IT system in Denmark and by the size of the organization at LAR.

The indicator about future-oriented behavior is quite equal for all firms except LAR, where it is slightly lower. One reason for the somewhat lower results at LAR is that it has larger groups with lower education especially at assembly line functions. The cultural construct about generosity shows the same result for all firms mainly because this is a firm strategy that the management wants all workers to act in compliance with.

### 4.4.9 *Results from individual firms – LAR*

For LAR, the total (266) observations can be divided into assembly line functions with 162 observations and support functions with 104 observations and we can do correlation and regression analysis for each group. The correlation matrix for the two result variables *Speed of production* and *Result from quality control* are shown in Table 4.13. We analyze if it is possible to find relationships between

*Table 4.13* Correlation matrix for result, communication and competence variables for LAR

| | | *Comm. up to manager* | *Comm. to own group* | *Group member initiatives* | *Educational average* | *Technical level* | *Training last month* |
|---|---|---|---|---|---|---|---|
| Speed prod ok (total LAR) | Correlation | .151* | .202** | .205** | .347** | −0.064 | 0.102 |
| | Sig. (2-tailed) | 0.013 | 0.001 | 0.001 | 0.000 | 0.301 | 0.096 |
| | N | 266 | 266 | 266 | 266 | 266 | 266 |
| Res from control (total LAR) | Correlation | −.343** | −0.110 | −.241** | 0.041 | −0.074 | 0.082 |
| | Sig. (2-tailed) | 0.000 | 0.072 | 0.000 | 0.509 | 0.227 | 0.183 |
| | N | 266 | 266 | 266 | 266 | 266 | 266 |
| Speed prod ok (assembly line) | Correlation | 0.132 | 0.103 | −0.013 | .159* | −0.048 | −.188* |
| | Sig. (2-tailed) | 0.093 | 0.194 | 0.869 | 0.044 | 0.545 | 0.017 |
| | N | 162 | 162 | 162 | 162 | 162 | 162 |
| Res from control (assembly line) | Correlation | −.312** | −0.115 | −.364** | 0.108 | −0.102 | −.177* |
| | Sig. (2-tailed) | 0.000 | 0.147 | 0.000 | 0.170 | 0.198 | 0.024 |
| | N | 162 | 162 | 162 | 162 | 162 | 162 |
| Speed prod ok (support functions) | Correlation | .218* | .389** | .423** | .503** | 0.008 | 0.147 |
| | Sig. (2-tailed) | 0.026 | 0.000 | 0.000 | 0.000 | 0.938 | 0.137 |
| | N | 104 | 104 | 104 | 104 | 104 | 104 |
| Res from control (support functions) | Correlation | −.414** | −0.116 | −0.056 | 0.043 | −0.064 | 0.172 |
| | Sig. (2-tailed) | 0.000 | 0.241 | 0.574 | 0.667 | 0.518 | 0.080 |
| | N | 104 | 104 | 104 | 104 | 104 | 104 |

Source: authors' data collection.

* Correlation is significant at the 0.05 level (2-tailed).

** Correlation is significant at the 0.01 level (2-tailed).

communication variables, competence variables and cultural variables and how they influence the results of production using the SPSS V23.0.0.2 system. We find a clear correlation between *Speed of production* and all three communication variables when we look at the LAR firm as a unit. This means that more communication is associated with speeds of production going more fluently. When we divide into subgroups we find significant correlations between communication and speed of production for the support functions while the significance of the results disappears for the assembly line functions. When we look at the other outcome variable, *Result from quality control*, we must take into consideration that this variable is defined by higher values produce worse results. Communication variables for the firm are significant with the expected sign. The two groups of production show significant results individually for the variable *Communication from the group leader to the boss.*

The next block of variables deals with competence using the variables *Educational average of workers in the group*, *Level of technical understanding* and *Participation in training* last month. Here we only find significant correlation coefficients for educational average, which means that the higher educational level is related to higher satisfaction regarding speed of production.

The cultural variables show interesting correlations with the outcome variables (see Table 4.14). We find strong correlations with the expected signs from the variables *Avoid uncertainty*, *Power unequal* and *Future orientation.* When we look at the different groups, the variable *Power unequal* still has a strong correlation for the support functions.

When we put the results into a regression model (using a customized linear regression model from SPSS) with *Speed of production* as the dependent variable and the three communication variables as independent, we only get a significant model with variable group members initiatives to the group leader as the independent variable (predictor), see Table 4.15. It is quite interesting to see that among the three communication variables this can be looked at as the strongest. The interpretation is that all communication is important but the initiatives upwards, from the workers in the group to the group leader, show stronger statistical power to explain speed of production than downward communication from the leader to the group. Another reason why the other two communication variables are not significant in the regression models is because of multicollinearity between all three communication variables.

We have calculated regression models for competence variables, (Table 4.16) and for the cultural variables, (Table 4.17). The model for the competence variables shows that the variables *Educational level* and *Participating in training* are both significant for explaining *Speed of production.* It is interesting that both variables are significant in the regression model because only one showed significant partial correlation.

For cultural variables, the regression model shows that the cultural factors *Avoid uncertainty*, *Power unequal* and *Future orientation* go into the regression model with significant results. We have also looked at the possibility of building regression models for the subgroups but these results are not discussed here.

*Table 4.14* Correlation matrix for cultural variables for LAR

| | | *Avoid uncertainty* | *Power unequal* | *Reward collective* | *Pride in firm* | *Equality men/women* | *Confrontational in firm* | *Future oriented* | *Generous* |
|---|---|---|---|---|---|---|---|---|---|
| Speed prod ok (total LAR) | Correlation | .363** | −.268** | 0.067 | −0.100 | −.157* | 0.035 | .175** | −0.055 |
| | Sig. (2-tailed) | 0.000 | 0.000 | 0.279 | 0.103 | 0.010 | 0.574 | 0.004 | 0.373 |
| | N | 266 | 266 | 266 | 266 | 266 | 266 | 266 | 266 |
| Res from control (total LAR) | Correlation | .152* | .204** | 0.006 | 0.058 | 0.042 | −0.102 | .229** | −0.102 |
| | Sig. (2-tailed) | 0.013 | 0.001 | 0.929 | 0.350 | 0.500 | 0.095 | 0.000 | 0.097 |
| | N | 266 | 266 | 266 | 266 | 266 | 266 | 266 | 266 |
| Speed prod ok (assembly line) | Correlation | .494** | −0.109 | −0.089 | −.246** | −.358** | 0.009 | .297** | −.164* |
| | Sig. (2-tailed) | 0.000 | 0.166 | 0.259 | 0.002 | 0.000 | 0.906 | 0.000 | 0.037 |
| | N | 162 | 162 | 162 | 162 | 162 | 162 | 162 | 162 |
| Res from control (assembly line) | Correlation | .229** | .401** | −0.034 | 0.055 | 0.034 | −.156* | .389** | −0.149 |
| | Sig. (2-tailed) | 0.003 | 0.000 | 0.665 | 0.485 | 0.672 | 0.047 | 0.000 | 0.059 |
| | N | 162 | 162 | 162 | 162 | 162 | 162 | 162 | 162 |
| Speed prod ok (support functions) | Correlation | 0.050 | −.541** | .200* | 0.018 | 0.136 | −0.062 | −.235* | 0.057 |
| | Sig. (2-tailed) | 0.611 | 0.000 | 0.041 | 0.853 | 0.170 | 0.530 | 0.017 | 0.567 |
| | N | 104 | 104 | 104 | 104 | 104 | 104 | 104 | 104 |
| Res from control (support functions) | Correlation | 0.015 | −0.121 | 0.123 | 0.097 | 0.115 | 0.074 | −0.112 | −0.025 |
| | Sig. (2-tailed) | 0.883 | 0.222 | 0.214 | 0.328 | 0.245 | 0.453 | 0.256 | 0.797 |
| | N | 104 | 104 | 104 | 104 | 104 | 104 | 104 | 104 |

Source: authors' data collection.

* Correlation is significant at the 0.05 level (2-tailed).

** Correlation is significant at the 0.01 level (2-tailed).

*Table 4.15* Regression results for speed of production and a communication variable for LAR

| | Model summary | | | | | |
|---|---|---|---|---|---|---|
| | *R* | *R square* | *Adjusted R square* | *Std. error of the estimate* | *F* | *Sig.* |
| | .205[a] | 0.042 | 0.038 | 1.027 | 11.563 | .001 |

| | *Coefficients*[b] | | | | |
|---|---|---|---|---|---|
| | *Unstandardized coefficients* | | *Standardized coefficients* | *t* | *Sig.* |
| | *B* | *Std. error* | *Beta* | | |
| (Constant) | 3.714 | 0.097 | | 38.197 | 0.000 |
| Group mem ini to you | 0.030 | 0.009 | 0.205 | 3.400 | 0.001 |

Source: authors' data collection.

a Predictors: (Constant), Group mem ini to you
b Dependent variable: speed prod ok (N = 266)

*Table 4.16* Regression results for speed of production and competence variables for LAR

| | Model Summary | | | | | |
|---|---|---|---|---|---|---|
| | *R* | *R Square* | *Adjusted R square* | *Std. error of the estimate* | *F* | *Sig.* |
| | .365[b] | 0.133 | 0.126 | 0.979 | 20.182 | .000 |

| *Model* | *Coefficients*[a] | | | | |
|---|---|---|---|---|---|
| | *Unstandardized coefficients* | | *Standardized coefficients* | *t* | *Sig.* |
| | *B* | *Std. error* | *Beta* | | |
| (Constant) | 2.875 | 0.185 | | 15.509 | 0.000 |
| Comp average | 0.325 | 0.053 | 0.350 | 6.098 | 0.000 |
| Group last month part training last month | 0.003 | 0.002 | 0.113 | 1.970 | 0.050 |

Source: authors' data collection.

a Dependent variable: Speed prod ok (N = 266)
b Predictors: (Constant), Comp average, Group part. training last month

*Table 4.17* Regression results for speed of production and cultural variables for LAR

| *Model summary* | | | | | | |
|---|---|---|---|---|---|---|
| *Model* | *R* | *R Square* | *Adjusted R square* | *Std. error of the estimate* | *F* | *Sig.* |
| | .493[c] | 0.243 | 0.234 | 0.917 | 28.017 | .000 |

| *Coefficients*[a] | | | | | |
|---|---|---|---|---|---|
| *Model* | *Unstandardized coefficients* | | *Standardized coefficients* | *t* | *Sig.* |
| | *B* | *Std. error* | *Beta* | | |
| (Constant) | 2.457 | 0.287 | | 8.563 | 0.000 |
| Avoid uncertainty | 0.265 | 0.045 | 0.319 | 5.876 | 0.000 |
| Power unequal | −0.224 | 0.040 | −0.318 | −5.610 | 0.000 |
| Future oriented | 0.246 | 0.058 | 0.240 | 4.226 | 0.000 |

Source: authors' data collection.

a Dependent variable: Speed prod ok (N = 266)
c Predictors: (Constant), Avoid uncertainty, Power unequal, Future oriented

### 4.4.10 Danpo

Previous analysis shows Danpo as the high-tech and capital-intensive producer with high speed on the assembly line compared to the other firms. The correlations between the outcome variable *Speed of production* and the *communication* and *competence* variables are shown in Table 4.18. The correlations are significant for all communication variables showing that the more communicative activities that take place, the better results for the *Speed of production* indicator we find. This result is equal in all directions from the *Group leader and up*, from the *Group leader to his own group* and *Initiatives from the group to the group leader.*

When we put this into a regression model, (see Table 4.19) we find that the variable *Group member initiatives to the group leader* is the one that is significant in the model, the two others do not enter into the model mainly because of multi-collinearity. But it is interesting to see that the indicator *Group member initiatives to the group leader* are relatively speaking stronger than the two others.

When we look at the correlations between *Speed of production* and competence variables we also find a significant correlation between all three competence variables. This means that higher knowledge levels develop in the same direction as the outcome results. Also, we have analyzed this with a regression model which shows that *Technical level* is the stronger variable and is significant in the model, see Table 4.20. This is quite interesting because Danpo has the most advanced technological equipment with the strongest technological competence variable.

*Table 4.18* Correlation matrix for result, communication and competence variables for Danpo

| | | *Comm. up to manager* | *Comm. to own group* | *Group member initiatives* | *Educational average* | *Technical level* | *Training last month* |
|---|---|---|---|---|---|---|---|
| Speed prod ok | Correlation | .448** | .435** | .616** | .322* | −.460** | .394* |
| | Sig. (2-tailed) | 0.001 | 0.006 | 0.000 | 0,045 | 0.003 | 0.013 |
| | N | 39 | 39 | 39 | 39 | 39 | 39 |

Source: authors' data collection.

* Correlation is significant at the 0.05 level (2-tailed).
** Correlation is significant at the 0.01 level (2-tailed).

*Table 4.19* Regression results for result and a communication variable for Danpo

| *Model summary* | | | | | |
|---|---|---|---|---|---|
| *R* | *R Square* | *Adjusted R square* | *Std. error of the estimate* | *F* | *Sig.* |
| .616[a] | 0.379 | 0.362 | 0.501 | 22.590 | ,000 |

| *Coefficients*[b] | | | | | |
|---|---|---|---|---|---|
| | *Unstandardized coefficients* | | *Standardized coefficients* | *t* | *Sig.* |
| | *B* | *Std. error* | *Beta* | | |
| (Constant) | 3.542 | 0.190 | | 18.667 | 0.000 |
| Group mem ini to you | 0.038 | 0.008 | 0.616 | 4.753 | 0.000 |

Source: authors' data collection.

a Predictors: (Constant), Group mem ini to you
b Dependent variable: Speed prod ok

*Table 4.20* Correlation matrix for result and cultural variables for Danpo

| | | *Avoid uncertainty* | *Power unequal* | *Reward collective* | *Pride in firm* | *Equality men/women* | *Confrontational in firm* | *Future oriented* | *Generous* |
|---|---|---|---|---|---|---|---|---|---|
| Speed prod ok | Correlation | ,536** | -,544** | 0,225 | 0,121 | 0,262 | 0,022 | 0,163 | 0,117 |
| | Sig. (2-tailed) | 0,000 | 0,000 | 0,168 | 0,461 | 0,108 | 0,893 | 0,321 | 0,477 |
| | N | 39 | 39 | 39 | 39 | 39 | 39 | 39 | 39 |

Source: authors' data collection.

* Correlation is significant at the 0.05 level (2-tailed).
** Correlation is significant at the 0.01 level (2-tailed).

Among the cultural variables *Avoid uncertainty* and *Power distance* were significant in the correlation analysis with the result variable with the expected signs, see Table 4.21. Danpo has a strong relationship with high scores on the indicator *Avoid uncertainty* and this variable is significant in the correlation matrix. The regression model is significant for *Power distance* (see Table 4.22). This indicator has very low

*Table 4.21* Regression results for result and competence variables for Danpo

| *Model summary* | | | | | | |
|---|---|---|---|---|---|---|
| | *R* | *R Square* | *Adjusted R square* | *Std. error of the estimate* | *F* | *Sig.* |
| | .460[a] | 0.211 | 0.190 | 0.565 | 9.916 | ,003 |

| *Coefficients*[b] | | | | | |
|---|---|---|---|---|---|
| *Model* | *Unstandardized coefficients* | | *Standardized coefficients* | *t* | *Sig.* |
| | *B* | *Std. error* | *Beta* | | |
| (Constant) | 5.238 | 0.293 | | 17.849 | 0.000 |
| Tech level | −0.571 | 0.181 | −0.460 | −3.149 | 0.003 |

Source: authors' data collection.

a Predictors: (Constant), Tech level
b Dependent variable: Speed prod ok

*Table 4.22* Regression results for speed of production and cultural variables for Danpo

| *Model summary* | | | | | | |
|---|---|---|---|---|---|---|
| | *R* | *R Square* | *Adjusted R square* | *Std. error of the estimate* | *F* | *Sig.* |
| | .544[a] | 0.296 | 0.277 | 0.534 | 15.556 | ,000 |

| *Coefficients*[b] | | | | | |
|---|---|---|---|---|---|
| *Model* | *Unstandardized coefficients* | | *Standardized coefficients* | *t* | *Sig.* |
| | *B* | *Std. Error* | *Beta* | | |
| (Constant) | 5.402 | 0.278 | | 19.439 | 0.000 |
| Power unequal | −0.636 | 0.161 | −0.544 | −3.944 | 0.000 |

Source: authors' data collection.

a Predictors: (Constant), Power unequal
b Dependent variable: Speed prod ok

absolute value in the Danish firm meaning that the power distance is low, but if the *Power distance* is reduced even more it is likely that the results also improve.

### 4.4.11 Ytterøy

Ytterøy is the smallest firm in the sample and can be looked at as a niche producer with a high cost level, medium technology equipment but a very specific adaptation to the market. This market orientation is pervasive at all levels of management. The communication variables show a very strong correlation with the outcome variable *Speed of production*. This means that better communication increases speed of production. Also, the competence variables show good correlation with the expected signs, see Tables 4.23 and 4.24.

Most of the cultural variables also show correlation, which is an indication that the firm can be looked at as one big family with a high degree of shared values. When we look at the regression results, we find the same result here as for the Danish firm that among the communication variables, *Communication up to the boss* is the strongest with significant results and a good model fit. For the competence variables, the Norwegian firm showed that *Education level* was the

*Table 4.23* Correlation matrix for result, communication and competence variables for Ytterøy

| | | *Comm. up to manager* | *Comm. to own group* | *Group member initiatives* | *Educational average* | *Technical level* | *Training last month* |
|---|---|---|---|---|---|---|---|
| Speed prod ok | Correlation | .885** | .739** | .733** | .443* | −.403* | .428* |
| | Sig. (2-tailed) | 0.000 | 0.000 | 0.000 | 0.014 | 0.027 | 0.018 |
| | N | 30 | 30 | 30 | 30 | 30 | 30 |

Source: authors' data collection.

* Correlation is significant at the 0.05 level (2-tailed).
** Correlation is significant at the 0.01 level (2-tailed).

*Table 4.24* Correlation matrix for result and cultural variables for Ytterøy

| | | *Avoid uncertainty* | *Power unequal* | *Reward collective* | *Pride in firm* | *Equality men/ women* | *Confron-tational in firm* | *Future oriented* | *Generous* |
|---|---|---|---|---|---|---|---|---|---|
| Speed prod ok | Correlation | .583** | -.684** | .530** | .503** | 0.034 | −.382* | .662** | .540** |
| | Sig. (2-tailed) | 0.001 | 0.000 | 0.003 | 0.005 | 0.858 | 0.037 | 0.000 | 0.002 |
| | N | 30 | 30 | 30 | 30 | 30 | 30 | 30 | 30 |

Source: authors' data collection.

* Correlation is significant at the 0.05 level (2-tailed).
** Correlation is significant at the 0.01 level (2-tailed).

strongest significant variable in the regression model. This indicated that knowledge was a significant factor for this firm. When it comes to cultural variables the best regression model showed that *Power unequal* and *Future orientated* were significant, see Tables 4.25, 4.26 and 4.27.

*Table 4.25* Regression results for speed of production and a communication variable for Ytterøy

| | | | *Model summary* | | | |
|---|---|---|---|---|---|---|
| | *R*[a] | *R Square* | *Adjusted R square* | *Std. error of the estimate* | *F* | *Sig.* |
| | .885 | 0.784 | 0.776 | 0.421 | 101.632 | .000 |

| | *Coefficients*[b] | | | | |
|---|---|---|---|---|---|
| *Model* | *Unstandardized coefficients* | | *Standardized coefficients* | *t* | *Sig.* |
| | *B* | *Std. Error* | *Beta* | | |
| (Constant) | 1.660 | 0.248 | | 6.702 | 0.000 |
| Comm number up to boss | 0.246 | 0.024 | 0.885 | 10.081 | 0.000 |

Source: authors' data collection.

a Predictors: (Constant), Comm number up to boss
b Dependent variable: Speed prod ok

*Table 4.26* Regression results for speed of production and competence variable for Ytterøy

| | | | *Model summary* | | | |
|---|---|---|---|---|---|---|
| *Model* | *R*[a] | *R Square* | *Adjusted R Square* | *Std. Error of the Estimate* | *F* | *Sig.* |
| 1 | .443 | 0.197 | 0.168 | 0.812 | 6.854 | .014 |

| | *Coefficients*[b] | | | | |
|---|---|---|---|---|---|
| *Model* | *Unstandardized coefficients* | | *Standardized coefficients* | *t* | *Sig.* |
| | *B* | *Std. Error* | *Beta* | | |
| (Constant) | −2.334 | 2.437 | | −0.958 | 0.346 |
| Comp average | 1.481 | 0.566 | 0.443 | 2.618 | 0.014 |

Source: authors' data collection.

a Predictors: (Constant), Comp average
b Dependent variable: Speed prod ok

*Table 4.27* Regression results for speed of production and cultural variables for Ytterøy

| *Model summary* | | | | | | |
|---|---|---|---|---|---|---|
| *Model* | *R*[a] | *R Square* | *Adjusted R Square* | *Std. Error of the Estimate* | *F* | *Sig.* |
| | .752 | 0.565 | 0.533 | 0.608 | 17.524 | .000 |

| *Coefficients*[b] | | | | | |
|---|---|---|---|---|---|
| *Model* | *Unstandardized coefficients* | | *Standardized coefficients* | *t* | *Sig.* |
| | *B* | *Std. error* | *Beta* | | |
| (Constant) | 2.068 | 1.459 | | 1.417 | 0.168 |
| Power unequal | −0.603 | 0.215 | −0.448 | −2.809 | 0.009 |
| Future oriented | 0.636 | 0.259 | 0.391 | 2.453 | 0,021 |

Source: authors' data collection.

a Predictors: (Constant), Power unequal, Future oriented
b Dependent variable: Speed prod ok

### *4.4.12 Crysbro*

Crysbro is situated in Kandy, the second largest city on Sri Lanka and is a medium sized producer with standard technology and produces mostly for the local market. When we look at the variable *Speed of production* and analyze the correlation with the communication variables we also find a positive correlation for the two variables *Communication up to the boss* and *Group leader speaks to his own group*. But we do not find a significant correlation for *Group members' initiatives to the group leader*. The correlations here are weaker, meaning that they are on the 5% level. The competence variables *Educational average* and *Technical level* both show strong significance with the outcome variable meaning that both education and technical competence go together with improved outcome. Many of the cultural variables show significance and it is interesting to see that the power distance variable is strongly significant together with the variable about future orientation, see Tables 4.28 and 4.29.

When we look at competence variables, we can build a very significant and interesting regression model where both variables *Competence average* and *Level of technology* are significant with the expected signs. When we look at the cultural variables, we can build a significant model with *Power unequal* and *Future oriented* as the two independent variables and *Speed of production* as the dependent, see Tables 4.30 and 4.31.

*Table 4.28* Correlation matrix for result, communication and competence variables for Crysbro

| | | *Comm. up to manager* | *Comm. to own group* | *Group member initiatives* | *Educational average* | *Technical level* | *Training last month* |
|---|---|---|---|---|---|---|---|
| Speed prod ok | Correlation | .361* | .333* | 0.278 | .807** | −.797** | |
| | Sig. (2-tailed) | 0.019 | 0.031 | 0.075 | 0.000 | 0.000 | |
| | N | 42 | 42 | 42 | 42 | 42 | |

Source: authors' data collection.

* Correlation is significant at the 0.05 level (2-tailed).
** Correlation is significant at the 0.01 level (2-tailed).

*Table 4.29* Correlation matrix for result and cultural variables for Crysbro

| | | *Avoid uncertainty* | *Power unequal* | *Reward collective* | *Pride in firm* | *Equality men/ women* | *Confron- tational in firm* | *Future oriented* | *Generous* |
|---|---|---|---|---|---|---|---|---|---|
| Speed prod ok | Correlation | 0.280 | −.633** | 0.208 | .341* | 0.174 | -0.294 | .615** | 0.115 |
| | Sig. (2-tailed) | 0.072 | 0.000 | 0.186 | 0.027 | 0.270 | 0.059 | 0.000 | 0.467 |
| | N | 42 | 42 | 42 | 42 | 42 | 42 | 42 | 42 |

Source: authors' data collection.

* Correlation is significant at the 0.05 level (2-tailed).
** Correlation is significant at the 0.01 level (2-tailed).

*Table 4.30* Regression results for speed of production and competence variables for Crysbro

| *Model summary* | | | | | | |
|---|---|---|---|---|---|---|
| | *R*[a] | *R Square* | *Adjusted R square* | *Std. error of the estimate* | *F* | *Sig.* |
| | .863 | 0.744 | 0.731 | 0.517 | 56.807 | .000 |

| *Coefficients*[b] | | | | | |
|---|---|---|---|---|---|
| *Model* | *Unstandardized coefficients* | | *Standardized coefficients* | *t* | *Sig.* |
| | *B* | *Std. error* | *Beta* | | |
| (Constant) | 3.322 | 0.731 | | 4.546 | 0.000 |
| Comp average | 0.562 | 0.138 | 0.483 | 4.077 | 0.000 |
| Tech level | −0.673 | 0.179 | −0.445 | −3.757 | 0.001 |

Source: authors' data collection.

a Predictors: (Constant), Comp average, Tech level
b Dependent Variable: Speed prod ok

*Table 4.31* Regression results for speed of production and cultural variables for Crysbro

| *Model summary* | | | | | | |
|---|---|---|---|---|---|---|
| | $R^a$ | *R Square* | *Adjusted R square* | *Std. error of the estimate* | *F* | *Sig.* |
| | .759 | 0.577 | 0.555 | 0.665 | 26.561 | .000[c] |

| *Coefficients*[b] | | | | | |
|---|---|---|---|---|---|
| *Model* | *Unstandardized coefficients* | | *Standardized coefficients* | *t* | *Sig.* |
| | *B* | *Std. error* | *Beta* | | |
| (Constant) | 0.802 | 1.223 | | 0.656 | 0.516 |
| Power unequal | −0.391 | 0.091 | −0.476 | −4.275 | 0.000 |
| Future oriented | 0.937 | 0.233 | 0.448 | 4.029 | 0.000 |

Source: authors' data collection.

a Predictors: (Constant), Power unequal, Future oriented
b Dependent Variable: Speed prod ok

### 4.4.13 KUPCO

KUPCO is a traditional white meat producing firm in Kuwait with most of the production for the local market. The correlation results for the variable *Speed of production* indicates that two of the communication variables *Number to speak up to the boss* and *Group initiatives to speak to the group leader* are significant with the expected signs. The cultural variables *Power distance* and *Future orientation* show strong correlation while *Avoid uncertainty* and *Generosity* show weaker correlation, see Tables 4.32 and 4.33. In the regression model *Power distance* and being *Generous* are the most significant cultural variables, see Table 4.34.

*Table 4.32* Correlation matrix for result, communication and competence variables for KUPCO

| | | *Comm. up to manager* | *Comm. to own group* | *Group member initiatives* | *Educational average* | *Technical level* | *Training last month* |
|---|---|---|---|---|---|---|---|
| Speed prod ok | Correlation | .742** | 0.050 | .547** | .579** | −.476** | |
| | Sig. (2-tailed) | 0.000 | 0.784 | 0.001 | 0.000 | 0.005 | |
| | N | 33 | 33 | 33 | 33 | 33 | |

Source: authors' data collection.

* Correlation is significant at the 0.05 level (2-tailed).
** Correlation is significant at the 0.01 level (2-tailed).

*Table 4.33* Correlation matrix for result and cultural variables for KUPCO

| | | *Avoid uncertainty* | *Power unequal* | *Reward collective* | *Pride in firm* | *Equality men/ women* | *Confron-tational in firm* | *Future oriented* | *Generous* |
|---|---|---|---|---|---|---|---|---|---|
| Speed prod ok | Correlation | .356* | –.569** | 0.045 | 0.171 | −0.160 | −0.159 | .482** | .393* |
| | Sig. (2-tailed) | 0.042 | 0.001 | 0.804 | 0.340 | 0.373 | 0.376 | 0.004 | 0.024 |
| | N | 33 | 33 | 33 | 33 | 33 | 33 | 33 | 33 |

Source: authors' data collection.

* Correlation is significant at the 0.05 level (2-tailed).
** Correlation is significant at the 0.01 level (2-tailed).

*Table 4.34* Regression results for speed of production and cultural variables for KUPCO

| *Model summary* | | | | | | |
|---|---|---|---|---|---|---|
| | *R*[a] | *R Square* | *Adjusted R square* | *Std. error of the estimate* | *F* | *Sig.* |
| | .686 | 0.471 | 0.435 | 0.626 | 13.341 | .000c |

| *Coefficients*[b] | | | | | |
|---|---|---|---|---|---|
| *Model* | *Unstandardized coefficients* | | *Standardized coefficients* | *t* | *Sig.* |
| | *B* | *Std. error* | *Beta* | | |
| (Constant) | 2.629 | 1.067 | | 2.463 | 0.020 |
| Power unequal | −0.442 | 0.104 | −0.562 | −4.232 | 0.000 |
| Future oriented | 0.591 | 0.205 | 0.383 | 2.884 | 0.007 |

Source: authors' data collection.

a Predictors: (Constant), Power unequal, Future oriented
b Dependent Variable: Speed prod ok

### *4.4.14 Summing up some results from the firms*

In this chapter we have a large number of statistical results from the firms. We have many observations from LAR and smaller numbers from the other firms. We are aware of the objections that can be raised towards different types of statistical analysis, especially regressions based on Likert scale data collection, although similar types of regressions are done in a large amount of scientific work every year. We do not want to draw strong conclusions based on one significant/not significant coefficient, therefore we will use the large number of results as a basis for more general conclusions about possible structures in the material. The first conclusion is that production was going reasonably well in all the five firms, but there were potentials for improvements. The results from the competence variables showed what we could expect from the knowledge indexes – lower levels in less developed countries. The correlation and regression results showed that the effects of the knowledge economy are there. We found in many cases that an increase in the knowledge level indicated that production would be more efficient and this contributed to improved competitiveness. We see this for firms both with lower and higher educational levels.

We found large differences in communication structure and effects. An increase in communication activities improves productivity for firms that have an advanced communication level. But we also find the same effects for KUPCO and Crysbro, meaning that improving communication for firms that initially are not doing so well can improve their situation. Culture is a strong driver, stronger than we had expected. Especially the indicator power distance, which again is related to trust, shows that a reduction of power distance will positively influence productivity, even if the power distance initially is high. In general, one interesting conclusions is that we find the knowledge economy is entering in all firms, but in different ways. Our impression is also that path dependency had stronger effects than we anticipated.

## References


Ajith Kumar, J., & Ganesh, L. S. (2009). Research on knowledge transfer in organizations: A morphology. *Journal of Knowledge Management, 13*(4), 161–174.

Alavi, M., & Leidner, D. E. (2001). Review: Knowledge management and knowledge management systems: Conceptual foundations and research issues. *MIS Quarterly*, 107–136.

Argote, L., & Ingram, P. (2000). Knowledge transfer: A basis for competitive advantage in firms. *Organizational Behavior and Human Decision Processes, 82*(1), 150–169.

Baker, K. A. (2002). *Organizational communication*. Maxwell, AL: Air Force University Press.

Bañegil Palacios, T. M., & Sanguino Galván, R. (2007). Intangible measurement guidelines: A comparative study in Europe. *Journal of Intellectual Capital, 8*(2), 192–204.

Barney, J. B. (1991). Firm resources and sustained competitive advantage. *Journal of Management, 17*(1), 99–120.

Barney, J. B., Ketchen, D. J., & Wright, M. (2011). The future of resource-based theory revitalization or decline? *Journal of Management, 37*(5), 1299–1315.

Bounfour, A., & Edvinsson, L. (2012). *Intellectual capital for communities*. London and New York: Routledge.

Cañibano, L., Sánchez, M. P., García-Ayuso, M., & Chaminade, C. (2002). *Guidelines for managing and reporting on Intangibles (Intellectual Capital Report)*. Madrid: Vodafone Foundation.

Conrad, C., & Poole, M. S. (2012). *Strategic organizational communication: In a global economy*. New York: John Wiley & Sons.

Curado, C., & Bontis, N. (2006). The knowledge-based view of the firm and its theoretical precursor. *International Journal of Learning and Intellectual Capital, 3*(4), 367–381.

Daft, R. (1983/2006). *Organization theory and design* (9th ed.). Boston: Cengage Learning.

Duan, Y., Nie, W., & Coakes, E. (2010). Identifying key factors affecting transnational knowledge transfer. *Information & Management, 47*(7), 356–363.

Dutta, S., Lanvin, B., & Wunsch-Vicent, S. (2015). *The global innovation index 2014: The human factor in innovation*. Fontainebleau, Ithaca, and Geneva: Cornell University, INSEAD, and WIPO.

Edvinsson, L., & Malone, M. S. (1997). *Intellectual capital: Realizing your company's true value by finding its hidden brainpower.* London: HarperCollins.

Fang, Y., Jiang, G. L. F., Makino, S., & Beamish, P. W. (2010). Multinational firm knowledge, use of expatriates, and foreign subsidiary performance. *Journal of Management Studies*, *47*(1), 27–54.

Gourlay, S. (2004). Knowing as semiosis: Steps towards a reconceptualization of 'tacit knowledge'. In H. Tsoukas & N. Mylonopoulos (Eds.), *Organizations as knowledge systems* (pp. 86–105). London: Palgrave Macmillan.

Gourlay, S. (2006). Towards conceptual clarity for 'tacit knowledge': A review of empirical studies. *Knowledge Management Research & Practice*, *4*(1), 60–69.

Grant, R. M. (1996). Toward a knowledge-based theory of the firm. *Strategic Management Journal*, *17*, 109–122.

Hamel, G. (1991). Competition for competence and interpartner learning within international strategic alliances. *Strategic Management Journal*, *12*(S1), 83–103.

Hickie, D. (2006). Knowledge and competitiveness in the aerospace industry: The cases of Toulouse, Seattle and North-West England. *European Planning Studies*, *14*(5), 697–716.

Hislop, D. (2013). *Knowledge management in organizations: A critical introduction.* Oxford: Oxford University Press.

Hofstede, G. H. (1980). Culture and organizations. *International Studies of Management & Organization*, *10*(4), 15–41.

Hofstede, G. H., & Hofstede, G. (2001). *Culture's consequences: Comparing values, behaviors, institutions and organizations across nations.* Boston, MA: SAGE Publications.

House, R., Javidan, M., Hanges, P., & Dorfman, P. (2002). Understanding cultures and implicit leadership theories across the globe: An introduction to project GLOBE. *Journal of World Business*, *37*(1), 3–10.

Huggins, R. A., & Izushi, H. (2007). *Competing for knowledge: Creating, connecting and growing.* London and New York: Routledge.

Itami, H. (1987). *Mobilizing invisible assets.* Cambridge, MA: Harvard University Press.

Jelavic, M. (2011). Socio-technical knowledge management and epistemological paradigms: Theoretical connections at the individual and organisational level. *Interdisciplinary Journal of Information, Knowledge, and Management*, *6*(1), 1–16.

Jensen, H. S. (2008). Management and learning in the knowledge society. *The Journal of Regional Analysis & Policy*, *38*(2), 130–137.

Kaplan, R. S., & Norton, D. P. (2004). The strategy map: Guide to aligning intangible assets. *Strategy & Leadership*, *32*(5), 10–17.

Lai, J., Lui, S. S., & Tsang, E. W. (2016). Intrafirm knowledge transfer and employee innovative behavior: The role of total and balanced knowledge flows. *Journal of Product Innovation Management*, *33*(1), 90–103.

Mahroeian, H., & Forozia, A. (2012). Challenges in managing tacit knowledge: A study on difficulties in diffusion of tacit knowledge in organizations. *International Journal of Business and Social Science*, *3*(19).

MERITUM Project. (2002). *Guidelines for managing and reporting on intangibles.* Madrid: Fundacion Airtel Movil.

Meyer, K. E., Mudambi, R., & Narula, R. (2011). Multinational enterprises and local contexts: The opportunities and challenges of multiple embeddedness. *Journal of Management Studies*, *48*(2), 235–252.

Nonaka, I., & Takeuchi, H. (1995). *The knowledge-creating company: How Japanese companies create the dynamics of innovation.* Oxford: Oxford University Press.

Nonaka, I., Toyama, R., & Konno, N. (2000). SECI, Ba and leadership: A unified model of dynamic knowledge creation. *Long Range Planning*, *33*(1), 5–34.

Penrose, E. (1959). *The theory of the growth of the firm*. New York: Wiley.

Polanyi, M. (1958). *Personal knowledge towards a post-critical philosophy*. London: Routledge and Kegan Paul Ltd.

Prahalad, C., & Hamel, G. (1990). The core competence of the corporation. *Harvard Business Review, May–June 1990*, 79–90.

Saliola, F., & Zanfei, A. (2009). Multinational firms, global value chains and the organization of knowledge transfer. *Research Policy, 38*(2), 369–381.

Signorini, P. E. (2008). European and regional disparities in human capital: The case of Italy. In C. Mazza, P. Quattrone, & A. Riccaboni (Eds.), *European universities in transition: Issues, models and cases* (pp. 258–269). Cheltenham and Northampton, MA: Edward Elgar.

Simon, H. A. (1991). Bounded rationality and organizational learning. *Organization Science, 2*(1), 125–134.

Sonnier, B. M. (2008). Intellectual capital disclosure: High-tech versus traditional sector companies. *Journal of Intellectual Capital, 9*(4), 705–722.

Spraggon, M., & Bodolica, V. (2012). A multidimensional taxonomy of intra-firm knowledge transfer processes. *Journal of Business Research, 65*(9), 1273–1282.

Stephan, J. (2009). *Understanding the relationship between knowledge and competitiveness in the enlarging European union*. Project no: CIT5–028519. Halle: Halle Institute for Economic Research (IWH).

Sveiby, K. E. (2001). A knowledge-based theory of the firm to guide in strategy formulation. *Journal of Intellectual Capital, 2*(4), 344–358.

Teece, D. J., Pisano, G., & Shuen, A. (1997). Dynamic capabilities and strategic management. *Strategic Management Journal, 18*(7), 509–33.

Tsoukas, H. (2005). Do we really understand tacit knowledge? In S. Little & T. Ray (Eds.), *Managing knowledge: An essential reader* (pp. 107–126). London: SAGE Publications.

Tuan, L. T. (2011). Human resource management in knowledge transfer. *International Business and Management, 2*(2), 128–138.

Venzin, M., Von Krogh, G., & Roos, J. (1998). Future research into knowledge management. In G. Von Krogh, J. Roos, & D. Kleine (Eds.), *Knowing in firms: Understanding, managing and measuring knowledge* (pp. 26–66). London: SAGE Publications.

Walter, G. (2005). Competitiveness: A general approach. *Russian-European Centre for Economic Policy, RECEP S REPORTS*, (2). Moscow: RECEP.

Westeren, K. I. (Ed.). (2012). *Foundations of the knowledge economy*. Cheltenham and Northampton, MA: Edward Elgar Publishing.

Westeren, K. I. (2013). *Kunnskap og konkurranseevne*. Bergen: Fagbokforlaget.

Westeren, K. I. (2015). Routines – Do they stimulate or hinder learning and innovation in industrial production. In C. Karlsson, B. Johansson, & R. Stough (Eds.), *Innovation and entrepreneurship in the global economy – Knowledge, technology and internationalization*. Cheltenham and Northampton, MA: Edward Elgar Publishing.

Williamson, O. E. (1996). *The mechanisms of governance*. Oxford: Oxford University Press.

World Bank. (2012). *Knowledge Economy Index (KEI) 2012 Rankings*. Retrieved from http://siteresources.worldbank.org/INTUNIKAM/Resources/2012.pdf.

World Economic Forum (Mercer). (2015). *The human capital report 2015*. Geneva, Switzerland: World Economic Forum.

World Economic Forum. (2016). *The global competitiveness report 2015–2016*. Geneva, Switzerland: World Economic Forum.

# 5 Innovations, knowledge and competitiveness

## 5.1 Introduction

The discussions and analyses of the concepts entrepreneurship and innovation have been some of the most focused and fundamental themes in scientific research and economic policy in the last decades and it is interesting to observe the extensive attention these concepts have received from the public and media. Today the innovation concept is used in many circumstances and in many connections. We have literature on business innovation, on regional and national innovation systems and innovation in the public sector. And we have discussions about innovation and entrepreneurship as one of the most important initiatives of industrial policies in Europe, USA and the rest of the world. This book is centred around knowledge and competitiveness and in this chapter, we will first give a presentation on the origins of the innovation concept – what can be learned from Schumpeter – and see from the start how close the innovation concept was linked to the economic development of the society. Then we will see how the innovation concept can be operationalized today and use this for an analysis of an innovation in the white meat producing firms in the project.

The next discussion will be about innovative initiatives. First, we will present some of the literature in this field – what happens on the way from creativity to innovations. We have collected data from our white meat producers about innovative initiatives. The data reflects how employees contribute with innovative suggestions for improvement. Then we will also shed some light on the (possible) link between knowledge generation and utilization to innovative initiatives. This chapter will be ended by a part on innovation management. Innovations in firms are essential but they must have a system for management of the innovation process to improve competitiveness.

## 5.2 Innovations – essential for economic development in society and for the firm

### *5.2.1 What can we learn from Schumpeter*

The scientific literature and applied projects centred around innovation and entrepreneurship often refer to the work of Joseph A. Schumpeter and his three famous books, *The theory of economic development* (1934), *Business cycles*(1939) and *Capitalism, socialism and democracy* (1950). Here we will give a presentation of how Schumpeter developed concepts like the entrepreneur, innovation and creative destruction and see how this fits into his more general analysis of the development of the capitalist economic system and how it relates to the business sector. We must be aware that Schumpeter did not use the word innovation very often, he spoke more about entrepreneurial activities, new combinations and creative destruction. Schumpeter's project was to analyze the main questions about the development of the capitalistic system and the role of the business sector as a part of the economy. His work became what we can call a third direction in economic theory in the first part of the twentieth century. The first is neoclassical equilibrium theory building on Walras and the second is Marxian economic theory. Schumpeter started his scientific writings around 1900 with his first main book in German, *Theorie der wirtschaftlichen Entwicklung*, (Schumpeter 1911). The first German edition of this book was much longer and had one chapter not included in the 1934 English translation of the book (entitled *The theory of economic development*). The main idea of this book, which continued in all his later scientific production, established a theory of disequilibrium based on the foundations of the capitalist economy where the market as an institution plays an important role together with private ownership. Schumpeter fundamentally disagreed with Walras, who theorized that the capitalist economy would develop into an equilibrium situation. He also disagreed with the Marxian economic structure based on disequilibrium development with its subsequent fundamental contradictions to the structure of the capitalist system.

When we look at the work of Schumpeter, he often used examples from production sectors and individual firms, but we must remember that his primary reasoning used the economic system as the point of departure. This can be understood by looking at the title of his first book in the English translation where he used the word 'Development'. Schumpeter said that development is what we are getting when we look at what is arising from initiatives within the economic system, Schumpeter (1911/2002). The alternative to development is what Schumpeter called adaptation which is change that is not qualitatively new and that (normally) emerges in response to forces outside the economy.

It is interesting to see how this use of the innovation concept that started in the German version of the book from 1911, was still considered when Schumpeter developed his central concepts of entrepreneurship, innovation and creative destruction. Schumpeter, in his book about 'Development' proposed that what he called ordinary economic theory (what we today would call neoclassical economics) was not capable of explaining economic development. Schumpeter linked his concepts together when he introduced the term entrepreneur for the economic actor who caused development. Schumpeter also argued about the principle of rational behavior. He said that this works well when the situation is like a static economy. But when we have the introduction of something new, then rational behavior in the traditional way will not always give the correct answer.

When we come to what creates development, the theory of Schumpeter is individualistic. In the 1911 edition of *Theorie* he spoke about man of action (*Man der Tat*) and described him as someone who does not accept reality as it is. It is this man of action that defines the entrepreneur. Schumpeter formulated something like 'He' (the man of action) takes pleasure in a social power position and in creating, (Schumpeter, 1911, in Swedberg, 2007).

Schumpeter's theory that says that the person who makes the new combinations is the entrepreneur. The use of the expression, *new combinations* is central for Schumpeter. When we look at entrepreneurs, from Thomas Edison to Steve Jobs, they all are faced with a large number of possible combinations, meaning that there are many possible ways to do things that have not been tried before. But the central ability of the entrepreneur is to choose the right combinations and put them into reality in an organization like a firm. In Schumpeter's 'Theory of economic development' we find his list of the types of new combinations:

1 The introduction of a new good or a new quality of a good.
2 The introduction of a new method of production which need by no means to be founded upon a scientifically new discovery, and can also exist in a new way of handling a commodity commercially.
3 The opening of a new market, that is, a market into which the particular branch of manufacturer of the country in question has not previously entered.
4 The conquest of a new source of supply of raw materials or half manufactured goods.
5 The carrying out of the new organization of an industry, like the creation of a monopoly position (for example trough thrustification) or the breaking up of a monopoly position.

(Schumpeter 1934: 66)

Most articles or books about innovation and entrepreneurship use this citation from Schumpeter's book. From Schumpeter's perspective it is interesting to note how he emphasizes that the points 1–5 are linked together while many other writers using this typology are very occupied by looking at how to delineate one type of innovation from the other. By looking at how this typology links together the development of innovations in the firm, we can first look at a new source of supply or a new method of production or a combination of these two that for the firm can be combined into a new good. This good opens a new market possibility which again may change the market organization of the industry. So, if we follow Schumpeter's advice it is much more fruitful to see how the different types of innovations can be linked together than how it is possible to separate one from the other.

Schumpeter also reflected on why only a minority of business leaders could be entrepreneurs. Schumpeter had not a developed a theory of knowledge and knowledge creation or about how people could convert tacit to explicit knowledge. Schumpeter talked more about intuition without going into much detail. But he also talked about what kind of qualifications an entrepreneur must have in addition to the skill of finding the right combinations. He emphasized the ability the entrepreneur must have to cooperate with people and he also mentioned the ability to withstand the resistance from the society. This resistance has at least two sources and the first comes from inside the firm where the entrepreneur tries to changes and developments. Here the central point for the entrepreneur is to have his employees change routines. The routine concept is important to Schumpeter as well as the processes about how to change them. Routines are often founded in the existing economic rationality and culture, but for the entrepreneur to be successful the routines need to be changed.

One other type of resistance comes from the environment of the firm, such as the legal control of the firm for fulfilling standards of production and quality control. Another task is security of production which is sometimes linked to an employer's organization. It is quite interesting to notice that many of these types of resistance to entrepreneurial management that Schumpeter wrote about in the first decades of 1900's are still found in the research about innovative activities today. This will be discussed in the empirical part of this chapter and in other parts of the book.

From his works Schumpeter also saw the difference between what one could call economic combinations and technological combinations. The much-used citation about new combinations is the following: 'The carrying out of new combinations we call enterprise, the individuals who's function is to carry them out we call entrepreneurs' (Schumpeter, 1934: 74).

Linked to the concept of the economic combinations, Schumpeter claimed that the entrepreneur also must make a profit for the development to be called an innovation – the combination must be an economic combination. If we look at this from today's structure and development of society several questions can be asked. One may ask if we talk about profit in the short run or in the longer run. Many innovative firms have negative economic development during the first years, then later become profitable. During that time the product, the process and the market may have changed considerably so the net profits are made because of new developments after what we first called the innovation.

Another argument is made about level of profit and market prices compared to what society needs. We have examples that products from the private sector, (e.g. in medicine and health care), are based on innovations which are not profitable in the private market but then the public sector picks up and uses this in developed versions with subsidized pricing in public hospitals or health institutions. One can say that this adds to the surplus of the society. A third argument is that many innovations and entrepreneurial activities based on new combinations will fail but the new developments these failures create may be produced with profits based on the failed innovations. There is no doubt that Schumpeter had an important and interesting point of view when he linked profit/economic surplus to the entrepreneurial activity and innovation but how to measure and evaluate this is not so easy.

### *5.2.2 Creative destruction*

Before we go into a discussion about the next central concept from Schumpeter, creative destruction, it is important to know Schumpeter believed in capitalist production as the fundamental mode of production with private ownership, competition and the market as the central regulator of economic activity and distribution. Schumpeter fundamentally disagreed with the traditional (neoclassical) explanation about how the capitalist system developed. For his disequilibrium theory, the concept of creative destruction was fundamental. In the book *Capitalism, socialism and democracy*, Schumpeter (1950: 82) he presented the concept of creative destruction:

> The opening of new markets, foreign or domestic, and the organizational development from the craft shop and factory to such concerns as U.S. steel illustrates the same process of industrial mutation – if I may use that biological term – that incessantly revolutionizes the economic structure from within, incessantly destroying the old one, incessantly creating a new one. This process of creative destruction is the essential fact about capitalism. It is what capitalism consists in and what every capitalist concern has got to live in.

When we apply the concept of creative destruction at the sectorial level we have seen several changes in sectorial technologies. For example, the production of watches is one example where technology totally has changed routines and production technologies and at the same time destroyed the old ways of doing production. We have also seen creative destruction applied to the development of the economy and production more in general. An example is found in the 'back office' revolution of IT technologies. This started in the financial sector where they changed from more manual procedures in bookkeeping to electronic and IT-based systems. Also, in one of the white meat producing firms we have seen a change from quality control based on human vision to using X-ray equipment. The conclusion is that the concept of creating destruction can be applied on many levels from one single product to the more fundamental changes of the economic system and societal production.

In a paper by Andersen, *et al.* (2006) they talk about creative destruction taking part as a sequence of events. First, we have the initial equilibrium where the starting point is an economic system based on stable routine behavior. Then the initial equilibrium breaks down when innovators start up their enterprises based on new innovative products and processes. When combined with increased value-added and/or reduced unit cost this produces a surplus, normally as a profit, for the firm and for society. This process of innovation also leads to the demand of new skills and new transfer of knowledge because of new routines. These innovations also lead to an upswing in the economy but the upswing will after some time fade out because the innovations also will sharpen the competitive process of the market.

This argument was one of the bases for Schumpeter's conclusion about the wave movements of the economy. One argument that may make this situation a little more complicated is that there is no reason to assume that the innovations and startup of new enterprises in one sector will be coordinated with what happens in other sectors. Schumpeter was fully aware of the characteristics of market behavior, that changes in one sector or one type of production could spread quickly to one sector, but may have little effect on the other part of the economy.

### *5.2.3 The link between innovation and competitiveness*

In the 1980's we saw a rising interest in competitiveness both in a theoretical and firm perspective. One background factor was a change in perspective to a more market oriented way of organizing society led by a change in policy in Europe and the United States influenced by Reagan and Thatcher. This new interest in competitiveness was found on different levels such as the firm, the region and the nation. The background for this was highly influenced by Michael Porter and his work on competitiveness (Porter, 1985; 1986; 1990; 1998). Together with this rising interest in competitiveness we saw an extended use of concepts like innovation, creativity and entrepreneurship. In Porter's work, competitiveness is closely linked to cluster development. That raises the question as to where innovation comes into this picture. In later years we have seen comments about Porter's work on this aspect, for example by Simmie (2006) and in Nooteboom (2006: 137) 'Second, while it is often claimed that clusters yield innovations, it has not been made clear how that works, in terms of firms acting in clusters, and it is not clear that clusters always contribute to innovations'.

Porter also saw innovation as an important task for the firm and he often built this into his analysis of competitiveness. When it comes to the point about relating and supporting industries Porter, *et al.* (2004: 38) said the following about how innovation and innovative activities spread among firms 'Local sourcing from capable suppliers based in the region enhances productivity and improves the capacity for innovation through allowing quicker and less costly communication, fostering the flow of ideas, and enhancing flexibility.'

There are many results showing that when firms get support from others to facilitate the process of innovation this again leads to a stronger competitive situation for the firm, see Tidd, *et al.* (2001).

When we look at developments after year 2000 the focus of the innovation concept has widened out, at least in three directions, to include global challenges like climate changes, population ageing, and scarcities of water and raw materials. Globalization of the world economy has brought new economies (such as the BRIC countries) closer to a front role in innovation development. This is one of the reasons for using a firm from Brazil as an example in the case study in this chapter. Another aspect for a new perspective on innovation is linked to the ongoing economic crisis which began in 2008. We see how countries like Greece are severely suffering from austerity plans, but at the same time the economic situation requires an increased speed in innovative developments. This also raises questions about the links between innovative development and income distribution, see Porter and Kramer (2011).

The discussions about the innovation concept after Schumpeter have gone in many directions and in the coming discussions we will build on what we often call the Oslo Manual, OECD (2005: 48–51):

> Four types of innovations are distinguished: product innovations, process innovations, marketing innovations and organizational innovations.
>
> A **product innovation** is the introduction of a good or service that is new or significantly improved with respect to its characteristics or intended uses. This includes significant improvements in technical specifications, components and materials, incorporated software, user friendliness or other functional characteristics.
>
> A **process innovation** is the implementation of a new or significantly improved production or delivery method. This includes significant changes in techniques, equipment and/or software.
>
> A **marketing innovation** is the implementation of a new marketing method involving significant changes in product design or packaging, product placement, product promotion or pricing.
>
> An **organizational innovation** is the implementation of a new organizational method in the firm's business practices, workplace organization or external relations.

Compared to Schumpeter's point of departure it is only the understanding of the organizational innovation that has changed content.

When discussing the innovation process, we will break it down into three steps starting with the invention that is based on idea generation. The next step is the actual innovation and the third is the commercialization. We will also stress the point of view coming from Schumpeter that an innovation must be able to create a surplus for the firm and society. When it comes to establishing innovation models and analyzing them in a historical perspective the most used source is Rothwell (1992; 1994). Rothwell established generations of innovation models. In the early 1990s, he ended up with five generations of models. Later work (Ortt and van der Duin, 2008) suggested that we may have six generations of models where the sixth is linked to the concept of open innovations (Chesbrough, *et al.* 2006).

### *5.2.4 Case study of an innovation in production of white meat*

The Danish chicken slaughter firm Danpo produces 184,000 chickens every day five days a week. In 2010–2011 the firm started to test out a system for classification and grading of chicken carcasses integrated in their chicken meat production. In 2012 the firm invested in the equipment and made it operational as a part of the production process.

The system is called VTS 2000 is a fully automatic system for classification and grading of chicken carcasses delivered from e+v Technology GmbH in Germany, documentation of the VTS 2000 can be found at www.eplusv.de/start_E.htm. The system is based on digital video image analysis. The major components are:

- The cameras
- The lamps
- Optical sensors
- Image analysis computers
- 2 stainless steel boxes

The logic behind the system is that the classification is done after the chickens are slaughtered, washed and hung on the transportation system inside the firm. The transport line takes the chicken through a system of two boxes with cameras (see Figures 5.1 and 5.2). Inside each box there is a high-speed video camera that

*Figure 5.1* Stainless boxes, part of VTS 2000

Source: www.eplusv.de/start_E.htm

*Figure 5.2* VTS 2000 box with camera and lamp

Source: www.eplusv.de/start_E.htm

captures images, one from front and one from the rear of every chicken. The computer program automatically analyzes each image and calculates carcass weight and chest fillet weight. The system also does other measurements and calculates several other parameters, which will be explained later.

Before the introduction of the system Danpo conducted a research project where they first sent the chickens through the VTS 2000 measuring system and after that did manual control. A report from these test procedures was published as Danish Technological Institute, DMRI (2010). Based on these results and other tests using the system on 30,000 chickens, the system is able to calculate the carcass weight with a precision of less than 1 gram, total fillet weight with a precision of less than 2 grams and calculating other parameters with satisfactory statistical test results.

The main reasons for the firm to introduce the system were the following:

- To establish a new payment system between the firm and breeders (the suppliers of chickens).
- Being able to give signals back to the breeder about health, feed and other parameters.
- Being able to use the system for better production planning and production monitoring inside the firm.
- Being able to use the system for better market planning.

Two firms have considered installing this type of equipment in Denmark, Danpo and Rose Poultry. Danpo has a proactive approach to the use of the system and Danpo has tried to exploit opportunities optimally. Rose Poultry has only looked at the possibilities but so far not bought or done tests with the system. One reason for this is that the system puts demands on both the knowledge and competence of those who use it and it also sets requirements for cooperation and knowledge transfer between departments within the firm and with the firm and outside partners.

This type of equipment based on scanning (taking pictures of animals) after they have been slaughtered has been used in the Danish food industry for many years, especially in pig and cattle meat production. The new challenge when it comes to chicken is that the software and classification systems are totally different since a chicken weighs only a fraction compared to pigs and cattle. Also, the speed of production per unit is very much faster and the system must be calibrated for photographing and scanning slaughter lines with a speed up to 12,000 chickens per hour. The firm required accurate measurement results for at least 98% of the chickens on the transport line to be able to successfully use the equipment.

The initiative for the firm to install the equipment came mainly from e+v Technology GmbH because of their marketing and their efforts to convince the firm about the benefits and possibilities for increased productivity. Use of the equipment did not come as a result of demands from within the firm or its own efforts to develop technology. The cooperation with the Danish Meat Research Institute (DMRI) research institute was also crucial for the firm's decision to install the technology.

As described, the technology includes cameras, lamps and light sensors, and boxes where the system is installed. Furthermore, all the camera systems are connected to a computer which is a standard PC with a relatively high performance, but not more advanced than a regular standard PC one can buy in a store. The distinctive and unique part of the system from the supplier is the software. It is the software that represents the innovative part of the technology. The software does the interpretation from pictures of the results. The actual scanning is read by the software and places several points on the image which represents the different parts of the chicken, see Figure 5.3.

Behind these points lie routines in the software that provide an interpretation so that the system can calculate the weight, size, color and many other characteristics tied to the scans which are used to calculate various interesting variables. For the system to work with the required accuracy, it must be calibrated. This is done by Danpo and they normally calibrate every night after production for the day is completed. These are automated procedures that are supplied by the vendor as a part of the software. The programming code is kept secret by e+v firm. The employees at Danpo only relate to the results and to check if there are any problems or discrepancies.

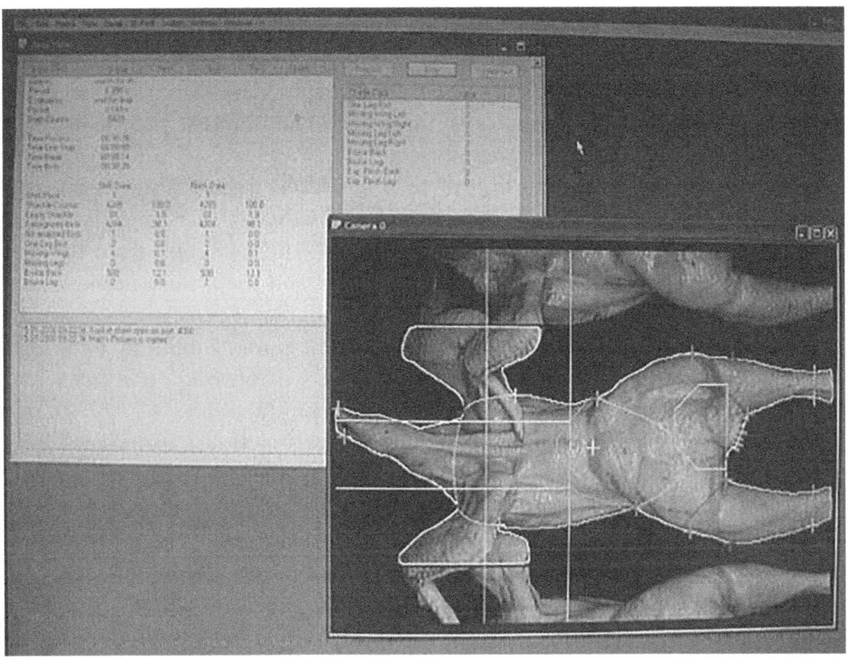

*Figure 5.3* Program window from computer

Source: www.eplusv.de/start_E.htm

What is commonly known about the software is that it is based on a very large number of scans of chickens. The vendor does regular upgrades of the software which is based on manual analyses of a large number of chickens. Based on these results the e+v firm calibrates the algorithms that calculate the different variables. In short, one can say that the innovative technology lies in the construction of the computer programs and especially the construction of algorithms in the program and how these are updated and tested on actual data. The innovative part for the firm is the use of the results and how this is done in relation to feedback to suppliers (breeders), the firm's own production planning and quality control, and market planning.

The experiences that Danpo has had so far using the equipment show the importance of management functions with focus on the importance of understanding of how the computer program, registration and algorithms work and how this is integrated in production. To get the best results it is important to focus on transfer of knowledge within the firm and to external partners. The use of the equipment has so far required no need for separate external training programs from the supplier other than what has been part of normal maintenance and upgrading.

Maintenance of the system has been limited in the sense that the equipment has had very few operational problems. On the other hand, to have a maintenance contract with the manufacturer is relatively costly compared to the value of the investment. A visit of two days from the manufacturer for maintenance costs about €10,000. The price for the purchase of equipment was approximately €250,000. The financing of the equipment was undertaken as a part of the firm's capital expenditures for investment purposes and it was not necessary to use special funds or other external financing. The purchase was financed by normal internal investment capital sources.

The livestock department in the firm especially wanted the equipment because this department has the contact with individual farmers (breeders). One important task here is to find an operational mode for payments from the firm to the breeder. Calculation of weight is essential and the system now plays an important part in this.

It has been known for three to four years in the poultry industry in Scandinavia that Danpo has this equipment, but as far as we know, no other firms have started to use the system as an integrated part of production.

As stated earlier, the three mains indicators the system calculates are carcass weight, chest fillet weight and a parameter called fillet yield. The experience the firm has had so far is that the breeders with the highest quality also have the largest coefficient for fillet yield defined as breast fillet as a percentage of the total weight of the chicken. Other parameters analyzed are the following:

1 Ammonia combustion.

   The system analyzes and detects patches on the chicken skin which come from the ammonia in faeces of chickens so that it looks like a burn.

2 Broken wing(s).

Here the criteria also are 0 or 1, either the chicken has a broken chicken wing or it has not. An interesting observation here is whether the wing was broken before the chicken came to the firm or if the wing was broken as part of the production process in the firm.

3 Detection of chickens hanging by one leg only.

During the manufacturing process the chickens are hung up on the transportation system and it is interesting to know how many are hanging by one leg only. This is detected by the image scanning and analysis by the software. This information is then used to calibrate and maintain the production system in the firm.

4 Chickens with or without head.

Normally the head of the chicken shall be removed before the chicken has come as far as the camera boxes on the production line. Chicken with head is detected and registered by the scanning system. This is also an indication that there is a technical problem in the production system of the firm.

5 Injuries and stains.

The analysis of the scanned images can also show if the chicken has damage or stains, detected as red or blue spots on the chicken. The interesting phenomena to observe relating to this are if there is blood retention in the meat. The indicator of injury and stains is of greater interest primarily for the analysis of breast fillets and is an indicator of the health and welfare of the chicken more in general.

6 Breast fillet indicators.

This is a criterion which is calculated as the proportion the breast fillet has as a part of the entire weight of the chicken. This criterion is important in several contexts. The firm uses this number as a quality indicator and this number is included in the formula on which the calculation of the payments between breeder and the firm is settled. This is logical since breast meat has a much higher price than the rest of the chicken.

### *5.2.5 The innovation in Danpo in a theoretical perspective*

What is described in the case study fits into Schumpeter's description and from the Oslo Manual that can be called a process innovation. This innovation was from the start essentially motivated by improving quality control, speed of production and payments and contracts with the breeders. Market development has gone in the direction of traceability and the system can be used to identify from which breeder the chicken comes from, this again can be used in marketing

The new way of evaluating product quality control by using IT technology adds a new aspect to the production process. The production is done in a technically new way which needs changes in routines, changes in knowledge level and transfer and allows an increase in the speed of production. The new technology is known from other types of meat production but the two novelty features are the speed of taking pictures and the size of the birds compared to other animals. The innovative aspect from a technical point of view lies in the software which operates the system.

One other interesting aspect with the case study is that there are two firms in Denmark producing white meat and these firms are about the same size and compete in the same markets. But the new quality control technology is only utilized in the Danpo firm and so far, not by the other. From the financial point of view this is interesting to notice because the cost of buying, installing and running this technology is quite low compared to other machinery and capital costs. From the Schumpeter point of view, we see in this case an interesting example of creative destruction. The employees must change from human quality control (actually using their eyes to look at the chickens) to IT technology. This means that the firm still must have employees doing quality control, but now looking at pictures and interpreting calculated results instead of looking at actual animals.

Most innovation studies emphasize that the innovation is context specific and this is the case also for the Danpo firm. But the interesting fact is that the other competing Danish firm has a context which is quite equal to the Danpo firm even though the innovation has not taken place in this firm. We will not go further into the analysis of why the other firm (Rose Poultry) has not introduced this technology, but just conclude that it was a strategic managerial decision to introduce this technology in the Danpo firm.

In the analysis of firms, we find in the literature several possible approaches to the analysis of the strategies of firms like the market-based, the resource-based view of the firm and the dynamic capabilities view of the firm. In relation to this study, the dynamic capabilities view of the firm seems most appropriate. In one of the founding articles written by Teece (2007), he specifies three distinct processes for the firm to utilize its innovative developments:

- Sensing opportunities
- Ceasing opportunities
- Reconfiguring the resource base

In this case study three central features of firm management were emphasized:

- How the supply chain was working
- How the product quality control was working
- How quality control could be used for direct market information

In recent years food markets indicate that consumers are more conscious about who is producing the food they are eating. For different types of meat and cheese (and other products as well) it has been a market characteristic to identify the producer, show some pictures and verify that this producer obeys ecologic standards, animal health standards and so on. For bulk production of chicken today it is more or less impossible to know the breeder and where the bird actually came from.

In the Danpo case the market argument was that if there was a complaint or a problem with quality the firm now could trace the meat to the producer. One argument for the innovation was how to relate the supply chain to product and quality control. The second main argument was that the speed of the quality control would be higher and the accuracy better. This was also an argument for reduced unit cost from the production point of view. With this new technology, it was possible to better integrate the quality control technology with the use of other (e.g. slaughter processing) technology in the production to increase the speed of the production line.

A third use of the technology was for the payments from the firm to the breeders. With the new technology, it was possible to make much more accurate estimations of the weight of the chickens, so the reliability of the information for the weight of chicken meat the breeder sent to the firm was better. The conclusion here is that the 'sensing' of the possibilities originally came from the producer of the technology but through the research test project the firm was able to transform the information into the management system to analyze the possibilities.

The process of seizing of the possibilities starts where the sensing ends, as the step from planning and calculations to testing the system in actual production. To do this the firm conducted a project together with a research institution. The firm had to be certain that the technology would work according to what the producer of the technology said. The total production line for white meat production is dependent on every part being able to keep the speed and continuity at a high level. Also, it was essential to have higher speed quality control with the IT system compared manual visual control.

In this project, the seizing of opportunities together with the reconfiguration of the resources are linked together because the new technology presupposed new routines, not only in production but in many aspects of the production. This is quite normal and to a large extent parallel with the reasoning by Schumpeter that an innovation process normally links together all aspects from types of innovation.

It is interesting to notice that the key features from the work by Teece (2007) are relevant in this case study using the concept of dynamic capabilities and three keywords like sensing, seizing and reconfiguring the opportunities and actual processes within the firm. Another interesting and relevant aspect of innovation theory is profitability. In this case the investment was quite low in monetary terms compared to other costs of the production process. The new technology seems to open more new possibilities for increased profits than actual results the first one or two years. According to the firm, the investment will be paid off in 2–3 years. From the firm's point of view this technology opens new possibilities to make profits in different ways by reducing unit cost of production and improving the market situation.

## 5.3 Innovative behavior

### *5.3.1 Innovative behavior – a theoretical introduction*

Innovation using different perspectives is the theme of Chapter 5. How Schumpeter developed the innovation concept was introduced and discussed in Chapter 5.2. This is essential for our understanding of innovations as a process also today. We must be aware that Schumpeter had an individualistic approach to what innovation is and spoke about this in his trilogy of books, (Schumpeter, 1934; 1939; 1950). It is how the individual carries out new combinations that are essential to innovation as a phenomenon. We are aware that later in his authorship Schumpeter (1950) also put emphasis on how institutions could influence the innovation process but Schumpeter never left the individual aspect as a creative necessity.

Schumpeter also discussed the phases or stages of the innovation process starting with the idea and creation phase, followed by the actual development of the innovation, and then how the innovation is put to work and managed as a part of firm operations. This was called innovation management, see Chapter 5.4. One often cited scientific work discussing the different phases of innovation putting stress on the creative face comes from Amabile (1988).

During the 1990's we saw an emerging number of studies trying to explain what they called innovative behavior in organizations, e.g. Kanter (1988), West and Farr (1990), and Scott and Bruce (1994). Based on West and Farr (1989; 1990), Yuan and Woodman (2010) have the following definition of the innovative behavior: 'We define innovative behavior as an employee's intentional introduction or application of new ideas, products, processes, and procedures to his or her work role, work unit, or organization' (Yuan and Woodman, 2010: 324).

One fundamental idea of this definition is that the behavior of all employees is intentional. This raises questions like how can we analyze innovative behavior and how can we explain why some employees are more innovative than others? On the following pages, we will present some ideas about what determines innovative behavior and in the last section of this chapter we will present some results based on our authors' data collection.

Adapted from Scott and Bruce (1994: 583), an often used and cited approach for what determines innovative behavior is found in Figure 5.4. Other authors have given illustrations about the same phenomena but presented it in different ways (see Janssen, *et al.*, 2004: 132, Yuan and Woodman, 2010: 326 and Montani, *et al.* 2014: 9). It is interesting to see how these presentations have similarities and differences but at the same time are trying to analyze the same phenomena – innovative behavior in organizations.

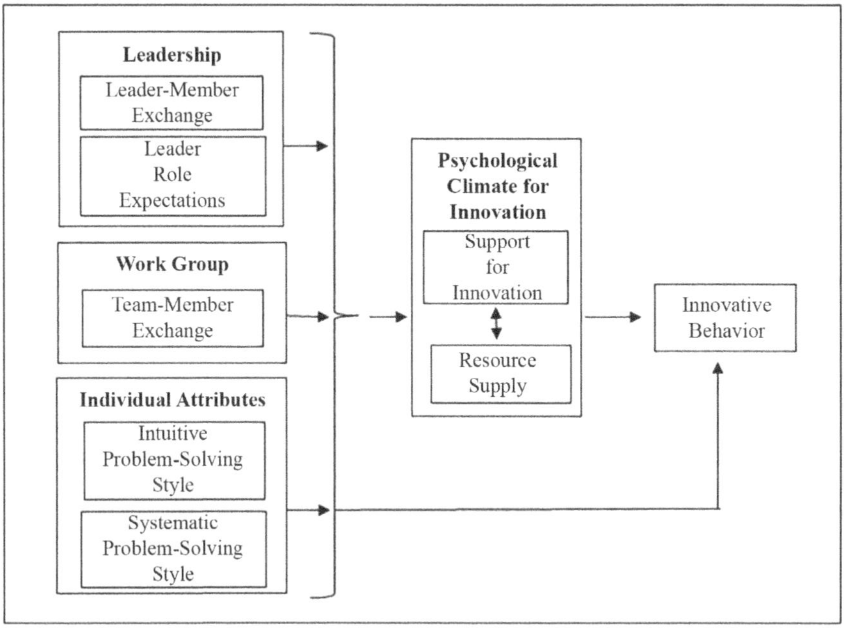


*Figure 5.4* Determining innovative behavior (adapted from Scott and Bruce (1994: 583), slightly simplified).

Practitioners and scientific analysts agree that innovative behavior challenges organizations in one way or another. Studies like Janssen (2000) looked at innovative behavior as a three-stage process where the first stage was idea generation, the second, idea promotion and the third, idea realization. In theory, there are at least two ways of measuring innovative behavior. One is to construct an indicator consisting of several characteristics that are relevant to the employees. Second is to do actual counting of the number of innovative initiatives as they appear in organizations.

The data collection in this project was based on counting. The first counting operation was done by registering the number of all ideas from each part of the organization (like all groups) and then asking about how many times an original idea was created. The next step was to find out how many of the creative ideas were formalized (meaning written down) and the third step was to count how many formalized ideas were acted upon. In Chapter 5.2 we had a more holistic view of innovation like Schumpeter's. Here we will look at innovative behavior in more detail in this chapter and see what characteristics support or hinder this.

When we analyze innovative behavior, it is important to be aware on which level in the organization we put focus. Normally we look at the individual level, the work group/team level and the organizational level. Of course, there is interaction between levels, but as we will see from the data collection in this project, production takes place in teams, which consist of individuals. The results are important for all including on the organization level. Most studies consider that organizations like firms are divided into groups (or departments) and in each group, there is one (sometimes more than one) person that has managerial responsibility. But also of fundamental importance are the individual attributes for both the leader and the participants in the group. The outcome variable which is innovative behavior can be made operational by looking at six characteristics (see Scott and Bruce 1994). This was developed further by Janssen (2000) using nine work behavior items for innovative behavior:

> (1) Creating new ideas for difficult issues (idea generation); (2) Searching out new working methods, techniques, or instruments (idea generation); (3) Generating original solutions for problems (idea generation); (4) Mobilizing support for innovative ideas (idea promotion); (5) Acquiring approval for innovative ideas (idea promotion); (6) Making important organizational members enthusiastic for innovative ideas (idea promotion); (7) Transforming innovative ideas into useful applications (idea realization); (8) Introducing innovative ideas into the work environment in a systematic way (idea realization); (9) Evaluating the utility of innovative ideas (idea realization).
>
> Janssen (2000: 292)

When we do actual research in firms or other types of organizations we often start by considering Janssen's (2000) work behavior item (characteristic) number one: 'Creating new ideas for difficult issues'. To do this in practice we can characterize all members in the group on a Likert scale from one to five, where one means that the person does not contribute to the creation of new ideas at all while five means a substantial contribution. This type of research procedure is well-known and commonly used in social science, but is not without problems. For example, one person in a group comes up with only one idea one year. But this idea is fundamental to the firm and lots of changes happen, including contributing to better competitiveness and higher profits. On the other hand, another person might propose, more or less every day, new ideas that challenge the organization and keep discussions going about how to produce and innovate but with no significant outcomes. The question then is how to characterize these two people on the Likert scale.

Many studies take as the starting point the model by Scott and Bruce (1994) in Figure 5.1. Scott and Bruce (1994) focus on leadership, group and individual levels. On the leadership level, it is the way the leader exchanges his views with the group and role expectations from the group members that are important. The processes inside the group are also crucial, together with the individual attributes of the group members.

The exchange that takes place on the different levels is filtered through what they call the psychological climate for innovation. This concept consists of factors like support for innovation and resource supply. In analyzing this filtering process together with how the factors could influence innovative behavior directly, Scott and Bruce (1994) explained how and why innovative behavior occurred. The model by Scott and Bruce (1994) was also useful because it put focus on work group processes and in this respect referenced Leader-Member Exchange (LMX) theory. To analyze the data collected in this project, LMX theory was of special interest and relevance and in the next section we will give an introduction and discussion about this.

When we look at other presentations about how to analyze innovative behavior we have mentioned Janssen, *et al.* (2004). Janssen, *et al.* (2004) started with the outcome – individual innovations – and analyzed how new ideas transferring to innovative behavior could have different outcomes in organizations. They said that innovative behavior normally was positive for the organization but analyzed how moderating factors could influence from the positive and negative side how the ideas develop to innovation. For our results, special interest from the analysis by Janssen, *et al.* (2004) is how the leaders (supervisors) of the group have essential influence over the idea generation process.

Yuan and Woodman (2010) also tried to explain innovative behavior. In the project discussed in this book we have used skill variables like education and organizational variables like (power) distance. One result from Yuan and Woodman (2010) was that the importance of the supervisor and his relationship to the rest of the group was fundamental. This corresponded with the results from the project reported in this book. Yuan and Woodman (2010) also did more detailed statistical analysis trying to identify paths. This suggested several interesting results but some of them seemed quite context dependent.

An article on the same subject but with a slightly different approach by Montani, *et al.* (2014) is interesting because it considered some of the aspects presented earlier but also added some new ones. In this model the factor called psychological climate for innovation was looked at as one of the fundamental drivers for innovative work behavior, where this was an intermediate stage variable (like a filtering variable) in the model of Scott and Bruce (1994).

The model by Montani, *et al.* (2014) also added new interesting aspects to the way they looked at learning and goal orientation as fundamental drivers for innovative work behavior. This means that knowledge level and skills were assumed to play a role. These factors had a direct impact on what they called envisioning and resulting innovative work behavior. Another driving factor is called task variety. This is also interesting because groups often need to deal with different tasks that require big differences in the kind of innovative solutions that can be relevant. The definition of innovative work behavior in Montani, *et al.* (2014) was using Janssen's (2000) nine work behavior items for innovative behavior.

### *5.3.2 Leader-Member Exchange (LMX) theory*

Leadership is one of the most studied social sciences topics after WW2. Following up the presentation about innovative behavior in Chapter 5.3.1, we will here focus on Leader-Member Exchange (LMX) theory because this is centred on the interaction between a leader and the subordinates (or members) of the group. This focus fits the framework for this book and the data collection in this project can be looked at as a point of departure for traditional industrial production that takes place in departments or groups. All groups have a leader function and in most groups in this project there is one single leader. The leader role is essential for production management and communication. The group leader has the central position as a knowledge broker between the management of the firm and the way tasks are performed by the members of the group.

When LMX theory took the approach of the vertical dyad linkage and was first developed by Dansereau, *et al.* (1975), Graen and Cashman (1975) and Graen (1976). Before 1975 the traditional assumption was that the leader treated the group as one unit without differentiating between members. The LMX theory directed attention to the differences that might exist between the leader and different members of the group. The relationship the leader had to one member was called dyadic and could often be very different from the relationship the leader had with other members of the group.

The LMX theory also drew on social exchange theory, see Blau (1964), where the employment relationship was looked at as an exchange between the leader and the group member. In this theory exchange was often divided into two types, economic exchange and social exchange. Early LMX studies by Liden and Graen (1980) and Graen and Uhl-Bien (1995), they focused on the differences between types of links or relationships between members of the group and the group leader. The studies spoke about in-group members where these were selected because of their skills, level of trust granted by the supervisor and motivation to take responsibility within the unit. These members contributed to the functioning of the group and firm beyond their formal tasks. In return, they received more attention and support from the group leader. The out-group members were characterized by a more formal exchange with their group leader and this often resulted in more routine oriented tasks.

LMX theory looked at the relationship between the leader and each of the group members as an exchange relationship. One important task was then to find what kind of dimensions or indicators that could be used to characterize this relationship. An article by Liden and Maslyn (1998) summarized the discussion during the 1990s and presented a model that has been widely used and extended. They argued that the LMX relationship has four dimensions (or indicators).

*Dimension one – affect*

This dimension refers to mutual attraction felt by the member and the leader mainly based on the interpersonal relationship rather than the professional.

*Dimension two – loyalty*

This dimension is defined by support for the objectives the member is supposed to perform. This dimension is also relevant from the point of view how the group leader is supporting, defending and contributing to the member's knowledge to find solutions to problems.

*Dimension three – contribution*

This dimension captures the perception of amount, direction and quality of all professional activities the members do to reach the goal of the group and organization. The contribution can go beyond the tasks assigned in the formal contract of employment because the member has the motivation and resources for such activities.

*Dimension four – professional respect*

This dimension reflects that each group member has built a reputation both inside and outside of the organization in relation to his job performance. The professional respect can be built up based on data from inside the organization or by documentation and information contributed by others.

This four-scale set of dimensions has been elaborated and changed several times. One operational version called the LMX-7 instrument builds on Graen and Uhl-Bien (1995) and has been presented and discussed in leadership literature such as Northouse (2007).

Graen and Uhl-Bien (1995) also widened the focus for use of the LMX model. In the beginning, the focus was on the interpersonal links. Since the middle of the 1990's, the focus shifted to look at productivity, culture and other characteristics of organizations. There have been some attempts to summarize the status of LMX theory, see Gerstner and Day (1997) and Dulebohn, *et al.* (2012).

One strength of the LMX theory is the focus and attention to the significance of communication in leadership. Here communication is a medium through which leaders and subordinates develop, grow and maintain beneficial exchanges. When this communication is accompanied by features such as mutual trust, respect and devotion it leads to effective leadership. This we also find as a result in the empirical part of this chapter.

### *5.3.3 Empirical results*

In the earlier two sections of this chapter we have discussed what innovations can be and how it can be measured from different sources and viewpoints. The questions about innovative behavior we have used in this study are the following:

1 Has anyone in the group come up with suggestions for changes in routines within your area of responsibility? – Suggested changes in routines
2 Have there been formal (written) suggestions from members of your group to change routines? – Formalized suggested changes in routines
3 Have any of the suggestions been acted upon? – Suggestions acted upon

The registration alternatives for question 1 and 2 are:

- The last week (numeric value: 1)
- The last month (numeric value: 2)
- The last three months (numeric value: 3)
- Any time in the past we can remember (numeric value: 4)
- Cannot remember any suggestion any time (numeric value: 5)

The results for the firms are shown in Table 5.1. First, we looked at the mean of how many times the employers through the group leader made suggestions for changes in routines. The first question makes no claims or assumptions about what kind of suggestion that is put forward. But it must be understood and interpreted by the group leader as a change that is relevant to the kind of tasks the group is supposed to perform. The numeric values are counted in the way that is explained above. This means that lower numbers indicate a higher level of innovative behavior in the firm.

The second question is about formalized suggestions. The criterion is that the suggestion must be written down so the group leader has something formal to send to other parts of the organization. The last question is about how many of the formalized suggestions have been acted upon. Here the data material has been recalculated to show the percentages.

*Table 5.1* Innovative behavior counted as changes in routines at Danpo, LAR, Ytterøy, Crysbro and KUPCO

| | *Suggested changes in routines* | *Formalized suggested changes in routines* | *Proposals acted upon* |
|---|---|---|---|
| Danpo A, N = 21 | 1.90 | 2.10 | |
| Danpo S, N = 18 | 1.28 | 1.22 | |
| Danpo T, N = 39 | 1.62 | 1.69 | 85% |
| LAR A, N = 162 | 2.09 | 2.67 | |
| LAR S, N = 104 | 1.24 | 1.55 | |
| LAR T, N = 266 | 1.75 | 2.21 | 63% |
| Ytterøy A, N = 12 | 2.17 | 2.17 | |
| Ytterøy S, N = 18 | 1.67 | 2.06 | |
| Ytterøy T, N = 30 | 1.87 | 2.10 | 82% |
| Crysbro A, N = 24 | 3.69 | 3.89 | |
| Crysbro S, N = 18 | 2.17 | 3.00 | |
| Crysbro T, N = 40 | 2.98 | 3.45 | 42% |
| KUPCO A, N = 15 | 3.20 | 3.40 | |
| KUPCO S, N = 18 | 2.78 | 3.01 | |
| KUPCO T, N = 33 | 2.94 | 3.18 | 37% |

Source: authors' data collection.

Abbreviations: A: Assembly line functions; S: Supply functions; T: Total; N: Number of observations.

When we look at innovative activities like suggestions for changes in routines we can divide the firms into two groups, the first one being Danpo, LAR and Ytterøy. They all have a high activity with the value of 1.62 in Danpo, 1.75 in LAR and 1.87 at Ytterøy as average for all functions in the firms. As expected we found higher activities (lower numerical values) in support functions compared to assembly line functions. The firms Crysbro and KUPCO had similar overall averages around three. But the structure of the firms differed where Crysbro had a high activity of innovative behavior in support functions and low in assembly line functions while KUPCO had more equal results for the different functions.

Another interesting aspect was to see how the innovative behavior took place during the different stages of the process. As expected, some suggestions for change in routines disappeared when we asked about formalizations. The process from suggestions to formalization and action was quite strong in Danpo, LAR and Ytterøy, which means that a high share of the suggestions were formalized and acted upon. At Crysbro the innovation process was weaker. Support functions were quite active at the suggestion stage, but loose in strength when it came to formalization. At KUPCO the process was more on the average but the level of suggestions in general was low. Both Crysbro and KUPCO had lower percentages for suggestions to be acted upon compared to the other firms.

We have also calculated correlations for the two variables about changes in routines and three groups of variables (the definitions and interpretations of these variables are discussed more in detail in Chapter 4):

An outcome variable (a question to the group leader):

1. To your knowledge was the speed of production satisfactory today?

Communications variables (questions to the group leader):

2. How many times did you (the group leader) speak with your leader (a person in the firm managerial leader team) today?
3. How many times today did you (the group leader) take the initiative to speak to members of your group?
4. How many times today did a member of the group take the initiative to speak to you?

Skills variables:

5. Average educational level of workers in group.
6. Average competence for workers (in the group) about technology.
7. Number of group members who have participated in courses/training in the last month.

We also calculated the correlations for cultural variables.

When we look at the results in Table 5.2 it is interesting to see that most results followed the expected patterns when it came to the relationship between

*Table 5.2* Correlations between innovative behavior and outcome, communication and skills variables

| | | *Speed of prod. ok* | *Comm. up to manager* | *Comm. to own group* | *Group member initiatives* | *Educational average* | *Technical level* | *Training last month* |
|---|---|---|---|---|---|---|---|---|
| Suggested changes in routines | P Correlation | −0.467** | −0.289 | −0.089 | −0.315 | −0.259 | 00.204 | −0.197 |
| | Sig. (2-tailed) | 0.003 | 0.075 | 0.591 | 0.051 | 0.112 | 0.213 | 0.230 |
| | Danpo: N | 39 | 39 | 39 | 39 | 39 | 39 | 39 |
| Formalized suggested changes in routines | P Correlation | −0.568** | −0.408** | −0.325* | −0.316* | −0.566** | 0.390* | −0.459** |
| | Sig. (2-tailed) | 0.000 | 0.010 | 0.043 | 0.050 | 0.000 | 0.014 | 0.003 |
| | Danpo: NN | 39 | 39 | 39 | 39 | 39 | 39 | 39 |
| Suggested changes in routines | P Correlation | −0.043 | −0.041 | −0.012 | −0.078 | −0.202** | -0.026 | −0.064 |
| | Sig. (2-tailed) | 0.499 | 0.519 | 0.852 | 0.214 | 0.001 | 0.682 | 0.309 |
| | LAR: N | 255 | 255 | 255 | 255 | 255 | 255 | 255 |
| Formalized suggested changes in routines | P Correlation | −0.106 | −0.105 | −0.009 | −0.238** | −0.268** | 0.198** | −0.135* |
| | Sig. (2-tailed) | 0.091 | 0.096 | 0.892 | 0.000 | 0.000 | 0.001 | 0.032 |
| | LAR: N | 255 | 255 | 255 | 255 | 255 | 255 | 255 |
| Suggested changes in routines | P Correlation | −0.543** | −0.572** | −0.652** | −0.609** | −0.688** | 0.645** | −0.631** |
| | Sig. (2-tailed) | 0.002 | 0.001 | 0.000 | 0.000 | 0.000 | 0.000 | 0.000 |
| | Ytterøy: N | 30 | 30 | 30 | 30 | 30 | 30 | 30 |
| Formalized suggested changes in routines | P Correlation | −0.650** | −0.571** | −0.739** | −0.730** | −0.677** | 0.594** | −0.633** |
| | Sig. (2-tailed) | 0.000 | 0.001 | 0.000 | 0.000 | 0.000 | 0.001 | 0.000 |
| | Ytterøy: N | 30 | 30 | 30 | 30 | 30 | 30 | 30 |
| Suggested changes in routines | P Correlation | −.531** | −.316* | −.523** | −.563** | −.699** | .554** | −.806** |
| | Sig. (2-tailed) | 0.000 | 0.041 | 0.000 | 0.000 | 0.000 | 0.000 | 0.000 |
| | Crysbro: N | 42 | 42 | 42 | 42 | 42 | 42 | 42 |

| | | | | | | | | |
|---|---|---|---|---|---|---|---|---|
| Formalized suggested changes in routines | P Correlation | −.424** | −0.062 | −0.096 | −0.255 | −0.411** | 0.350* | −0.642** |
| | Sig. (2-tailed) | 0.005 | 0.696 | 0.543 | 0.103 | 0.007 | 0.023 | 0.000 |
| | Crysbro: N | 42 | 42 | 42 | 42 | 42 | 42 | 42 |
| Suggested changes in routines | P Correlation | −0.178 | -0.206 | -0.092 | -0.200 | -0.185 | 0.229 | −0.370* |
| | Sig. (2-tailed) | 0.321 | 0.249 | 0.610 | 0.264 | 0.303 | 0.200 | 0.034 |
| | KUPCO: N | 33 | 33 | 33 | 33 | 33 | 33 | 33 |
| Formalized suggested changes in routines | P Correlation | −0.424* | −0.401* | −0.359* | −0.255 | −0.118 | 0.099 | −0.373* |
| | Sig. (2-tailed) | 0.014 | 0.021 | 0.040 | 0.153 | 0.514 | 0.585 | 0.033 |
| | KUPCO: N | 33 | 33 | 33 | 33 | 33 | 33 | 33 |

Source: authors' data collection.

* Correlation is significant at the 0.05 level (2-tailed).
** Correlation is significant at the 0.01 level (2-tailed).

P Correlation: Pearson Correlation, all calculations are done using the SPSS system.

communication and innovative behavior. What we expected was that a strong communication process had an influence to extend the level of innovative initiatives. Of course, correlation coefficients only tell us if the factors vary in the same direction or not. As we argued in Chapter 4, communication is an interactive and multidimensional process and can have both internal and external links before the written suggestions are there.

In Danpo and Ytterøy and it is interesting to see that the correlations for the communication variables got stronger when we changed from the variable *changes in routines* to *suggested formalized changes in routines.* At LAR, we only found one significant correlation and that was between the variables *formalized suggested changes in routines* and *group members initiatives to the group leader.* It was the upward communications process that showed the stronger results. For both Crysbro and KUPCO firms the calculations showed the expected pattern. At the Crysbro firm the results changed considerably from the variables *changes in routines* to *formulized changes in routines.*

When we look at skills we see the expected results that higher skills go together with more formulized suggestions for changes in innovations. As stated in Chapter 4 the variable about technical level is measured in an inverse way so the lower number indicator expresses higher technical levels. In general, we find support for the view that higher skills lead to higher levels of all innovative behavior. Higher skills also contribute to a higher degree of formalized changes in routines.

We will only give some more general statements about the outcome variable and innovative behavior. Higher values on the outcome variable mean that production is going more smoothly with less production stops or other interruptions in production. Most firms show significant correlations between smoother production and increases in innovative behavior. This supports the argument that a positive 'atmosphere' in production supports innovative behavior. This correlates with some of the articles cited in earlier sections of this chapter (e.g. Scott and Bruce, 1994).

The results for correlations between the cultural variables and the variables about changes in routines are shown in Table 5.3. How cultural variables are constructed and how they can be interpreted is discussed in detail in Chapter 4.4.8. In this section, we will concentrate on the most important one – Power unequal – because this relates to power distance and trust in the organization. This variable is based on the statement:

> Do you expect and agree that power should be unequally shared?

This means that the higher the indicator values, the higher the power distance the respondent wants to express. According to Hofstede and Hofstede (2001) higher power distance can be interpreted as reduced trust. And as we have discussed in the earlier sections of this chapter trust is a central concept to explain innovative behavior in general and in LMX theory.

*Table 5.3* Correlations between innovative behavior and cultural variables

| | | *Avoid uncertainty* | *Power unequal* | *Reward collective* | *Pride in firm* | *Equality men/ women* | *Confrontational in firm* | *Future oriented* | *Generous* |
|---|---|---|---|---|---|---|---|---|---|
| Suggested changes in routines | P Correlation | −0.196 | 0.029 | −0.105 | −0.085 | 0.140 | -0.009 | -0.175 | -0.249 |
| | Sig. (2-tailed) | 0.231 | 0.861 | 0.523 | 0.607 | 0.395 | 0.959 | 0.287 | 0.126 |
| | Danpo: N | 39 | 39 | 39 | 39 | 39 | 39 | 39 | 39 |
| Formalized suggested changes in routines | P Correlation | −0.395* | 0.323* | −0.425** | −0.115 | −0.030 | 0.105 | -0.247 | -0.306 |
| | Sig. (2-tailed) | 0.013 | 0.045 | 0.007 | 0.484 | 0.858 | 0.524 | 0.129 | 0.058 |
| | Danpo: N | 39 | 39 | 39 | 39 | 39 | 39 | 39 | 39 |
| Suggested changes in routines | P Correlation | 0.077 | −0.008 | −0.069 | −0.146* | 0.076 | -0.078 | -0.334** | 0.033 |
| | Sig. (2-tailed) | 0.222 | 0.902 | 0.272 | 0.020 | 0.224 | 0.215 | 0.000 | 0.598 |
| | LAR: N | 255 | 255 | 255 | 255 | 255 | 255 | 255 | 255 |
| Formalized suggested changes in routines | P Correlation | −0.019 | 0.125* | -0.162** | −0.185** | −0.092 | 0.021 | -0.217** | -0.072 |
| | Sig. (2-tailed) | 0.761 | 0.047 | 0.010 | 0.003 | 0.143 | 0.735 | 0.000 | 0.254 |
| | LAR: N | 255 | 255 | 255 | 255 | 255 | 255 | 255 | 255 |
| Suggested changes in routines | P Correlation | −0.437* | 0.583** | −0.232 | −0.496** | −0.404* | 0.325 | -0.433* | -0.204 |
| | Sig. (2-tailed) | 0.016 | 0.001 | 0.218 | 0.005 | 0.027 | 0.080 | 0.017 | 0.279 |
| | Ytterøy: N | 30 | 30 | 30 | 30 | 30 | 30 | 30 | 30 |
| Formalized suggested changes in routines | P Correlation | −0.511** | 0.598** | −0.247 | −0.433* | −0.305 | 0.395* | -0.592** | -0.336 |
| | Sig. (2-tailed) | 0.004 | 0.000 | 0.189 | 0.017 | 0.101 | 0.031 | 0.001 | 0.070 |
| | Ytterøy: N | 30 | 30 | 30 | 30 | 30 | 30 | 30 | 30 |
| Suggested changes in routines | P Correlation | −0.235 | 0.769** | −0.185 | −0.464** | −0.254 | 0.235 | -0.462** | -0.073 |
| | Sig. (2-tailed) | 0.134 | 0.000 | 0.241 | 0.002 | 0.105 | 0.134 | 0.002 | 0.646 |
| | Crysbro: N | 42 | 42 | 42 | 42 | 42 | 42 | 42 | 42 |

*(Continued)*

*Table 5.3* (Continued)

| | | *Avoid uncertainty* | *Power unequal* | *Reward collective* | *Pride in firm* | *Equality men/ women* | *Confrontational in firm* | *Future oriented* | *Generous* |
|---|---|---|---|---|---|---|---|---|---|
| Formalized suggested changes in routines | P Correlation | 0.103 | 0.483** | −0.137 | −0.367* | −0.023 | 0.061 | −0.236 | 0.233 |
| | Sig. (2-tailed) | 0.517 | 0.001 | 0.386 | 0.017 | 0.884 | 0.703 | 0.132 | 0.138 |
| | Crysbro: N | 42 | 42 | 42 | 42 | 42 | 42 | 42 | 42 |
| Suggested changes in routines | P Correlation | −0.302 | 0.409* | −0.118 | −0.222 | −0.181 | −0.221 | 0.025 | 0.178 |
| | Sig. (2-tailed) | 0.087 | 0.018 | 0.514 | 0.215 | 0.315 | 0.217 | 0.889 | 0.322 |
| | KUPCO: N | 33 | 33 | 33 | 33 | 33 | 33 | 33 | 33 |
| Formalized suggested changes in routines | P Correlation | −0.109 | 0.420* | −0.277 | −0.186 | −0.082 | 0.054 | −0.091 | 0.077 |
| | Sig. (2-tailed) | 0.547 | 0.015 | 0.118 | 0.301 | 0.648 | 0.764 | 0.616 | 0.672 |
| | KUPCO: N | 33 | 33 | 33 | 33 | 33 | 33 | 33 | 33 |

Source: authors' data collection.

* Correlation is significant at the 0.05 level (2-tailed).
** Correlation is significant at the 0.01 level (2-tailed).

P Correlation: Pearson Correlation, all calculations are done using the SPSS system.

For Danpo and LAR we find significant correlations with the expected sign first when we look at formalized suggested changes in routines. It is when we have singled out the most serious innovative ideas that trust becomes important. For KUPCO and Crysbro trust was always important in the innovation process, but remember that these two firms had a lower innovative activity than the other firms. Danpo showed significant correlations also for the indicators *avoid uncertainty* and *reward collective actions.* This is logical because the firm has an advanced technological level with large negative consequences if something goes wrong. This is also reflected in the way that collectiveness is important – the technological solutions include all departments – one department is dependent on successful implementations of the technology in the other.

The Norwegian firm Ytterøy has a higher contribution of positive cultural components than the others. This is because this firm has been able to create a 'positive family feeling'. This is also important for the firm's economic ability to survive. The firm is a niche producer with a high cost level and must be able to follow the market and innovate in the way the market demands. This must reflect a clear understanding through all stages of production.

## 5.4 Innovation management

### *5.4.1 Introduction*

There are numerous models and suggestions about how to manage innovations. We begin looking at the concepts of Tidd and Bessant (2013) where they outlined how innovation can be analyzed as a core process within an organization. They use four keywords or key areas to look at this; the first is *searching* which means how the organization must look for opportunities for innovation. The next step is to *select* what the organization can and will do and why. In a general analysis where we do not specify what kind of organization we are looking at we must consider that different organizations have different goals. In our study we look at firms. Then the objective of the firms is to strengthen and improve competitiveness and earn profits at the same time. The third step is about *implementation*; how the firm will manage the process so the innovation is working successfully in the firm. For the fourth and final step, they use the word *capture*. This is the process about how the firm will benefit from the innovation and implement this into the general strategy of the firm.

For our purpose, it is preferable to go into more detail about how we analyze the innovation processes for a firm. It is interesting to see how different studies and articles rely on the same factors. In this respect, we will look at work by Adams, *et al.* (2006), Dodgson (2000) and Hidalgo and Albors (2008). The article by Adams provides a literature review and summary of many studies which looked at innovation management, so one can say that the results by Adams are in a way, a state of the art. In our project, we will use the following list of indicators to analyze the innovation process:

A Inputs and resource situation: Manpower, capital and financial resources
B Knowledge management: Idea generation, knowledge repository and information flows
C The integration of innovation strategy and firm strategy
D Organization and culture
E Technology and technological collaboration
F The use of IT-based solutions
G Commercialization: Market research, market testing, marketing, and sales
H Complexity and risk

In our empirical example, we will continue to use the firms from the food processing industry (white meat production) and that raises the question about innovation in low-tech industries compared to high-tech industries. Fagerberg, *et al.* (2006) discussed this theme in *Handbook of innovations* and the question is, are there are significant differences between innovation management and innovation processes in low-tech, medium-tech and high-tech firms? Many writers use the book from OECD (1994) to see which firms are classified as producing with low, medium or high levels of technology. The OECD classification is based on industrial sectors. In food processing industries we find a very large difference in technology between the large-scale producers of white meat based on medium- and high-technology equipment compared to the low-scale ecologic producer where everything takes place outdoors on a farm. When it comes to the market it is not so easy to taste the difference between the two types of white meat but the ecological argument is important in marketing. In pharmaceutical production, a sector that often is looked at as high-tech, we have copy producers of established medicines that take place with (normally) only medium level of technology. On the other side, we have leading edge firms when it comes to research and development where the level of technology and knowledge is very much higher than in the copy firms. So, the differentiation between low-tech and high-tech based on sector classification is problematic.

We have other attempts to classify industrial production using criteria and characteristics other than OECD, including a suggestion from Pavitt (1984). His categories were named (1) supplier-dominated, (2) scale-intensive (3) information-intensive (4) science-based (5) specialized-supplier. This suggestion gives solutions to some problems; for example, we can have science-based production for quite normal consumer goods while still looking at production based on specialized input factors.

If we then return to the classification by OECD and look at low and medium technology firms, a more general conclusion is the following. Low and medium level technology firms seem to have more easily definable products which means that they use innovations to develop product differentiation and cost efficiency. For high-tech firms the innovation process is linked to fundamentally new technologies and their entry into completely new markets with new products satisfying new needs. Low and medium technology industries are often more labor-intensive and therefore innovations into more advanced technology dominated production is an interesting option. Low and medium technology industries also depend more on how the vertical integration of the production chain is constructed resulting in a drive for innovative activities.

### *5.4.2 Indicators to analyze the innovation process*

*A Inputs and resource situation*

The situation more in general for the firm when innovation takes place is of vital importance for the success of the actual innovation process. This is analyzed by many studies and one group of research looked at how much the firm spent for research and development activities compared to the total cost of production. This is often called R&D intensity. Several studies find results indicating that higher R&D intensity is a success factor for innovation processes, but there is no univocal relation for this, see Cohen, *et al.* (1987) and Cassiman and Veugelers (2006). One study by Stock, *et al.* (2001) examined the relationship between absorptive capacity and new product development. They found an inverted U-shape which means that there are diminishing returns for large increases R&D intensity. Other studies like Parisi, Schiantarelli and Sembenelli (2006) found the same result, that R&D spending is positively associated with the probability of innovations. What we can expect when firms use money for research and development purposes are results that show improved productivity. Whether this has decreasing returns or not when we come to high levels of R&D intensity is questionable; here the results go in different directions.

The more fundamental questions about input factors and how they influence the innovation ability of the firm can be analyzed by looking at labor and capital. There have been several studies investigating how the qualifications of the employees in firms influence the firm's ability to innovate. Items of specific importance are the skills, experience and education level of the employees. Here we find results indicating that higher employment levels and skills increase the propensity for firms to innovate, but this conclusion is not always straightforward. A study by Westeren (2012) showed that increasing skills as a separate factor was not sufficient to influence innovation positively, there must be management of the information flows that contribute as an important driver for increased innovations.

One study by Baumol (2004) discussed the importance of education for innovation. The study concluded that a higher level of education in general was a stimulus for innovation but this was not a one-sided story. One question Baumol raised was whether a higher educational level stimulated creativity or not. Baumol found, like many others, that some of the most famous innovators did not have a high educational level in the field where they did the innovation. This of course goes back again to the argument that innovations to a high degree are context specific. When we look at capital as a factor of production we also have many studies showing that firms with updated capital equipment are more likely to be innovative than firms with more average equipment. We also find the same result when we analyze the influence of fixed capital investments, they are promoting the possibility of innovative behavior in firms, see Parisi, *et al.* (2006). As background factors, high quality of labor and capital positively influence innovations but the interesting question is, which circumstances promote the best results?

### *B Knowledge management and innovations*

Knowledge management and innovation have grown into a scientific field of its own with numerous books and publications including Nonaka and Takeuchi's (1995) book about the knowledge-creating firm. Other contributions are found in Eardley and Uden (2011) and Lundvall and Nielsen (2007). There are also several country studies and firm studies, examples include Brand (1998), Westeren (2012) and Håkansson and Waluszewski (2014).

When we talk about the links between knowledge management and innovations we first need define what we mean by the concept of knowledge capital. In Chapter 4 of this book we divided knowledge capital into (1) Human capital, (2) Structural capital and (3) Relational capital.

The next question then is how to manage knowledge capital. We normally divide this into processes. The first is identification and here we must look at knowledge in relation to the production processes that are central for the value creation of the firm. The next item is measurement where the firm must find a useful and operational set of indicators to measure what the knowledge capital consists of. Knowledge management then is the management system that the firm uses to operate the knowledge capital in such a way that the firm can achieve the objectives that usually are to maximize profits and strengthen competitiveness.

One central task regarding knowledge management is how to develop indicators for the measurement of knowledge when we look at this for the purpose of analyzing the competitiveness of the firm. A summary of the indicators presented in Chapter 4 gives the following groups:

- Indicators related to outcome
- Indicators relating to workers competence
- Indicators related to technology
- Indicators related to communication and communicative skills
- Indicators related to the context
- Indicators related to culture

In the actual management of knowledge to develop the firm's innovative possibilities it is necessary to distinguish between explicit and tacit knowledge. As stated in Chapters 1 and 4, the definition of explicit knowledge is what can be codified and stored and this is not controversial. There are several definitions and interpretations of the concept of tacit knowledge. In this book we build on the work of Polanyi (1958; 1966), see Chapter 4.

One central discussion in theory and practice is how the conversion of knowledge from tacit to explicit knowledge can trigger innovations. In a case study by Westeren (2012) we can see how a firm can contribute to conversions from tacit to explicit knowledge and in the process of doing this we see how innovations occur. To explain why this happens we need to look at the knowledge transfer system in the firm and how this is managed. The study identifies the knowledge brokers in the firm. The communicative skills of these brokers are central to the employees' ability to contribute to new innovations.

There are many studies either based on single firms or groups of firms like Alegre, *et al.* (2013), Mundra, *et al.* (2011), and Gloet and Samson (2012) finding that the more professional and well-designed systems there are for knowledge management, the higher the probability to see innovations occur. At the same time, these studies also show that innovations to a high degree are context dependent. One interesting result when we put many of these studies together is that there seems to be little difference between low-tech and high-tech production sectors, implying that more professional knowledge management has a positive effect on all innovations.

### C *The integration of innovation strategy and firm strategy*

Earlier in this chapter we discussed how the innovation process has changed with emphasis on innovation as a knowledge and technology feature. Now the innovation process for a majority of firms is a fundamental part of firm strategy. Recent literature on this question suggests that innovation must be included in all main goal formulation and solutions for action even though we talk about a main strategy formulation for the firm, which is to develop competitive strength and improve profitability at the same time, Simons (2013) and Teece (2010).

We can say that all eight points in our list of analysis for analyzing innovation management are about how to integrate an innovative strategy in the total firm strategy management. If we look at one of the later more famous strategy formulations for firms, lean management, we find that innovation plays an important part but other aspects must also be integrated together with innovative behavior. A study by Hsu (2011) presented interesting points of view on how competitive product design and innovation strategies go together based on a study of computer and consumer electronic industries. The study showed that the firms had quite different strategies with respect to production marketing and cooperative contracts with other firms. For some firms, technology innovations were central for business development while for other firms, marketing sales and cooperation in markets were the main factor for the firm. For other firms their position in the vertical supply chain was decisive for their innovation strategy. This showed that the integration of innovative strategy into the general business strategy for the firms varied greatly even in the same production sector. So, to assume we find one single prescription is not likely.

Studies from other sectors (e.g. the wood sector industry by Nybakk, *et al.*, 2011) showed in principle the same results that innovation was seen as an important and decisive factor for business and competitive developments. Operationally, to develop this the innovation strategy is normally derived from the more fundamental situation of the firm and the overall business plan. The more general results show that firms which are able to successfully integrate the innovation strategy into the firm's total strategy normally are more profitable with a relatively stronger competitive situation.

### *D Innovativeness, organization and culture*

In the original work from Schumpeter (1934; 1939; 1950) he mentioned organizational innovations as one category. Schumpeter's focus and examples were related to conditions outside the firm like a new market organization. The focus on organizational innovations inside the firm emerged after WW2. In the discussion here we will use the interpretation from the Oslo Manual (OECD 2005) where organizational innovations included responsibilities, accountability, command lines and information flows in the firm. Organizational innovations may change:

- The number of hierarchical levels
- The divisional structure of functions
- The separation between different functions
- The vertical structure of the firm – outsourcing/insourcing of activities

Successful innovation management is normally dependent on having an organization that reflects the goals and possibilities of the firm and integrates the innovation policy into the firm's goals. The traditional model for business organization was based on a hierarchical model where the manager had control over the system that normally was divided into departments and department leaders who again had responsibility for managing their part of the production process. This model has been challenged because firms now need to have innovations on all levels in the organization. Articles dealing with these aspects include early contributions from Monge, *et al.* (1992), Lam (2006), and von Held (2012) where the focus was to combine innovation and creativity with social network studies.

The first keyword in this discussion is about different types of network models. There is a large literature on development from hierarchical organizations to network based organizational models. The main achievement from the point of view of innovation is that creative ideas can be linked by different networks to different people and show different possibilities without everything going through one established hierarchical model. This argument again is linked to the knowledge management argument that knowledge workers now have a greater demand for autonomy than earlier. An article by Jensen (2008) is about how the autonomy pyramid is turned upside down with the introduction of what can be called the knowledge economy and the knowledge organization. One argument from Jensen is that many people at different levels in the organization may have more knowledge than the responsible manager. This knowledge contributes to innovativeness in such a way that it is counterproductive to have a hierarchal system. If the network organization is too loosely coupled such that core knowledge and competences are without managerial control, there could be negative consequences. One study by Haeussler (2006) based on biotechnology firms in Germany showed that managers did not have to worry as much as one would think about a rather loosely coupled network organizations.

Another argument that has changed organizational thinking is what can be called the learning organization. Studies by Senge and Suzuki (1994) and Lundvall and Borrás (1997) suggested that organizations improved in flexibility and innovativeness when the organizational structure had learning processes on every level. Another argument for change in organizational structure that promotes innovativeness is the development of project based organizations. Because of factors like managerial freedom, risk reduction and possibilities for making contacts independently we have seen many innovative processes taken out of the firm and organized on a project basis.

In general, we can say that culture has a two-sided function in society, it is the glue that holds society together and it is culture that forms the background for the decision-making of the individual. Early studies by Hofstede (1980; 1991) considered the impact of culture on firm organization and change. The GLOBE project House, *et al.* (2004) also looked at the links between culture and innovation. One study by Ozgen, *et al.* (2011) gave an analysis of the impact of cultural diversity on innovation based on data from the Netherlands. This study started by recognizing the fact that people with different cultural backgrounds have both advantages and problems when they come to a new country and want to start up new firms with innovating activities. The advantages are that they bring with them new ideas, new values and they see new possibilities that are not always seen by the inhabitants of the country. On the other hand, there is often a recourse gap because people with a different cultural background do not always have the financial resources and networks that are necessary to do successful innovations.

Another way of looking at culture as an important factor is that we now have people from different countries working in firms. One effect of this is that communication seems to be crucial because of language differences. A study by Westeren (2012) found results showing that different language backgrounds influenced the possibilities for the transition of tacit to explicit knowledge as a factor to enhance innovation. The knowledge level, possibilities and background to be innovative, were normally quite high for people coming from other countries with high education and expertise. But they needed an information broker in the firm to pick up the ideas and assist them with implementation in the firm. Another cultural factor is the male/female division. In the food producing firms we investigated in this project, many of the supervisors and others in leading managerial positions were men while the industrial workers have a high share of women. In two of the firms, the one in Norway and the one in Denmark, the situation is that many of the workers come from countries where the language is totally different from Scandinavian languages. This is a great challenge for the managerial system, especially at the supervisor level.

### E *Technology and technological collaboration*

One of the most researched themes within the field of innovation management is about technology and how different technologies contribute to the firm's competitive situation via the innovation processes. In this research tradition, we also find the concepts of incremental and radical innovations, Damanpour and Aravind (2012). The radical innovations are quite easy to delineate because they represent production processes and products that are fundamentally new to the market and to the firms. The question about incremental innovations is more difficult to delineate because the criteria from the Oslo Manual says that for a change to be an innovation it needs to be new to the firm and contribute to new combinations.

Research on differences between small or large firms indicates that small firms are more likely to develop new radical technologies. One of the most famous stories here is about the development of the Apple computer. Following Christensen and Bower (1996), they found that large firms were often developing new technologies when their old ones were threatened. One of the most recent famous books on the subject is by Clayton M. Christensen about the innovators dilemma (2013).

It is not the intention in this chapter to give a complete discussion on this subject but one other point deserves to be mentioned and that is about technological collaboration. The formation of the concepts and analysis of what is now called systems of innovation started in the 1990's with books by Edquist (1997) and Lundvall (1992). Here we talk about national and regional systems of innovation. One of the main reasons for doing this is to analyze how within a triple helix model the public sector and other institutions can contribute to innovative activities. This again improves the competitiveness of firms, thereby strengthening national productivity in the globalized economy.

### F *The use of IT-based solutions*

Innovation-based IT solutions are normally looked at as a positive factor that contributes to innovative activities in firms. When we look at the link between IT and productivity we often cite the so-called Solow paradox with the following sentence 'You can see the computer age everywhere but in the productivity statistics', Solow (1987: 36).

However, most studies and articles find a positive relationship between IT and productivity on the firm level, see Hall, *et al.* (2012). But when we come to the analysis of the link between IT and innovation the results are more difficult to interpret. Most IT systems for firms are designed for the production activities of the firm and not to enable innovation. When we look at IT, it is interesting to see how flexible the system is because normally innovative activities change something. Polder, *et al.* (2012) found that ICT was an important driver in innovation based on data from the Netherlands.

However, in which way can we look at ICT investments as a possible determinant for innovation? The question here is whether the investment in IT equipment came before the innovation as an enabler or if it came after the innovation because of new needs. One must also be aware of the facts that new IT systems normally require a higher level of competence and in the process of gaining this competence the firm can see possibilities for innovation. The general conclusion here is that innovative activities are context specific and it is not easy to draw very specific conclusions. The more general picture looks like ICT investments are important both as one enabler and as a result of innovative behavior.

### G *Markets and innovations*

The discussion of the link between markets and innovation relates back to Schumpeter (1934) where he came with the point of view that large firms operating in a concentrated market were a powerful engine of progress for economic development and for innovative behavior. One of the most discussed hypotheses associated with Schumpeter is that the probability to experience innovation behavior increases with market concentration. The point of view from Schumpeter is problematic when it comes to economic policy and rules for preventing monopolistic behavior by firms. One of the most famous results of the general neoclassic economy is that monopolistic behaving firms reduce welfare for society. On the other hand, Schumpeter argued that such firms will stimulate innovative processes.

Another way to look at this is how firms can successfully market their innovations. We have many examples about how market innovations have succeeded and failed; see the books by Trott (2008) and Tidd and Bessant (2013). We will not go through this literature in detail but be aware that some of the ideas from Schumpeter remain. Several firms have a market strategy to use innovation to create monopoly-like situations like niche products that are sheltered from competition. This line of thought can also be traced back to Porter where one of his general suggestions for developing competitiveness is product differentiation.

### H *Risk and innovation*

Management of risk in industrial production is a field of its own and has gained a lot of interest in recent years. We have seen the link between innovation and risk from the start of innovation theory with Schumpeter, because for Schumpeter it was important to look at innovation and possibilities for new combinations as a part of the same picture. Schumpeter spoke about the entrepreneur as the person who could choose the right combinations when multiple combinations were possible.

In the later years, we have seen books and articles about innovation and risk and the more general statement by Pavit (2006) is the following:

> Innovation processes involve the exploration and exploitation of opportunities for new or improved products, processes or services....novation is inherently uncertain given the impossibility of predicting accurately the cost and performance of a new artifact, and the reactions of users to it.
>
> Pavit (2006: 88)

Many studies have quite similar results about the attitude of taking risk among entrepreneurs. The studies show that innovators to a high degree are risk averse. The results from a study by Duarte (2010) showed that 67% of the firms had a high level of risk aversion, 28% were risk averse, 3% were moderate risk takers, while only 2% of the innovators in the study were characterized as risk takers. Similar results can be found in Dollinger (2003).

Another perspective for looking at risk and innovations is how the firm manages the risk they must take to implement innovative changes in processes, products and market. There are several methodologies to deal with this and one model is called supply chain innovation and risk assessment, which is an aid for firms to balance and manage risk. This is most relevant for firms where supply chain management is an important part of production like in white meat production.

### 5.4.4 *Case studies*

In the theoretical part, we presented a list with eight indicators that have been used to analyze management of the innovation process. In this empirical part, we will use two of the producers of white meat, LAR in Paraná in Brazil and Danpo in Denmark. The finished product – the white meat as a commodity – is to a large degree the same, but the production technology, the skills of the labor force and the market conditions are different as earlier documented. In this picture, we have analyzed how the firms manage the innovation processes. The 8-indicator list presented earlier is based on several studies from different lands and industries and comprises a quite complete list. In the discussion based on the two firms here we may find that not all of the eight indicators have the same relevance. We have investigated the firms for many years doing interviews and field studies about their organization of production, innovations, of the vertical integration and market relations and in this respect the study of innovations and innovative processes has had a central place. In our study of innovations, we have had the same problem as in many other similar studies – namely to define and identify what is an innovation. We have used the Oslo Manual (OECD, 2005) – but as in any innovation study it is necessary to use interpretation and judgement to decide operational criteria for what is an innovation.

It is important to consider that the Danpo firm has a highly advanced level of technology in production. The system of quality control is based on a digital video image analysis of every chicken that is produced. The market strategy for the firm is focused on the national market in Denmark and it is from this market the firm makes most of its profits. There are large fluctuations in demand from the national market from week to week and month to month. The firm produces a much higher volume than is needed for the national market which the firm exports mainly to Germany. The firm takes into consideration that the price for exports is lower than the price for deliveries to the national market, so one can say that the firm uses exports as a strategy to even out the fluctuations in the national market.

As explained earlier, LAR is a Brazilian firm situated in Paraná, Brazil. Compared to the Danish producer, LAR has a medium level of technology but a more labor-intensive production than Danpo. The main innovative side of the firm is how it does vertical integration, see Chapter 3. The firm has an integrated system from the production of eggs, to chicken, to the slaughter and the firm is able to have high quality meat production with relatively low costs for the feed. The market situation for the firm is an export share of about 50–60%. The strategy of the firm is to increase the export share and use exports as the main factor contributing to the profits of the firm. The main export markets are China, Europe, Japan and Russia.

In our analysis of innovation management in the firms we will use the eight indicators presented earlier (see Table 5.4).

### *5.4.5 Concluding remarks*

Innovation management has grown into a scientific field of its own. The focus has for many years been on what an innovation is and what contribution an innovation can make to the competitiveness of the firm. How the firm should be successful in doing the innovation process first gained attention in the last decades before the turn of the century. Dealing with innovations we must bear in mind that innovations are context specific so it is difficult to find general conclusions about the innovation management process. Our two investigated firms have a similar product but operate under different (home) market, technology and cultural conditions. One interesting similar factor is the importance of knowledge management for the success of innovation management. The two firms do knowledge management operationally quite differently but the dependence on having a system that transmits the correct knowledge at the correct time with a correct interpretation is essential.

Another item that is important and done successfully for both firms is the integration of the innovation strategy in firm strategy. Here we see that this is done consciously and connected to the top management level. Culture is more important than firms often are aware of. In medium and large firms, it is nearly unavoidable that subcultures occur. And when the firm changes the procedures and routines from direct human quality control (using eyes) to interpretation of computer produced pictures, this also challenges the cultural dimension of the workers.

The empirical part also warns that technology and networks may challenge the innovation process. Examples from the empirical studies show that the computer software equipment in the Danpo case was kept secret by the firm that

*Table 5.4* Innovation management in Danpo and LAR

| *Factors* | *Comments* |
|---|---|
| 1. Inputs and resource situation | Danpo is depending on a high level of expertise of labor especially at the group leader/supervisor level in production and for the specialized personnel responsible for operating the new technology.<br><br>For LAR, it is important to have a satisfactory level of expertise and education for the group leader/supervisor and production workers. Since the innovative strength lies in the vertical chain it is also important to have a corresponding level of knowledge through the chain so that the knowledge flows pass from one part of the chain to the next without misunderstandings and obstacles.<br><br>For both firms, it is important that there are people with decision-making capabilities who always look for innovative activities.<br><br>Financial resources are not a problem for any of the firms to do the innovating activities. |
| 2. Knowledge management | Knowledge management is essential for the success of the innovating activities in both firms.<br><br>In Danpo the new technology is essential not only in the production line making quality control more efficient but in all important parts of production. A central aspect for the success of the organization of production based on the new technology is that the knowledge matches and flows. By match we mean that the knowledge has the right level and right focus.<br><br>LAR also takes knowledge management seriously because the departments are interconnected and have frequent meetings for coordination of knowledge dissemination. We found two areas of special importance, the first was the link between the sales department and production planning and control. The second was the general management of knowledge through the vertical chain. |
| 3. The integration of innovation strategy and firm strategy | The main innovating activity in LAR is supply chain management, so the innovation strategy must be the central part of the firm strategy. The firm has control of the different stages of production. For LAR a little less than 50% of the total cost makes up for the share of live chicken. A favorable cost situation for the production is based on high efficiency in feed production (the main ingredient in the feed is soya and corn) is taken care of by the way the firm manages the vertical deliveries, see Chapter 2.<br><br>For Danpo the situation and challenges are different compared to LAR when it comes to the integration of innovation strategy into the firm strategy. Danpo has to successfully integrate a technology strategy into the firm strategy. The focus at Danpo is then how much the innovation contributes to profits and to strengthening the competitive situation. The integration to a large degree is about optimization of production and quality control. The market situation for the firm is that both factors are central for reducing costs and improving quality control. |

| *Factors* | *Comments* |
|---|---|
| 4. Organization and culture | For LAR the organizational setup is the innovative idea. On the cultural side there are several challenges, one is the cultural differences between the breeders and the industrial system.<br>In Danpo the new technological solution creates a new organizational setup. This changes some of the communication lines but this is taken care of by the firm. The most important organizational and cultural challenge is that a large share of the production workers comes from countries with a non-Scandinavian background. |
| 5. Technology and technological collaboration | The technological solution is the main part of the innovation at Danpo. The technological part of the innovation lies in the software of the system. But to make this innovative for the firm the main job is to integrate this with the other parts of the technological equipment.<br>For LAR the strategy is a partnership or integration between agribusiness and production equipment. All parts of the vertical chain receive technical support and training from the firm. LAR is working to pursue a strategy of automation quite intensely because they have a labor-intensive production. |
| 6. Use of IT-based solutions | As already mentioned, the innovation in Danpo is IT-based. In addition to that it was important to integrate the new IT systems into the existing systems of the firm. For some parts of the system this demanded new solutions.<br>Also, LAR is dependent on the IT systems function as a link between the levels in the vertically integrated system. |
| 7. Commercialization and market | Danpo has the home market in Denmark as its main market but the importance of quality control is essential for both home and export markets.<br>LAR is constantly monitoring the internal and external market. The sales strategy is based on scenarios starting from the premise that both the internal and the international market demand must be met. The firm does not have its own international brand. In the world markets the products are marketed through distributors in packages, sizes and different standards depending on the market. |
| 8. Complexity and risk | The project risk for the innovating activities for Danpo has two aspects. From the financial point of view the risk is low – the cost of the new equipment is relatively low. From the production planning point of view the risk is high. The firm is dependent on the equipment working at the speed of the production line. The firm is dependent on few and only short stops in the production line.<br>At LAR the project risk is low. Experience shows that vertical integration works – the essential part is the optimization. |

produced the equipment. In all network theory, we say that trust is fundamental. When Danpo gets a software upgrade they find the quality satisfactory in use but they do not know in detail what has been done. But so far, we have not seen that this has challenged the trust between the software firm and Danpo.

There is no doubt a need for more studies about innovation management both in theory and practice. What this study reveals is not just the need to know more about innovation, but also more specifically what results can be generalized and what results are so context specific that they only shed light on the examined case. Another question that also needs more attention is the types of relationships between knowledge and innovations management.

## References

Adams, R., Bessant, J., & Phelps, R. (2006). Innovation management measurement: A review. *International Journal of Management Reviews*, *8*(1), 21–47.

Alegre, J., Sengupta, K., & Lapiedra, R. (2013). Knowledge management and innovation performance in a high-tech SMEs industry. *International Small Business Journal*, *31*(4), 454–470.

Amabile, T. M. (1988). A model of creativity and innovation in organizations. In B. Staw & L. L. Cummings (Eds.), *Research in organizational behaviour* (Vol. 10, pp. 123–167). Greenwich: JAI Press.

Andersen, E. S., Dahl, M. S., Lundvall, B. Å., & Reichstein, T. (2006). *Schumpeter's process of creative destruction and the Scandinavian systems: A tale of two effects*. Paper for the DRUID Conference, 18–20 June 2006.

Baumol, W. J. (2004). *Education for innovation: Entrepreneurial breakthroughs vs. corporate incremental improvements* (No. w10578). Cambridge, MA: National Bureau of Economic Research.

Blau, P. M. (1964). *Exchange and power in social life*. New Brunswick, NJ: Transaction Publishers.

Brand, A. (1998). Knowledge management and innovation at 3M. *Journal of Knowledge Management*, *2*(1), 17–22.

Cassiman, B., & Veugelers, R. (2006). In search of complementarity in innovation strategy: Internal R&D and external knowledge acquisition. *Management Science*, *52*(1), 68–82.

Chesbrough, H., Vanhaverbeke, W., & West, J. (Eds.). (2006). *Open innovation: Researching a new paradigm*. Oxford: Oxford University Press.

Christensen, C. M. (2013). *The innovator's dilemma: When new technologies cause great firms to fail*. Cambridge, MA: Harvard Business Review Press.

Christensen, C. M., & Bower, J. L. (1996). Customer power, strategic investment, and the failure of leading firms. *Strategic Management Journal*, *17*(3), 197–218.

Cohen, W. M., Levin, R. C., & Mowery, D. C. (1987). Firm size and R&D intensity: A re-examination. *Journal of Industrial Economics*, *35*(4), 543–65.

Damanpour, F., & Aravind, D. (2012). Managerial innovation: Conceptions, processes, and antecedents. *Management and Organization Review*, *8*(2), 423–454.

Dansereau Jr., F., Graen, G., & Haga, W. J. (1975). A vertical dyad linkage approach to leadership within formal organizations: A longitudinal investigation of the role making process. *Organizational Behavior and Human Performance*, *13*(1), 46–78.

Danish Meat Research Institute (DMRI). (2010). *Vision classification and value-based payment of broiler chickens*. Final report Project No. 1379720. Copenhagen: DMRI (Danish Meat Research Institute).

Dodgson, M. (2000). *The management of technological innovation: An international and strategic approach*. Oxford: Oxford University Press.

Dollinger, M. J. (2003). *Entrepreneurship: Strategies and resources*. London: Pearson.

Duarte, N. (2010). Business strategies on innovation, risk and proactivity. In *Proceedings of the 5th WSEAS International Conference on Economy and Management Transformation* (Vol. 1, pp. 302–307).

Dulebohn, J. H., Bommer, W. H., Liden, R. C., Brouer, R. L., & Ferris, G. R. (2012). A meta-analysis of antecedents and consequences of leader-member exchange: Integrating the past with an eye towards the future. *Journal of Management, 38*(6), 1715–1759.

Eardley, A., & Uden, L. (Eds.). (2011). *Innovative knowledge management: Concepts for organizational creativity and collaborative design*. Hershey, PE: IGI Global.

Edquist, C. (Ed.). (1997). *Systems of innovation: Technologies, institutions, and organizations*. London: Pinter.

Fagerberg, J., Mowery, D. C., & Nelson, R. R. (Eds.). (2006). *The Oxford handbook of innovation*. Oxford: Oxford University Press.

Gerstner, C. R., & Day, D. V. (1997). Meta-analytic review of leader-member exchange theory: Correlates and construct issues. *Journal of Applied Psychology, 82*, 827–844.

Gloet, M., & Samson, D. (2012). Knowledge management and innovation performance in Australian service sector organizations. *System Science (HICSS), January 2012*, 4032–4041.

Graen, G. B. (1976). Role-making processes within complex organizations. In *Handbook of industrial and organizational psychology* (p. 1245). Chicago: Rand McNally.

Graen, G. B., & Cashman, J. F. (1975). A role-making model of leadership in formal organizations: A developmental approach. *Leadership frontiers*.

Graen, G. B., & Uhl-Bien, M. (1995). Relationship-based approach to leadership: Development of leader-member exchange (LMX) theory of leadership over 25 years: Applying a multi-level multi-domain perspective. *The Leadership Quarterly, 6*(2), 219–247.

Haeussler, C. (2006). 'Take and give' versus 'knowledge catching' – Empirical analysis of the management of knowledge flows. *Working paper*, Ludwig-Maximilian University of Munich, Munchen.

Håkansson, H., & Waluszewski, A. (Eds.). (2014). *Knowledge and innovation in business and industry: The importance of using others*. London: Routledge.

Hall, B. H., Lotti, F., & Mairesse, J. (2012). Evidence on the impact of R&D and ICT investments on innovation and productivity in Italian firms. *Economics of Innovation and New Technology, 1*, 29.

Hidalgo, A., & Albors, J. (2008). Innovation management techniques and tools: A review from theory and practice. *R&D Management, 38*(2), 113–127.

Hofstede, G. H. (1980). *Culture's consequences: International differences in work-related values*. Beverly Hills, CA: SAGE Publications.

Hofstede, G. H. (1991). *Cultures and organizations: Software of the mind*. London: McGraw-Hill.

Hofstede, G. H., & Hofstede, G. (2001). *Culture's consequences: Comparing values, behaviors, institutions and organizations across nations*. Beverly Hills, CA: SAGE Publications.

House, R. J., Hanges, P. J., Javidan, M., Dorfman, P. W., & Gupta, V. (Eds.). (2004). *Culture, leadership, and organizations: The GLOBE study of 62 societies*. Beverly Hills, CA: SAGE Publications.

Hsu, Y. (2011). Design innovation and marketing strategy in successful product competition. *Journal of Business & Industrial Marketing, 26*(4), 223–236.

Janssen, O. (2000). Job demands, perceptions of effort reward fairness and innovative work behaviour. *Journal of Occupational and Organizational Psychology, 73*(3), 287–302.

Janssen, O., Van de Vliert, E., & West, M. (2004). The bright and dark sides of individual and group innovation: A special issue introduction. *Journal of Organizational Behavior, 25*(2), 129–145.

Jensen, H. S. (2008). Management and learning in the knowledge society. *Journal of Regional Analysis and Policy, 38*(2), 130–137.

Kanter, R. M. (1988). When a thousand flowers bloom: Structural, collective, and social conditions for innovation in organization. In B. M. Staw & L. L. Cummings (Eds.), *Research in organizational behavior* (Vol. 10, pp. 169–211). Greenwich, CT: JAI Press.

Lam, A. (2006). Organizational innovation. In J. Fagerberg, D. C. Mowery, & R. R. Nelson (Eds.), *The Oxford handbook of innovation*. Oxford: Oxford University Press.

Liden, R. C., & Graen, G. (1980). Generalizability of the vertical dyad linkage model of leadership. *Academy of Management Journal, 23*(3), 451–465.

Liden, R. C., & Maslyn, J. M. (1998). Multidimensionality of leader-member exchange: An empirical assessment through scale development. *Journal of Management, 24*(1), 43–72.

Lundvall, B. A. (Ed.). (1992). *National systems of innovation: Towards a theory of innovation and interactive learning*. London: Pinter.

Lundvall, B. Å., & Borrás, S. (1997). *The globalising learning economy: Implications for innovation policy*. Brussels: European Commission.

Lundvall, B. Å., & Nielsen, P. (2007). Knowledge management and innovation performance. *International Journal of Manpower, 28*(3/4), 207–223.

Monge, P. R., Cozzens, M. D., & Contractor, N. S. (1992). Communication and motivational predictors of the dynamics of organizational innovation. *Organization Science, 3*(2), 250–274.

Montani, F., Odoardi, C., & Battistelli, A. (2014). Individual and contextual determinants of innovative work behaviour: Proactive goal generation matters. *Journal of Occupational and Organizational Psychology, 87*(4), 645–670.

Mundra, N., Gulati, K., & Vashisth, R. (2011). Achieving competitive advantage through knowledge management and innovation: Empirical evidences from the Indian IT sector. *The IUP Journal of Knowledge Management, 9*(2), 7–26.

Nonaka, I., & Takeuchi, H. (1995). *The knowledge-creating company: How Japanese companies create the dynamics of innovation*. Oxford: Oxford University Press.

Nooteboom, B. (2006). Innovation, learning and cluster dynamics. In P. Cooke, R. L. Martin, & B. T. Asheim (Eds.), *Clusters and regional development: Critical reflections and explorations* (pp. 137–163). London: Routledge.

Northouse, P. G. (2007). *Leadership: Theory and practice*. Thousand Oaks, CA: SAGE Publications.

Nybakk, E., Crespell, P., & Hansen, E. (2011). Climate for innovation and innovation strategy as drivers for success in the wood industry: Moderation effects of firm size, industry sector, and country of operation. *Silva Fennica, 45*(3), 415–430.

OECD. (1994). *The measurement of scientific and technical activities*. Paris: OECD.

OECD. (2005). *Proposed guidelines for collecting and interpreting technological innovation data* (Oslo Manual, 3rd revised ed.). Paris: OECD.

Ortt, J. R., & van der Duin, P. A. (2008). The evolution of innovation management towards contextual innovation. *European Journal of Innovation Management, 11*(4), 522–538.

Ozgen, C., Nijkamp, P., & Poot, J. (2011). *The impact of cultural diversity on innovation: Evidence from Dutch firm-level data* (No. 6000). Discussion paper series//Forschungsinstitut zur Zukunft der Arbeit, Bonn.

Parisi, M. L., Schiantarelli, F., & Sembenelli, A. (2006). Productivity, innovation and R&D: Micro evidence for Italy. *European Economic Review, 50*(8), 2037–2061.

Pavitt, K. (1984). Sectoral patterns of technical change: Towards a taxonomy and a theory. *Research Policy, 13*(6), 343–373.

Pavitt, K. (2006). Innovation processes. In J. Fagerberg, D. C. Mowery, & R. R. Nelson (Eds.), *The Oxford handbook of innovation* (pp. 86–114). Oxford: Oxford University Press.

Polanyi, M. (1958). *Personal knowledge*. Chicago: University of Chicago Press.

Polanyi, M. (1966). *The tacit dimension*. Chicago: University of Chicago Press.

Polder, M., Zand, F., van Leeuwen, G., & van Beers, C. (2012). *Complementarities between information technologies and innovation modes in the adoption and outcome stage: A Micro-econometrics analysis for the Netherlands*. The Hague: Statistics Netherlands.

Porter, M. E. (1985/2008). *On competition*. Cambridge, MA: Harvard Business Review Books.

Porter, M. E. (Ed.). (1986). *Competition in global industries*. Cambridge, MA: Harvard Business Review Books.

Porter, M. E. (1990). *Competitive advantage of nations: Creating and sustaining superior performance*. New York, NY: The Free Press.

Porter, M. E. (1998). Clusters and the new economics of competition. *Harvard Business Review, 76*(6), 77–90.

Porter, M. E., Ketels, C. H., Miller, K., & Bryden, R. (2004). *Competitiveness in rural US regions: Learning and research agenda*. Cambridge, MA: Institute for Strategy and Competitiveness, Harvard Business School.

Porter, M. E., & Kramer, M. R. (2011). Creating shared value. *Harvard Business Review, 89*(1/2), 62–77.

Rothwell, R. (1992). Successful industrial innovation: Critical factors for the 1990s. *R&D Management, 22*(3), 221–240.

Rothwell, R. (1994). Towards the fifth-generation innovation process. *International Marketing Review, 11*(1), 7–31.

Schumpeter, J. A. (1911). *Theorie der wirtschaftlichen Entwicklung*. Leipzig: Duncker & Humblot.

Schumpeter, J. A. (1911/2002). New Translation from *Theorie der wirtschaftlichen Entwicklung. American Journal of Economics and Sociology, 61*(2), 405–437.

Schumpeter, J. A. (1934). *The theory of economic development: An inquiry into profits, capital, credit, interest, and the business cycle*. Cambridge, MA: Harvard University Press.

Schumpeter, J. A. (1939). *Business cycles*. New York: McGraw-Hill.

Schumpeter, J. A. (1950). *Capitalism, socialism, and democracy* (3rd ed.). New York: Harper.

Scott, S. G., & Bruce, R. A. (1994). Determinants of innovative behavior: A path model of individual innovation in the workplace. *Academy of Management Journal, 37*(3), 580–607.

Senge, P. M., & Suzuki, J. (1994). *The fifth discipline: The art and practice of the learning organization*. New York: Currency Doubleday.

Simmie, J. (2006). Do clusters or innovation systems drive competitiveness. In P. Cooke, R. L. Martin, & B. T. Asheim (Eds.), *Clusters and regional development: Critical reflections and explorations* (pp. 164–187). London: Routledge.

Simons, R. (2013). *Levers of control: How managers use innovative control systems to drive strategic renewal*. Cambridge, MA: Harvard Business Press.

Solow, R. M. (1987). We'd better watch out. *New York Times Book Review* (July 12).

Stock, G. N., Greis, N. P., & Fischer, W. A. (2001). Absorptive capacity and new product development. *The Journal of High Technology Management Research, 12*(1), 77–91.

Swedberg, R. (2007). *Rebuilding Schumpeter's theory of entrepreneurship*. Conference on Marshall, Schumpeter and Social Science, March 17–18, 2007, Hitotsubashi University.

Teece, D. J. (2007). Explicating dynamic capabilities: The nature and microfoundations of (sustainable) enterprise performance. *Strategic Management Journal, 28*(13), 1319–1350.

Teece, D. J. (2010). Business models, business strategy and innovation. *Long Range Planning, 43*(2), 172–194.

Tidd, J., & Bessant, J. (2013). *Managing innovation, integrating technological, market and organizational change* (5th ed.). Chichester: Wiley.

Tidd, J., Pavitt, K., & Bessant, J. (2001). *Managing innovation* (Vol. 3). Chichester: Wiley.

Trott, P. (2008). *Innovation management and new product development.* New York: Pearson Education.

von Held, F. (2012). *Collective creativity: Exploring creativity in social network development as part of organizational learning.* New York: Springer.

West, M. A., & Farr, J. L. (1989). Innovation at work: Psychological perspectives. *Social Behavior, 4,* 15–30.

West, M. A., & Farr, J. L. (1990). Innovation at work. In M. A. West & J. L. Farr (Eds.), *Innovation and creativity at work: Psychological and organizational strategies* (pp. 3–13). Chichester, UK: Wiley.

Westeren, K. I. (Ed.). (2012). *Foundations of the knowledge economy: Innovation, learning and clusters.* Cheltenham: Edward Elgar Publishing.

Yuan, F., & Woodman, R. W. (2010). Innovative behavior in the workplace: The role of performance and image outcome expectations. *Academy of Management Journal, 53*(2), 323–342.

# 6 Competitiveness in the global chicken market

## 6.1 Introduction

Competitiveness has been the subject of debates on international trade since David Ricardo's theory of comparative advantage. His perspective is still relevant today. For Ricardo (1817), a country has comparative advantages in producing a good when the opportunity cost of production relative to others is lower in this country than in others (Krugman, *et al.* 2015). Heckscher and Ohlin (1991) on the other hand, emphasized the differences in relative costs of factors of production as a determining factor for international trade. According to Heckscher and Ohlin, a country tends to produce and export the products which require factors of production in relative abundance. In this case the pattern of international trade would be determined by the difference in the allocation of factors of production between countries. In this chapter, we will analyze characteristics of the international market for white meat from chicken focusing on competitiveness. We will look at the international market and also give more detailed points of view on the countries of special interest in this book, Denmark, Brazil, Norway, Sri Lanka and Kuwait.

Different indices are used to measure competitiveness according to the traditional theories of international trade e.g. Revealed Comparative Advantages Index (RCA); Balassa's (1965) Specialization Index (SI); Laursen's (2015) Revealed Symmetric Comparative Advantages Index (RSCA) and Coverage Index (CI).

Vernon (1966; 1979) argued that traditional theories of international trade failed to recognize that factors such as innovations, economies of scale, external economies and the uncertainties arising from imperfect information also affect trade between countries. The new theory of international trade, notably the works of Krugman (1979; 1980) and Helpman and Krugman (1985), has brought in important aspects of the effects of international trade by introducing increasing returns to scale, product differentiation and intra-industry trade to the agenda. We will argue here that increasing returns to scale and product differentiation by firms operating in monopolistic or oligopolistic markets increase competition as they provide consumers with a wider range of products at lower prices. In this case, economies of scale lead to falling prices.

International trade has been highlighted as one of the main factors affecting the economic growth of a country (Frankel, *et al.*, 1996; Frankel and Romer, 1999). The competitiveness of exports provides the inflow of foreign currency, which contributes to the increase of the GDP and a more dynamic development of the domestic market. The introduction of firms to the international market stimulates the introduction of new technologies and benefits from knowledge generated by innovation, key factors for the competitiveness, Grossman and Helpman (1991a; 1991b; 1995).

Researches by Bernard, *et al.* (1995), Bernard and Jensen (1999), Bernard, *et al.* (2003), Bernard, *et al.* (2007), and Melitz (2003) emphasized the microeconomic aspects that affect competitiveness and introduced the discussion about heterogeneous firms and international trade.

When the firm decides to internationalize it faces unrecoverable costs in activities such as transportation, marketing, distribution and costs related to the adaptation of the products to the requirements of the new markets. The firm must also allocate resources to enhance qualifications of personnel for external links like external sales and others. These costs form a barrier to entry and here we often see self-selection: the stronger and more productive firms are before the introduction, the greater are the chances for survival and thereby for participation in the international market. See Wagner (2007) and Sales and Westeren (2015) for a discussion of the self-selection hypothesis. We also assume that firms learn from export activities and that there is a dynamic effect: exporting firms learn from the introduction to international markets which leads to an increase in productivity, Keller (2004; 2010), Baldwin and Yan (2010), De Loecker (2007, 2013), and De Loecker and Warzynski (2012).

It is difficult to isolate the impact exporters make due to the introduction to the international market from other effects that also affect productivity in the firm, because while firms decide to export they also normally invest. Costantini and Melitz (2008) emphasized that access to new technologies, management methods and new products increased knowledge. At the same time, investments and innovations tended to increase productivity as a strategy for staying in the international market. In this way innovations can increase productivity and the probability of a firm to be successful in an internationalization process through exports, but it is necessary that the firm utilize the abilities and capacities to implement new technologies and knowledge developments.

There are different interpretations on how to measure competitiveness in an international perspective. Since this study aims to analyze international competitiveness in the global poultry market the following indicators of international competitiveness will be used:

- Revealed Comparative Advantage Index (RCA) proposed by Balassa (1965)
- The Balassa (1965) SI
- The Laursen (2015) Revealed Symmetric Comparative Advantage Index (RSCA)
- The Market Share (MS) index proposed by Krugman and Hatsopoulos (1987)

The following section will present the methodological procedures of the research. The next will give an overview of the global chicken market and an analysis of competitiveness using indicators. The following section will analyze the results from the case study in an international market perspective.

## 6.2 Methodological questions

This research has both a theoretical and applied perspective because it draws on the theory of international trade to analyze the international competitiveness of the chicken (white meat) sector complemented by a case study. It is also explanatory as it seeks to describe the characteristics of this sector and to explain the relationship between variables that affect competitiveness, Williams (2007).

### *6.2.1 Revealed Comparative Advantages Index (RCA)*

The RCA proposed by Balassa (1965) is used to reveal if a particular sector of a country has a comparative advantage in relation to another country or to the world. This index is often used to measure export competitiveness and is calculated based on the following expression:

$$RCA_{ij} = \frac{\frac{X_{ij}}{X_j}}{\frac{X_{iw}}{X_w}} \tag{1}$$

Where:

$X_{ij}$ = value of exports of sector *i* by country *j*;
$X_j$ = total value of exports by country *j*;
$X_{iw}$ = value of exports of sector *i* in world *w*;
$X_w$ = total value of world exports *w*.

The numerator of the expression (1) shows the share of exports of sector *i* in the total exports of country *j*, while the denominator of the expression represents the world participation of sector *i* in the total world exports *w*. The Balassa Comparative Advantage Index (RCA) can range from zero to infinity. Values greater than one indicate that the country has a comparative advantage revealed in the considered sector. On the other hand, a value below one indicates that the country under analysis presents a revealed comparative disadvantage (Benedictis and Tamberi, 2004).

### *6.2.2 Revealed Symmetric Comparative Advantage Index (RSCA)*

Laursen (2015) comments that the RCA result is not comparable at both sides. To neutralize the asymmetry present in the Revealed Comparative Advantage Index, it is recommended to calculate the Symmetric Comparative Advantage Index (RSCA), which is given by:

$$RSCA_{ij} = \frac{RCA_{ij} - 1}{RCA_{ij} + 1} \tag{2}$$

In which:

> $RSCA_{ij}$ is the Revealed Symmetric Comparative Advantage Index; and
> $RCA_{ij}$ is the Revealed Comparative Advantage Index.

The Revealed Symmetric Comparative Advantage Index varies within the range of -1 to +1. In this sense, when $0 \leq RSCA_{ij} \leq 1$ the country has a revealed comparative advantage in the sector in question. On the other hand, if $RSCA_{ij} \langle\ 0$ the country has a comparative disadvantage in the sector under analysis.

In relation to the efficiency of the Revealed Symmetric Comparative Advantage (RSCA), Laursen (2015) made a theoretical analysis of the properties of this index and empirically compared the RCA with RSCA through the normality test. The author concluded that studies that were based on RCA results may be inaccurate due to the asymmetry of this indicator. Therefore, the RSCA is more efficient and easier to interpret and in this study, will only show the results related to RSCA.

### 6.2.3 Commercial Coverage Rate (CR)

The Commercial Coverage Rate (CR) refers to the percentage of imports supplied by imports in a given sector. This indicator was proposed by Verdoorn (1960) and the sectorial level can be expressed as:

$$CR_i = \frac{X_i}{M_i} \qquad (3)$$

In which:

> $CR_i$ is the Commercial Coverage Rate in sector *i*;
> $X_i$ = total exports of sector *i*; and
> $M_i$ = total imports from sector *i*.

When $CR_i > 1$, the country under analysis has a strong sectorial commercial competitiveness, while a $TC_i < 1$ shows a commercial dependence in this sector.

### 6.2.4 Market share (MS)

It is one of the simplest and most widely used indicators of competitiveness. It is calculated from the following expression:

$$MS = \frac{X_{ij}}{X_{iw}} \qquad (4)$$

In which:

> $X_{ij}$ = value of exports of sector *i* by country *j*; and
> $X_{iw}$ = value of exports of sector *i* in the world *w*.

It should be noted that issues related to protectionism between countries, such as trade and tariff barriers, exchange rate variations, and other variables are not captured by these indicators. However, to the extent possible, information was sought in the literature to qualify the behavior of these indicators. Aspects referring to databases and variables will be dealt with below.

## 6.3 Databases and variables

This study is analyzing the international competitiveness of the global chicken market. To do this we have used the following databases:

- United Nations (FAOSTAT and FAOSTAT, online)
- United Nations Food and Agriculture Organization (FAO)
- EUROSTAT (ec.europa.eu/eurostat)
- Common Format for Transient Data Exchange (COMTRADE) and United Nations, COMTRADE (online)

We chose the period from 2000 to 2014 because we wanted to shed light on the main characteristics of the chicken market and developing trends recent years. Chicken production data were obtained from the FAOSTAT database and refer to total poultry meat produced by the country/world (in million tons).

Belova, *et al.* (2012) show that, in general, the share of chickens is dominant reaching approximately 90% of total poultry meat production. In the case of European Union countries, the EUROSTAT report shows that chicken meat made up 79.8% of the total poultry meat produced in 2014 (EUROSTAT, 2017). So, when analyzing the poultry industry, we have a very good proxy for the behavior of the chicken meat sector.

The subdivision of the poultry sector according to the classification of the Standard International Trade Classification Revision 3 (SITC Rev. 3) is shown in Table 6.1. All competitiveness indicators and analyses throughout the study will be performed according to this subdivision. This is one of the main contributions of this study because previous work using competitiveness indicators has been restricted to the analysis of aggregate data, as example (see Belova, *et al.* 2012).

*Table 6.1* Classification of the subsectors of poultry according to SITC Rev. 3

| *Codes* | *Products* |
|---|---|
| 0123 | Meat and edible offal of the poultry of subgroup 001.4, fresh, chilled or frozen |
| 01231 | Poultry not cut in pieces, fresh or chilled |
| 01232 | Poultry not cut in pieces, frozen |
| 01234 | Poultry cuts and other offal, fresh or chilled |
| 01235 | Poultry cuts and offal (other than liver), frozen |

Source: United Nations – Standard International Trade Classification (SITC Rev. 3), (2002).

At the end of the study of the international competitiveness of the chicken market we present the results of the case study of the five firms analyzed. The focus of the analysis will be on explaining how the behavior of these firms affects their competitiveness in the international market.

In the following section, we will present and discuss the evolution of the market and indicators of international competitiveness of the chicken market from 2000 to 2014.

## 6.4 International competitiveness of the chicken market between 2000 and 2014

This section will discuss the results of global poultry commerce and international competitiveness for the period from 2000 to 2014. First, the production of chicken meat from the ten largest producing countries and countries of interest in the years between 2000 and 2014 is highlighted. The world production of these countries has also been relativized by the population to obtain chicken production per capita. This information will be useful when analyzing global exports and imports, since low per capita production among the world's largest producers of chicken meat can signal the need for imports of this product to meet the demand. The data are shown in Table 6.2.

It is observed that the five largest countries producing chicken meat in 2014 were the United States of America, China, Brazil, mainland China and Russian Federation. Taken together these countries produced 55.33 million tons, or 52.2% of the world's production of chicken meat. France, the United Kingdom and Spain were among the top ten producers of chicken meat in the year 2000, but they lost successive positions between 2000 and 2005.

However, by comparing production by the total population of each country, Brazil (60.75 kg per capita), Netherlands (56.68 kg per capita), the United States (55.48 kg per capita), Argentina (45.00 kg per capita) and Poland (42.26 kg per capita) stood out with the highest per capita production worldwide. Between 2000 and 2014, world's production of chicken meat increased, with the exception of Denmark (-9.8 kg per capita) and Kuwait (-4.7 kg per capita). Brazil, Netherlands and the United States have a per capita production that corresponded to more than four times the world average in 2014. The highlights in the production of chicken meat in 2014 were the Russian Federation and Poland, which quadrupled their absolute and per capita chicken meat production in relation to the year 2000, reaching 26.78 kg per person.

The growth in the world demand for poultry meat has been maintained for decades due to the increase in per capita income of the population; population growth and the fact that chicken meat is a healthy and cheap source of protein compared to beef and pork meat, despite the increase in price (Belova, *et al.* 2012).

The evolution of the value of poultry exports and the market share of the ten largest exporting countries and countries of special interest in this research is shown in Table 6.3. The value of world poultry exports has increased from $8.3 billion to $21.5 billion, or about 243% in current prices between 2000 and 2014.

*Table 6.2* Production of chicken meat (million tons), population (millions of people) and chicken production per capita for the world's largest producers and countries of interest in the years between 2000 and 2014

| *Countries* | *2000* | | | *2014* | | | *Annual growth rate of production per capita (%)* |
|---|---|---|---|---|---|---|---|
| | *Production (million tons)* | *Population (millions of persons)* | *Production per capita* | *Production (million tons)* | *Population (millions of persons)* | *Production per capita* | |
| USA | 13,944.00 | 282.90 | 49.29 | 17,722.31 | 319.45 | 55.48 | 0.79 |
| China | 9,064.19 | 1,299.13 | 6.98 | 12,830.41 | 1,400.60 | 9.16 | 1.83 |
| Brazil | 5,980.60 | 175.79 | 34.02 | 12,519.48 | 206.08 | 60.75 | 3.94 |
| China mainland (*) | 8,364.00 | 1,269.97 | 6.59 | 12,257.00 | 1,369.44 | 8.95 | 2.07 |
| Russian Federation | 754.99 | 146.40 | 5.16 | 3,769.69 | 143.43 | 26.28 | 11.47 |
| Mexico | 1,825.25 | 102.81 | 17.75 | 2,879.69 | 125.39 | 22.97 | 1.73 |
| India | 864.00 | 1,053.48 | 0.82 | 2,730.04 | 1,295.29 | 2.11 | 6.49 |
| Japan | 1,194.52 | 125.71 | 9.50 | 2,128.19 | 126.79 | 16.78 | 3.87 |
| Iran (Islamic Republic of) | 803.00 | 65.85 | 12.19 | 2,069.40 | 78.14 | 26.48 | 5.31 |
| Indonesia | 803.95 | 211.54 | 3.80 | 1,939.23 | 254.45 | 7.62 | 4.75 |
| Argentina | 957.79 | 37.06 | 25.85 | 1.934.00 | 42.98 | 45.00 | 4.80 |
| Poland | 560.00 | 38.49 | 14.55 | 1,632.19 | 3.86 | 42.26 | 7.37 |
| Netherlands | 697.00 | 15.89 | 43.85 | 956.13 | 16.87 | 56.68 | 1.73 |
| Denmark | 187.48 | 5.34 | 35.12 | 142.80 | 5.65 | 25.29 | −2.17 |
| Kuwait | 32.96 | 1.93 | 17.08 | 46.19 | 3.75 | 12.31 | −2.16 |
| Norway | 43.09 | 4.49 | 9.59 | 94.76 | 5.15 | 18.41 | 4.44 |
| Sri Lanka | 63.17 | 18.78 | 3.36 | 143.92 | 20.62 | 6.98 | 4.99 |
| Other countries | 21,616.97 | 2,570.19 | 8.41 | 37,387.82 | 3,213.47 | 11.63 | 3.72 |
| **Total Worldwide** | **67,756.96** | **7,425.75** | **9.12** | **113,183.23** | **8,666.17** | **13.06** | **3.48** |

Source: developed by the author based on data from the Food and Agriculture Organization (FAO), FAOSTAT, 2017.

(*) For a detailed definition of China mainland, see the source.

*Table 6.3* Exports of poultry meat from the largest exporting countries and selected countries: total value and market share – 2000, 2005, 2010 and 2014

| *Countries* | *Value (US$ millions)* | | | | *Annual growth rate (%)* | *Market share (%)* | | | |
|---|---|---|---|---|---|---|---|---|---|
| | *2000* | *2005* | *2010* | *2014* | | *2000* | *2005* | *2010* | *2014* |
| Brazil | 879.35 | 3,496.23 | 5,952.03 | 7,050.14 | 14.89 | 10.56 | 26.93 | 27.57 | 24.69 |
| USA | 1,784.06 | 2,469.47 | 3,816.60 | 4,935.46 | 7.02 | 21.42 | 19.02 | 17.68 | 17.29 |
| Netherlands | 985.02 | 1,290.50 | 1,989.36 | 2,939.59 | 7.56 | 11.83 | 9.94 | 9.21 | 10.30 |
| Poland | 71.61 | 469.00 | 957.31 | 1,794.39 | 23.95 | 0.86 | 3.61 | 4.43 | 6.29 |
| Germany | 223.47 | 612.99 | 950.01 | 1,316.98 | 12.55 | 2.68 | 4.72 | 4.40 | 4.61 |
| France | 1,151.04 | 1,141.52 | 993.64 | 1,308.91 | 0.86 | 13.82 | 8.79 | 4.60 | 4.58 |
| Belgium | 363.15 | 638.97 | 873.11 | 1,021.46 | 7.14 | 4.36 | 4.92 | 4.04 | 3.58 |
| Hong Kong SAR | 571.21 | 164.37 | 865.47 | 804.84 | 2.31 | 6.86 | 1.27 | 4.01 | 2.82 |
| Turkey | 5.93 | 33.70 | 203.29 | 651.04 | 36.78 | 0.07 | 0.26 | 0.94 | 2.28 |
| China | 587.37 | 194.42 | 427.64 | 576.97 | -0.12 | 7.05 | 1.50 | 1.98 | 2.02 |
| Argentina | 10.83 | 109.91 | 379.24 | 546.68 | 29.88 | 0.13 | 0.85 | 1.76 | 1.91 |
| Denmark | 174.29 | 260.35 | 222.68 | 184.96 | 0.40 | 2.09 | 2.01 | 1.03 | 0.65 |
| Norway | 0.63 | 1.87 | 4.69 | 8.14 | 18.62 | 0.01 | 0.01 | 0.02 | 0.03 |
| Kuwait | 1.28 | n.d. | 2.07 | 3.95 | 7.77 | 0.02 | n,d, | 0.01 | 0.01 |
| Sri Lanka | 0.08 | 0.03 | 1.54 | 1.21 | 20.23 | 0.00 | 0.00 | 0.01 | 0.00 |
| Others | 1,518.64 | 2,099.86 | 3,951.54 | 5,404.90 | 8.83 | 18.24 | 16.17 | 18.30 | ***18.93*** |
| Total | 8,327.95 | 12,983.19 | 21,590.22 | 28,549.62 | 8.56 | 100.00 | 100.00 | 100.00 | 100.00 |

Source: developed by the author based on data from the United Nations, COMTRADE (2017). Database.

n.d. means no data available.

Cultural and religious barriers to the consumption of pork and beef also contribute to the expansion of poultry meat consumption, such as the cases in which pork is banned for Muslims and beef for Hindus.

Over the period from 2000 to 2014, the poultry market has been very dynamic. In 2000, Brazil was the fourth largest exporter of poultry in the world, exporting US$879 million (10.6% of the total). The evolution of Brazilian poultry exports showed an exceptional growth reaching US$8.1 billion in 2014, an increase of 702% between 2000 and 2014. This performance gave Brazil in 2005 the position of the world's largest poultry exporter, outperforming the United States and the Netherlands. Overall, the largest poultry exporter countries are Brazil, the United States, the European Union, China, Hong Kong, Turkey and Argentina.

In 2014 the global exports of poultry were strongly concentrated in four countries: Brazil (24.7%), the United States (17.3%), the Netherlands (10.3%) and Poland (6.3%), with a 58.6% share of total world exports. Poland has substantially increased its poultry exports becoming the fourth largest exporting country in 2014, worth US$1.8 billion, or a 6.9% share of the market.

France, China and Hong Kong did not take advantage of market growth and lost market shares in the period. In fact, in 2000, the combined share of these three countries was 27.7%, falling to 9.4% in 2014. Exports from Denmark, Norway, Sri Lanka and Kuwait totalled US $ 198.3 million in 2014, or about 0.7% of exports worldwide. Of these countries, it is only Denmark that has an export value of some significance.

The Bovine Spongiform Encephalitis (BSE) crisis, which occurred in the late 1990s, also boosted consumption of poultry meat and demand for quality, product certification and food safety, particularly in Europe. According to Magdelaine, *et al.* (2008) this was due to the consumers' wish for healthy food.

Davis (2015) pointed out that demand for chicken meat on the international market has also been shown to be sensitive to Highly Pathogenic Avian Influenza (HPAI) and Low Pathogenic Avian Influenza (LPAI) diseases. In response, several countries have been suspending imports.

To analyze the competitiveness of the world's largest exporters of poultry, the competitiveness indices of poultry exports from the same countries were calculated. The results are shown in Table 6.4. The Balassa Index (BI) shows whether a country specializes in the export of poultry. The index varies from −1 to 1. Values below zero show that the country in question has no specialization in poultry exports, while positive values indicate specialization in exports. The closer to 1, the higher the degree of specialization. Brazil, the United States, Poland, Turkey and Argentina have strong export specialization in poultry, while the Netherlands, Belgium, France, Sri Lanka and Norway have medium or weak specialization in poultry exports. France and Denmark have been losing specialization in exports over the period. Germany, Hong Kong, China, Kuwait and Sri Lanka are countries that do not have a specialization in the export of poultry.

The sectorial coverage rate (CR) is also calculated in Table 6.4. This rate shows whether the country under consideration is a net exporter or net importer.

*Table 6.4* International competitiveness indices for poultry meat exports from the largest exporting countries and selected countries – 2000, 2005, 2010 and 2014

| *Countries* | *Balassa Index (BI)* | | | | *Sectorial Coverage Rate (CR)* | | | | *RSCA* | | | | *Market share (MS)* | | | |
|---|---|---|---|---|---|---|---|---|---|---|---|---|---|---|---|---|
| | *2000* | *2005* | *2010* | *2014* | *2000* | *2005* | *2010* | *2014* | *2000* | *2005* | *2010* | *2014* | *2000* | *2005* | *2010* | *2014* |
| Brazil | 1.00 | 1.00 | 1.00 | 1.00 | 1.301.12 | 4.903.49 | 1.949.62 | 612.19 | 0.85 | 0.92 | 0.91 | 0.91 | 10.56 | 26.93 | 27.57 | 24.69 |
| USA | 0.98 | 0.95 | 0.91 | 0.91 | 90.83 | 36.57 | 21.42 | 22.04 | 0.27 | 0.36 | 0.35 | 0.33 | 21.42 | 19.02 | 17.68 | 17.29 |
| Netherlands | 0.64 | 0.45 | 0.50 | 0.50 | 4.59 | 2.66 | 3.03 | 3.03 | 0.56 | 0.49 | 0.47 | 0.54 | 11.83 | 9.94 | 9.21 | 10.30 |
| Poland | 0.73 | 0.73 | 0.91 | 0.93 | 6.41 | 6.36 | 22.22 | 27.02 | 0.27 | 0.61 | 0.62 | 0.69 | 0.86 | 3.61 | 4.43 | 6.29 |
| Germany | -0.54 | -0.32 | -0.15 | -0.16 | 0.30 | 0.52 | 0.74 | 0.73 | -0.53 | -0.34 | -0.32 | -0.28 | 2.68 | 4.72 | 4.40 | 4.61 |
| France | 0.65 | 0.38 | -0.10 | 0.01 | 4.65 | 2.21 | 0.82 | 1.02 | 0.49 | 0.35 | 0.15 | 0.20 | 13.82 | 8.79 | 4.60 | 4.58 |
| Belgium | 0.30 | 0.31 | 0.34 | 0.27 | 1.88 | 1.91 | 2.05 | 1.73 | 0.19 | 0.20 | 0.20 | 0.17 | 4.36 | 4.92 | 4.04 | 3.58 |
| Hong Kong SAR | -0.19 | -0.56 | -0.32 | -0.35 | 0.68 | 0.28 | 0.51 | 0.48 | 0.36 | -0.39 | 0.20 | 0.00 | 6.86 | 1.27 | 4.01 | 2.82 |
| Turkey | 0.72 | 0.99 | 0.99 | 1.00 | 6.09 | 132.85 | 235.61 | 581.84 | -0.72 | -0.47 | 0.11 | 0.46 | 0.07 | 0.26 | 0.94 | 2.28 |
| China | 0.10 | -0.26 | -0.38 | -0.21 | 1.22 | 0.58 | 0.44 | 0.66 | 0.28 | -0.67 | -0.68 | -0.73 | 7.05 | 1.50 | 1.98 | 2.02 |
| Argentina | -0.59 | 0.94 | 0.90 | 0.99 | 0.26 | 30.03 | 20.04 | 262.54 | -0.52 | 0.36 | 0.59 | 0.68 | 0.13 | 0.85 | 1.76 | 1.91 |
| Denmark | 0.57 | 0.25 | 0.17 | -0.02 | 3.65 | 1.66 | 1.41 | 0.96 | 0.46 | 0.43 | 0.23 | 0.04 | 2.09 | 2.01 | 1.03 | 0.65 |
| Norway | -0.26 | -0.32 | 0.53 | 0.53 | 0.58 | 0.51 | 3.30 | 3.27 | -0.98 | -0.97 | -0.92 | -0.93 | 0.01 | 0.01 | 0.02 | 0.03 |
| Kuwait | -0.96 | n.d. | -0.98 | -0.97 | 0.02 | n.d. | 0.01 | 0.01 | -0.90 | n.d. | -0.96 | -0.95 | 0.02 | n.d. | 0.01 | 0.01 |
| Sri Lanka | -0.88 | -0.92 | 0.08 | 0.23 | 0.07 | 0.04 | 1.16 | 1.59 | -0.98 | -0.99 | -0.77 | -0.87 | 0.00 | 0.00 | 0.01 | 0.00 |
| Other Countries | -0.51 | -0.59 | -0.52 | -0.51 | 0.32 | 0.26 | 0.31 | 0.32 | -0.51 | -0.55 | -0.50 | -0.48 | 18.24 | 16.17 | 18.30 | 18.93 |

Source: developed by the author based on data from the United Nations, COMTRADE Database (2017).

n.d. means no data available.

Countries that have a CR value greater than one are net exporters. Countries with CR values less than one are considered net importers. It is observed in the period of the analysis that Brazil 's sectorial coverage rate has been much higher than the average of the other exporting countries, revealing the country's strong competitiveness in relation to the other main competitors in the global market. The CR of the United States has declined over time, although exports have been much larger than imports. Poland, Turkey and Argentina have increased coverage rates which indicates increasing competitiveness in the international market. Germany, China, Hong Kong and Kuwait showed CR of less than one, which reveals a strong commercial dependence in this sector, as emphasized by Juchniewicz and Łukiewska (2015). After 2005, the sectorial coverage rates of Norway and Sri Lanka have become higher than one, indicating an increase in competitiveness, but since the export volumes are so small this does not mean much for international trade.

The RSCA shows that Brazil, the United States, Poland, France, Belgium and Denmark developed a comparative advantage in the poultry sector throughout the period, while Germany, Norway, Kuwait and Sri Lanka lose in competitiveness according to this indicator. Argentina and Turkey had a disadvantage in 2000, but became competitive over the rest of the period. Poland's competitiveness and specialization in this segment increased significantly, see Table 6.4.

Based on the combined results from Tables 6.2 to 6.4, it is concluded that Brazil, the United States, Poland, Turkey and Argentina are highly specialized countries in the production of chicken meat. Several EU countries are among the world's leading exporters but are not among the largest per capita producers in this market, with the exception of the Netherlands and Poland. France, Belgium, Hong Kong, China and Denmark lost competitiveness and market share over the period. On the other hand, Germany, which is not competitive from the point of view of international competitiveness indicators, has increased its market share.

It should be noted that, according to the Association of Poultry Processors and Poultry Trade in the EU Countries (AVEC, 2015), the per capita consumption of chicken meat is quite diverse among the member countries of the European Union. Average consumption for the EU countries reached 26.8 kg per capita in 2014.

However, in Germany, the largest EU country, annual consumption per capita was 19.5 kg, while in Portugal it reached 39 kg per capita in the same year (AVEC, 2015). The report shows that chicken meat consumption has expanded over time and that 76% of the EU market is supplied by the UK, Poland, Germany, France, Spain, Italy and the Netherlands. The rigid rules imposed on EU chicken producers, the increased intra-bloc consumption, and the pressure from consumers and NGOs to improve animal welfare have contributed to successive price increases, affecting competitiveness (AVEC, 2015).

The value of poultry imports and the market share for the top ten importing countries and countries of special interest is shown in Table 6.5. Total imports reached US $ 24.6 billion in 2014, an increase of 222.4% in current prices compared to the value from the year 2000. The five largest importers in the

*Table 6.5* Imports of poultry meat from the ten largest importing countries: total value and market share – 2000, 2005, 2010 and 2014

| *Countries* | *Value (US$ millions)* | | | | *Annual growth rate (%)* | *Market share (%)* | | | |
|---|---|---|---|---|---|---|---|---|---|
| | *2000* | *2005* | *2010* | *2014* | | *2000* | *2005* | *2010* | *2014* |
| Germany | 746.36 | 1,181.73 | 1,278.84 | 1,807.88 | 6.08 | 9.76 | 9.88 | 6.58 | 7.34 |
| United Kingdom | 864.57 | 1,437.39 | 1,573.41 | 1,744.52 | 4.79 | 11.31 | 12.02 | 8.10 | 7.08 |
| Saudi Arabia | 366.10 | 625.84 | 1,304.22 | 1,708.59 | 10.82 | 4.79 | 5.23 | 6.71 | 6.93 |
| Hong Kong SAR | 835.47 | 579.48 | 1,686.46 | 1,669.12 | 4.72 | 10.93 | 4.85 | 8.68 | 6.77 |
| Japan | 898.77 | 924.50 | 1,146.32 | 1,421.16 | 3.10 | 11.76 | 7.73 | 5.90 | 5.77 |
| Mexico | 257.07 | 532.85 | 821.42 | 1,337.96 | 11.62 | 3.36 | 4.46 | 4.23 | 5.43 |
| France | 247.28 | 517.04 | 993.64 | 1,286.69 | 11.62 | 3.23 | 4.32 | 5.11 | 5.22 |
| Netherlands | 214.80 | 486.05 | 657.27 | 969.73 | 10.57 | 2.81 | 4.06 | 3.38 | 3.94 |
| China | 480.67 | 334.38 | 962.91 | 878.30 | 4.10 | 6.29 | 2.80 | 4.95 | 3.56 |
| Russian Federation | 366.26 | 847.48 | 861.87 | 801.77 | 5.36 | 4.79 | 7.09 | 4.43 | 3.25 |
| Brazil | 0.68 | 0.71 | 3.05 | 11.52 | 20.81 | 0.01 | 0.01 | 0.02 | 0.05 |
| Denmark | 47.74 | 156.97 | 157.46 | 193.10 | 9.76 | 0.62 | 1.31 | 0.81 | 0.78 |
| Kuwait | 71.48 | n.d. | 176.83 | 286.70 | 9.70 | 0.94 | 0.00 | 0.91 | 1.16 |
| Norway | 1.08 | 3.67 | 1.42 | 2.49 | 5.75 | 0.01 | 0.03 | 0.01 | 0.01 |
| Sri Lanka | 1.17 | 1.51 | 1.33 | 0.76 | -2.85 | 0.02 | 0.01 | 0.01 | 0.00 |
| Other Countries | 2,244.46 | 4,328.41 | 7,808.42 | 10,522.70 | 10.85 | 29.36 | 36.20 | 40.18 | 42.70 |
| Total World | 7,643.95 | 11,957.99 | 19,434.88 | 24,643.01 | 8.12 | 100.00 | 100.00 | 100.00 | 100.00 |

Source: developed by the author based on data from the United Nations, COMTRADE Database (2017).

n.d. is no data available.

world during the period 2000–2014 were: Germany, the United Kingdom, Saudi Arabia, Hong Kong and Japan. Imports to these five countries totalled $3.7 billion (48.6% of total imports) in 2000. However, these imports have grown at a lower annual growth rate compared to the importing market (5.6% per year against 8.1% of total imports). The imports from these countries increased, but market share in imports declined gradually, reaching 33.9% of the total in 2014, see Table 6.5.

Also, we see in Table 6.5 that poultry imports to Mexico and France increased by approximately 420% between 2000 and 2014, or 11.6% per year in the period. Imports as a whole became less concentrated, so that the total share of other importing countries has expanded from 29.4% in 2000 to 42.7% in 2014. Imports to the five countries of interest (Brazil, Denmark, Kuwait, Norway and Sri Lanka) accounted for about 2% of total imports in 2014, Denmark (0.8%) and Kuwait (1.2%), while Brazil, Norway and Sri Lanka accounted for 0.6% of the imports in 2014. In the case of Sri Lanka, this was probably due to the import prohibition policy, which aimed to boost production in the domestic market.

According to SITC Rev. 3, worldwide exports and imports can be analyzed by sub-product, subdividing the market into its main segments: the market for fresh or chilled poultry meat and the frozen poultry market. United Nations data for the year 2014 show that the exports in the market of fresh and chilled poultry totalled US $ 7.41 billion, while that of frozen poultry reached US $16.96 billion. This corresponded respectively to 30.4% and 69.6% of the total worldwide exported by the sector. (United Nations, COMTRADE, 2017).

## 6.5 International competitiveness of chicken meat by subgroups

The poultry market can be subdivided into four categories, as presented in Table 6.1. This section provides an analysis for the year 2014 according to these subgroups. Data from the United Nations show that in the year 2014 the total value of world poultry exports was equal to US$24.37 billion. Subdividing this total into the subgroups of fresh or chilled poultry and frozen poultry, it is estimated that US$7.41 billion (30.40%) of total exports refer to fresh or chilled meat and US$16.96 billion (69.60%) of this value refers to the frozen poultry market. (United Nations, COMTRADE, 2017).

The value of world poultry exports in 2014 per subsector for the ten largest exporting countries of each product is shown in Table 6.1. As far as the whole fresh or chilled poultry market is concerned, the main exporting country was China, with a market value equal to US$256.6 million, or 19.46% of the total for this segment. Belarus and Poland were the world's second and third largest exporters of fresh poultry, respectively.

Five of the world's top ten exporters of whole fresh or chilled poultry are EU countries, which together exported $319.61 million, or 24.24% of that total. The United States and Saudi Arabia participated with about 3.2% and 3.3% of the total respectively. The total exports from the countries of interest in this study (Denmark, Brazil, Kuwait, Norway and Sri Lanka) were negligible for this segment, see Figure 6.1.

When analyzing the destinations of exports of whole, fresh or chilled poultry in the year 2014, it was observed that 93.2% of the Chinese exports were destined for the Hong Kong SAR. Belarus exports were destined for the Russian Federation, while exports from Poland were mainly destined for European Union countries (US$44.64 million or 68.5% of the total) and Czech Republic (US$44.42 million, or 31.34% of the total). (United Nations, COMTRADE, 2017).

The largest exporter of poultry cuts and other offal, fresh or chilled was the Netherlands, with approximately US$1.30 billion, or 19.4% of the total value exported by the sector (Figure 6.1). Netherlands exports were destined for European Union countries. The United Kingdom and Germany together imported US$820.43 million, or 63.23% of the total fresh or chilled poultry meat from the Netherlands (United Nations, COMTRADE). Despite having suffered outbreaks of Avian Influenza (AI) in 2003, the country is the largest chicken and egg producer in Europe, (Windhorst, 2016).

The United States is the 2nd largest exporter of cuts and other offal, fresh or chilled, with 16.55% of the total exported by the sector. Exports from the United States are concentrated in Mexico and Canada, accounting for 67.9% and 30.7% of total exports in 2014.

In general, it is concluded that the market for fresh or chilled poultry is heavily concentrated in intra-bloc exports. European Union countries export/import among themselves; The United States exports to NAFTA countries, while China destines its exports to Hong Kong and Macao.

In the market of frozen poultry not cut in pieces, Brazil is the absolute leader, with a total export of US$2.44 billion in 2014, or 52.17% of market share. In 2014, Brazil exported to 104 countries. Of the total value of Brazilian exports in the sector, US$1.76 billion (or 72.33% of the total) were exported to countries in the Arab world (see Figure 6.1). Saudi Arabia was the main importer of frozen whole poultry from Brazil, with US$479.96 million, or 32.86% of the total. (United Nations, COMTRADE, 2017).

France was the second largest exporter of frozen poultry not cut in pieces in the world in the year 2014 with $419.99 million, or about 9% of the total exported by the sector. Like Brazil, its exports are strongly concentrated in the Arab countries, which represented 81.11% of the total value exported by France in 2014. The European Union countries are also part of France's niche, as expected, but with less importance.

Exports of frozen poultry cuts and offal (other than liver) represent the main market in terms of value. In 2014, the value exported worldwide in this segment totalled US$15.78 billion, or 55.44% of the world's exports of poultry. Brazil and the United States lead the world's exports in the sector. In 2014, the combined value of exports from these countries was US$8.28 billion, or 52.45% market share.

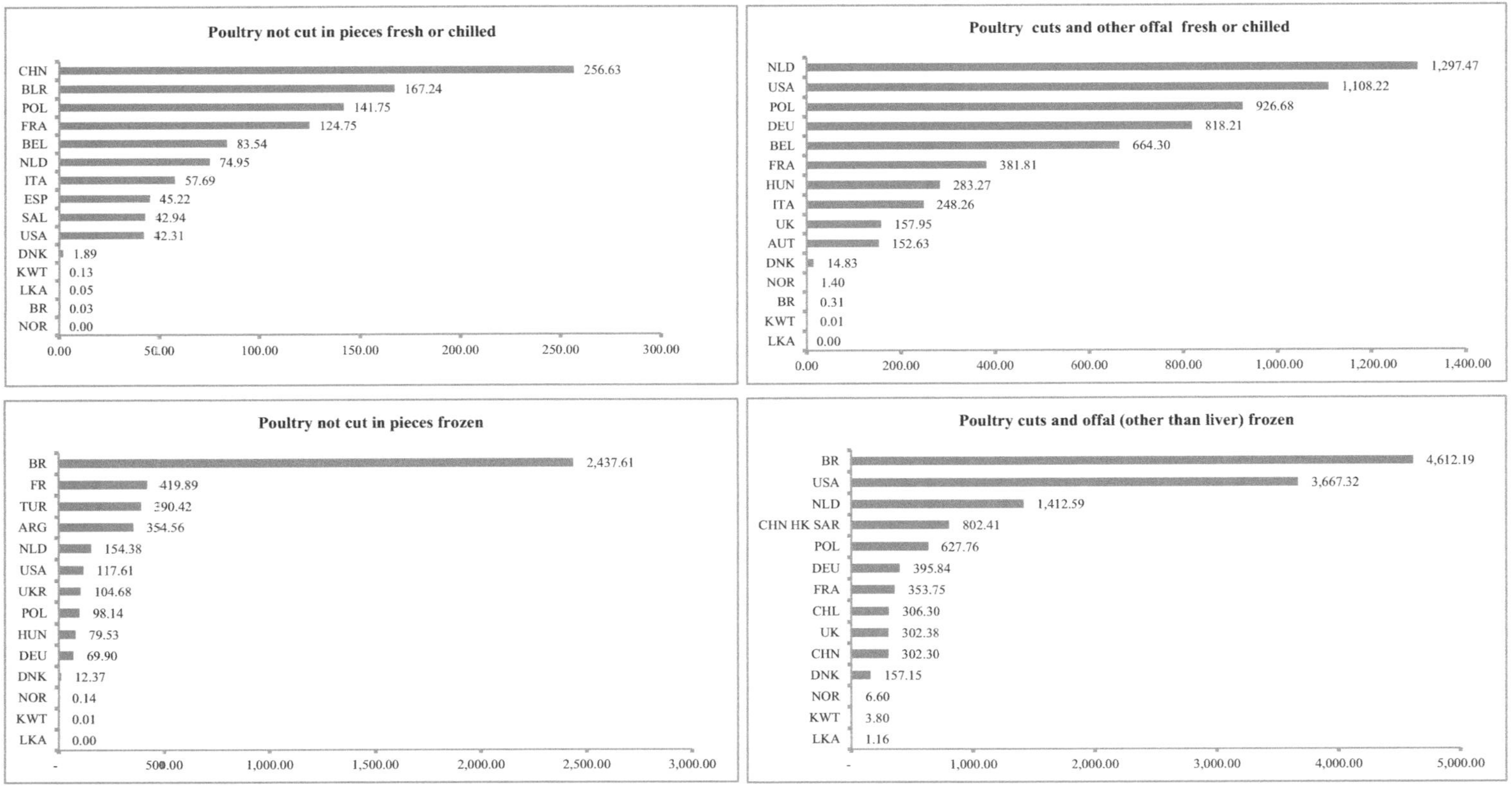


*Figure 6.1* Exports of poultry of the top ten exporters of fresh, chilled or frozen poultry from selected countries, 2014

Source: research results based on data from the United Nations, COMTRADE Database (2017).

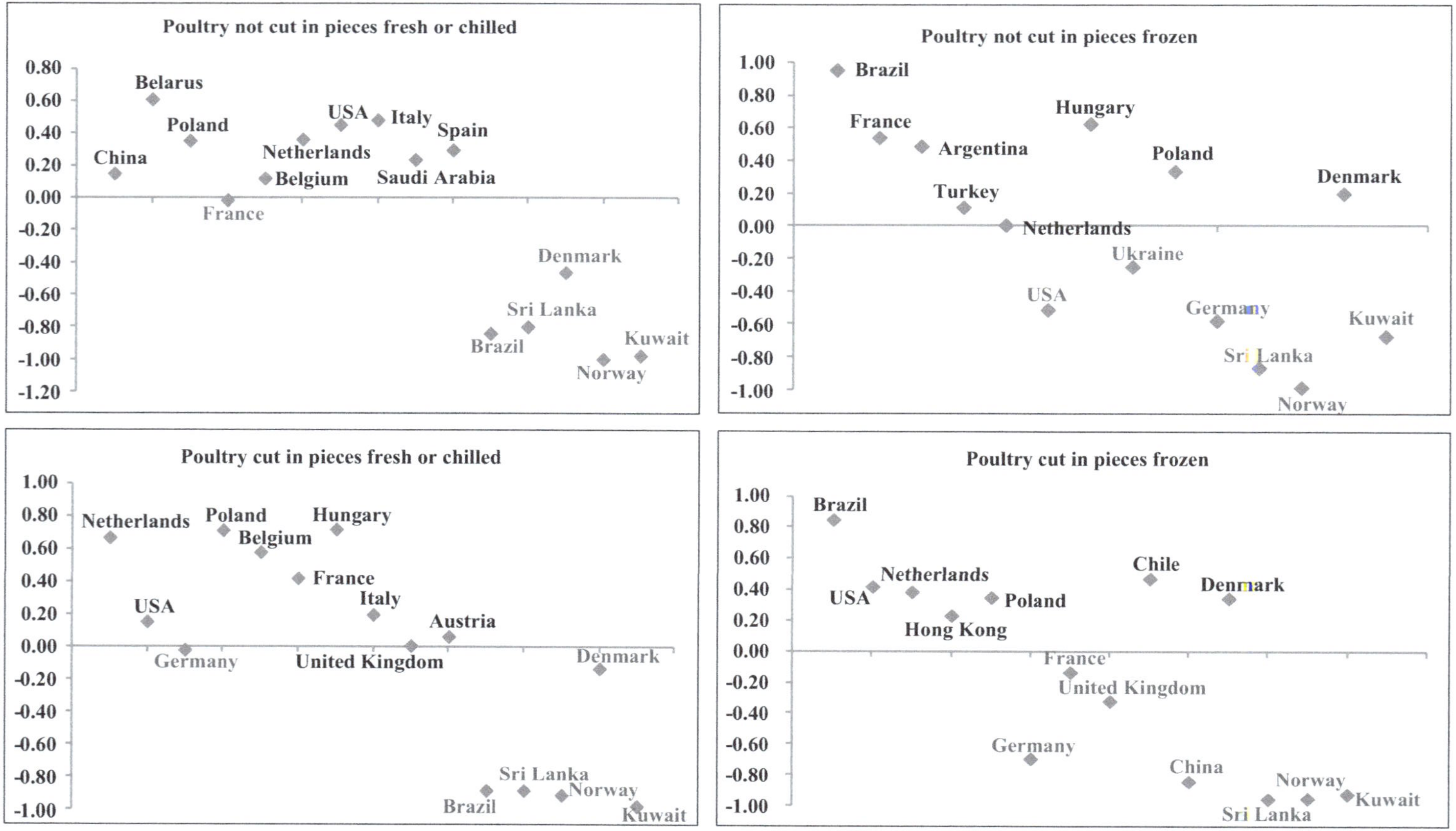


*Figure 6.2* RSCA of the world's top ten exporters of fresh, chilled or frozen poultry, selected countries – average for the period 2000–2014

Source: Research results based on data from the United Nations, COMTRADE Database (2017).

## 6.6 Competitiveness of the international chicken meat market: a case study at the firm level

Throughout this book, we have been discussing how the aspects of cost, contracts, innovation and knowledge can affect the competitiveness of firms in the chicken meat sector. In Chapter 3 we show that there were several degrees of vertical integration between firms and in Chapter 2 we see that how the supply work is of vital importance for the cost structure and competitive situation. In other case studies, Crysbro (Sri Lanka) and KUPCO (Kuwait) appeared integrated, LAR (Brazil) is also relatively integrated while the Nordic companies of Danpo (Denmark) and Ytterøy Chicken (Norway) were closer to a market solution.

When a firm established in the market has control of the supply chain, it becomes difficult for new firms to enter the region. If a new slaughterhouse decides to establish itself in the market, it will be necessary for it to build its own supply chain, from the fertile egg to the market. In Chapter 2 we saw that LAR was able to manage the vertical integration successfully ending up with the lowest unit costs in the sample. One reason is because Brazil is one of the leading world producers of corn and soybeans, the main components in chicken feed. LAR is located in Paraná State, the second largest producer of corn and soybeans in Brazil, and acquires these inputs at lower costs than those observed in the world market. This confers a comparative advantage of costs relative to other companies that are part of the research.

Hecksher and Ohlin (1991) trade theory argues that countries have competitiveness and export the intensive goods in the relatively abundant and cheap resource. Since the labor cost is relatively more expensive in the European countries compared to Kuwait, Sri Lanka and Brazil, it is natural that the Danish and Norwegian companies seek to make their production lines more technology-intensive. In Chapter 2 we see that Danpo is the most technology-intensive, while Crysbro and KUPCO have the lowest labor cost share in production.

The adoption of technology contributes to increased productivity, which is paramount to reducing production costs. However, the literature reveals that technology adoption requires more skilled workers (skills) and knowledge (Goldin and Katz, 1998; Autor, *et al.*, 2003; and Westeren, 2012).

It is not enough simply to adopt technology. In order to increase productivity, it is necessary to have people in the firms capable of handling and disseminating these innovations at the factory floor level. In this case, Danpo and Ytterøy have an advantage since its ratio of skilled to unskilled workers is higher, both in the administrative sector and in the production line. On the other hand, the challenges for Crysbro (Sri Lanka) and KUPCO (Kuwait) are much higher when compared to those for LAR (Brazil).

All aspects mentioned affect the firm's competitiveness in the international market. Most important here is whether the firm only operates in the domestic market and markets the surplus or by-products in the international market, or if the international market is more important than the domestic market.

Al-Nasser (2006) reported that consumption of chicken meat in Kuwait in 2006 was equal to 60.8 kg per capita while their domestic production of chicken in 2014 was equal to 14.85 kg per capita (FAOSTAT, online). Based on this information, Kuwait needs to import chicken meat to surpass domestic demand. KUPCO's production is totally geared to the local market and there are negligible exports.

All imports of chicken meat into Kuwait must have health certificates and halal certificates issued by an Islamic Centre in the country of origin. LAR in Brazil uses the halal process in 100% of their slaughter. This guarantees an advantage in relation to the countries that do not have the productive process certified by this type of slaughter.

In Sri Lanka, for religious reasons, chicken meat has preference over pork and beef. According to Alahakoon, *et al.* (2016), consumption of chicken meat per capita was 7.09kg in 2013, while consumption of beef and pork was equal to 1.8kg and 0.32kg per capita, respectively. In this chapter, we show that Sri Lanka is not competitive in the international chicken meat market. In this regard, the Sri Lanka government strongly regulates the import of chicken meat to protect local producers and foster the domestic industry.

In addition to the import control, the Sri Lankan government has adopted a controlled pricing system so that local companies take the price set by the government as given. In this case, to compete in the domestic market and to make a profit, Crysbro had to minimize production costs. The shortage of resources for investments in technology and cheap labor in the local market have made Crysbro an intensive company in low-wage labor. The strategy for survival in the domestic market has been the innovation of products, finding and acting in new niches in the domestic market. The international market is considered as secondary; the company exports only excess production not marketed in the domestic market.

As emphasized in this book, LAR is the largest company in this case study. LAR's production line is intensive in less-skilled laborers, whose salary is higher than those observed in Kuwait and Sri Lanka, but lower when compared to those observed in Nordic companies. LAR's production represents only 1.7% of the Brazilian total production, which is extremely competitive. Approximately 60% of production is focused on the domestic market, while exports represent 40% of total production.

Throughout this book it has been shown that the comparative advantages of LAR are associated with the purchase of inputs, identifying target markets and the management of the production chain and costs. It is interesting to note that what prevails in LAR in terms of innovation are the process innovations led mainly by the support of suppliers, customers and participation in international fairs in the sector. These results are in line with those observed by Sereia and da Camara (2015).

The use of labor in LAR is intense, and a significant part of the workers on the factory floor receive wages linked to the national minimum wage. The company is located in a region close to the Brazilian border with Paraguay, and the labor market suffers from the direct influence of wages across the border. This can be an obstacle both to the maintenance and to the future expansion of the company, should the economy in the border region demand workers in a greater proportion, attracted by wages.

In order to comply with the Brazilian government's legislation regarding sanitary export, safety and process standards, LAR maintains an average of 240 employees in its production line. At the same time, labor legislation adds 198 more people to the total number of workers. This means that approximately 10% of the workforce used by the company is linked to these two lines contributing to reduced productivity relative to other competitors in the international market.

LAR also serves markets niches of halal products and is certified by Mc Donald's. All its production is inspected by employees contracted by the clients to guarantee the accuracy of the processes.

Labor productivity is also related to the type of product produced. Comparing the Brazilian company with the other companies of this case study, in the products destined for the international market, 100% of the chicken breasts are deboned; 32% of the chicken legs are boned and there is 100% cut on the chicken wings. If on one hand the customization of production depresses labor productivity, on the other hand it provides the company an opportunity to enjoy a niche market in international trade, with added value to exported products.

Danpo (Denmark) has a combined focus with about 50% of the production for the domestic market and 50% for export. Danpo's export goes to European Union countries and mainly Germany. This means that Danpo's export is protected by EU rules and that the export ends up relatively close to the firm's production base. Looking at Chapter 2 we see that Danpo is reasonably competitive, but not with unit costs as low as LAR either through the vertical chain or in slaughter operations. So, within an international context Danpo is competitive inside the EU. This also corresponds with the impression that Danpo takes out a substantial part of its profit from the domestic market. Danpo looks well-prepared for international trends when it comes to traceability of products and an IT system functioning through the vertical chain geared to respond to rapid marked changes.

Ytterøy is a small niche oriented producer that rationalize production and market management processes in order to remain competitive in the domestic market. Ytterøy chicken uses the international market only to a very limited degree to export low value-added by-products that do not meet demand in the domestic market, such as feet, carcass and viscera.

### *6.6.1 Final considerations*

The objective of this chapter was to analyze the global competitiveness of the chicken meat market. Throughout the study it was observed that the world market is subdivided into two segments: the market for fresh or chilled chicken meat and the market for frozen chicken meat. The market for fresh or chilled chicken meat is dominated by European Union countries, although not all major actors have a comparative advantage revealed. On the other hand, the frozen poultry market has a diversified behavior, in which Brazil has the position of leadership.

The analysis for countries of interest in this research (Brazil, Denmark, Kuwait, Norway and Sri Lanka) showed that none of these actors has a comparative advantage in the export market of fresh or chilled meat. Denmark and Brazil were competitive in the subgroup of frozen poultry meat not cut in pieces, while only Brazil proved to be competitive in the market of frozen poultry meat cut in pieces.

The case study at the firm level revealed the importance of technology to increase labor productivity and to be able to manage a low cost the value chain independent of hierarchical or market-based structure. In general, it was observed that LAR is the only firm among those analyzed that can compete in an international market free of tariff or non-tariff barriers to trade. The major challenge is the adoption of more technology-intensive processes and, consequently, the investment in the training of its employees.

Finally, it is important that firms entering the international market remain attentive to exchange rate fluctuations. Unexpected currency depreciation can reduce the profit obtained from exports, making it an additional challenge for firms, particularly firms in transitional and developing economies.

## References

Alahakoon, A. U., Jo, C., & Jayasena, D. D. (2016). An overview of meat industry in Sri Lanka: A comprehensive review. *Korean Journal for Food Science of Animal Resources*, *36*(2), 137–144. doi:10.5851/kosfa.2016.36.2.137.

Al-Nasser, A. (2006). Poultry industry in Kuwait. *World's Poultry Science Journal*, *62*(4), 702–708. doi:10.1017/S004393390600122X.

Association of Poultry Processors and Poultry Trade in the EU Countries (AVEC). (2015). Annual Report. *AVEC.* Retrieved from www.avec-poultry.eu/system/files/archive/new-structure/avec/Annual_Report/2015/Annual%20Report%202015.pdf.

Autor, D. H., Levy, F., & Murnane, R. J. (2003). The skill content of recent technological change: An empirical exploration. *The Quarterly Journal of Economics*, *118*(4), 1279–1333.

Balassa, B. (1965). Trade liberalisation and 'revealed' comparative advantage. *The Manchester School*, *33*, 99–123. doi:10.1111/j.1467–9957.1965.tb00050.x.

Baldwin, J., & Yan, B. (2012). Export market dynamics and plant-level productivity: Impact of tariff reductions and exchange-rate cycles. *The Scandinavian Journal of Economics*, *114*(3), 831–855. doi:10.1111/j.1467–9442.2012.01716.x.

Belova, A., Smutka, L., Rosochatecka, E., & Bazina, A. (2012). Competitiveness of domestic production of poultry meat on the EU market and on the world market. *Agris On-line Papers in Economics and Informatics*, *4*(4), 11–25. Retrieved from http://purl.umn.edu/146273.

Benedictis, L. de, & Tamberi, M. (2004). Overall specialization empirics: Techniques and applications. *Open Economies Review*, *15*(4), 323–346. Retrieved from https://link.springer.com/article/10.1023/B:OPEN.0000048522.97418.99.

Bernard, A. B., Eaton, J., Jensen, J. B., & Kortum, S. (2003). Plants and productivity in international trade. *The American Economic Review*, *93*(4), 1268–1290.

Bernard, A. B., & Jensen, J. B. (1999). *Exporting and productivity*. National Bureau of Economic Research, no. w7135. Retrieved from www.nber.org/papers/w7135.

Bernard, A. B., Jensen, J. B., & Lawrence, R. Z. (1995). *Exporters, jobs, and wages in US manufacturing: 1976–1987*. Brookings Papers Microeconomics, pp. 67–119. Retrieved from www.brookings.edu/wp-content/uploads/1995/01/1995_bpeamicro_bernard.pdf.Bernard, A. B., Jensen, J. B., Redding, S. J., & Schott, P. K. (2007). Firms in international trade. *The Journal of Economic Perspectives, 21*(3), 105–130.

Costantini, J., & Melitz, M. (2008). The dynamics of firm-level adjustment to trade liberalization. In E. Helpman, D. Marin, & T. Verdier (Eds.), *The organization of firms in a global economy* (pp. 107–141). Cambridge, MA: Harvard University Press.

Davis, C. G. (2015). Factors influencing global poultry trade. *International Food and Agribusiness Management Review, 18*(A), 1–12. Retrieved from www.ifama.org/resources/Documents/v18ia/Davis.pdf.

De Loecker, J. (2007). Do exports generate higher productivity? Evidence from Slovenia. *Journal of International Economics, 73*(1), 69–98.

De Loecker, J. (2013). Detecting learning by exporting. *American Economic Journal: Microeconomics, 5*, 1–21. doi:10.1257/mic.5.3.1.

De Loecker, J., & Warzynski, F. (2012). Markups and firm-level export status. *The American Economic Review, 102*(6), 2437–2471. doi:10.1257/aer.102.6.2437.

EUROSTAT. (2017). *Meat production statistics*. Eurostat Statistics Explained. Retrieved from http://ec.europa.eu/eurostat/statistics-explained/index.php/Meat_production_statistics.

Frankel, J. A., & Romer, D. (1999). Does trade cause growth? *The American Economic Review, 89*(3), 379–399.

Frankel, J. A., Romer, D., & Cyrus, T. (1996). *Trade and growth in East Asian countries: Cause and effect?* National Bureau of Economic Research, no. w5732. Retrieved from www.nber.org/papers/w5732.

Goldin, C., & Katz, L. F. (1998). The origins of technology-skill complementarity. *The Quarterly Journal of Economics, 113*(3), 693–732.

Grossman, G. M., & Helpman, E. (1991a). Trade, knowledge spillovers, and growth. *European Economic Review, 35*(2–3), 517–526.

Grossman, G. M., & Helpman, E. (1991b). Quality ladders in the theory of growth. *The Review of Economic Studies, 58*(1), 43–61.

Grossman, G. M., & Helpman, E. (1995). Technology and trade. In G. M. Grossman & K. Rogoff (Eds.), *Handbook of international economics, 3* (pp. 1279–1337). Amsterdam: North-Holland.

Heckscher, E. F., & Ohlin, B. G. (1991). *Heckscher-Ohlin trade theory*. Cambridge, MA: The MIT Press.

Helpman, E., & Krugman, P. R. (1985). *Market structure and foreign trade: Increasing returns, imperfect competition, and the international economy*. Cambridge, MA: The MIT Press.

Juchniewicz, M., & Łukiewska, K. (2015). Competitive position of the food industry of the European Union on the global market. *Acta Scientiarum Polonorum. Oeconomia, 14*(3), 63–72. Retrieved from https://journals.indexcopernicus.com/api/file/viewByFileId/108305.pdf.

Keller, W. (2004). International technology diffusion. *Journal of Economic Literature, 42*(3), 752–782.

Keller, W. (2010). International trade, foreign direct investment, and technology spillovers. In B. H. Hall & N. Rosenberg (Eds.), *Handbook of the economics of innovation* (pp. 793–829). Amsterdam: Elsevier.

Krugman, P. R. (1979). Increasing returns, monopolistic competition, and international trade. *Journal of International Economics, 9*(4), 469–479.

Krugman, P. R. (1980). Scale economies, product differentiation, and the pattern of trade. *The American Economic Review, 70*(5), 950–959.

Krugman, P. R., & Hatsopoulos, G. N. (1987). The problem of US competitiveness in manufacturing. *New England Economic Review*, 18–29.

Krugman, P. R., Obstfeld, M., & Melitz, M. (2015). *International economics* (10th ed.). Boston, MA: Pearson Education.

Laursen, K. (2015). Revealed comparative advantage and the alternatives as measures of international specialization. *Eurasian Business Review, 5*(1), 99–115.

Magdelaine, P., Spiess, M. P., & Valceschini, E. (2008). Poultry meat consumption trends in Europe. *World's Poultry Science Journal, 64*(1), 53–64.

Melitz, M. J. (2003). The impact of trade on intra-industry reallocations and aggregate industry productivity. *Econometrica, 71*(6), 1695–1725.

Ricardo, D. (1817). *On the principles of political economy and taxation* (3rd ed.). Ontario: Batoche Books. Retrieved from http://socserv.mcmaster.ca/econ/ugcm/3ll3/ricardo/Principles.pdf.

Sales, M. F., & Westeren, K. I. (2015). Market and trade as drivers of innovation. *Journal of International Business and Economics, 15*(1), 49–58.

Sereia, V. J., & Camara, M. R. G da. (2015). Innovation in the agro-industrial poultry meat companies of Paraná. *REBRAE, 8*(3), 304–322.

United Nations Food and Agriculture Organization (FAO). COMTRADE. (2017). Retrieved from https://comtrade.un.org/.

United Nations Food and Agriculture Organization (FAO). FAOSTAT. (2017). Retrieved from www.fao.org/faostat/en/#home.

United Nations – Standard International Trade Classification (SITC Rev. 3). (2002). Retrieved from https://unstats.un.org/unsd/statcom/doc02/isic.pdf.

Verdoorn, P. J. (1960). The intra-bloc trade of Benelux. In E. A. G. Robinson (Ed.), *Economic consequences of the size of nations* (pp. 291–329). New York, NY: International Economic Association.

Vernon, R. (1966). International investment and international trade in the product cycle. *The Quarterly Journal of Economics, 80*(2), 190–207.

Vernon, R. (1979). The product cycle hypothesis in a new international environment. *Oxford Bulletin of Economics and Statistics, 41*(4), 255–267.

Wagner, J. (2007). Exports and productivity: A survey of the evidence from firm-level data. *The World Economy, 30*(1), 60–82.

Westeren, K. I. (2012). *Foundations of the knowledge economy: Innovation, learning, and clusters.* Cheltenham: Edward Elgar.

Williams, C. (2007). Research methods. *Journal of Business & Economics Research, 5*(3). Retrieved from www.cluteinstitute.com/ojs/index.php/JBER/article/view/2532/2578.

Windhorst, H. W. (2016). *The Netherlands – The leading country in European egg and poultry meat exports.* Retrieved from Zootecnica International Information website: http://zootecnicainternational.com/focus-on/netherlands-leading-country-european-egg-poultry-meat-exports/.

# 7 Summary, conclusions, and policy implications

The title of this book is about competitiveness and knowledge. The intention as stated in Chapter 1 is to find some answers to questions on relationships where knowledge is the central aspect for firms to develop competitiveness. In this chapter, we present a summary of the most central aspects addressed throughout the book followed by some conclusive statements that reflect policy implications.

## 7.1 Cost structure and competitive situation

It is a challenging ambition to combine theory and firm practice in the field of competitiveness and knowledge, especially when the firms in the study differ substantially in size, internal organization and market conditions. For the white meat production firms, the cost share of live chicken to total cost varies from 42% to 57%. This is fundamental to the cost structure of the firms. Throughout the book we see how knowledge creation, transfer and management play a part in this.

Labor cost affects the cost structure through the total vertical chain. We expected to find differences in labor cost shares between firms but some of the differences were large. Wage level played a role here. We did not get data for wage per hour for the firms in Brazil, Kuwait and Sri Lanka but estimates from 'unofficial' sources indicate the average wage rate for production workers in US dollars to be five times higher in Norway/Denmark compared to Brazil. The wage rates were lower in Kuwait and Sri Lanka compared to Brazil. When we looked at the more technical term 'Firm Production in Metric Tons/employee' we found that LAR utilized about 2.5 times more manpower hours per produced ton of white meat than Danpo.

LAR was the most cost-efficient producer when looking at total production cost for chicken delivered at the factory door (USD 1.44/KG). Danpo and Crysbro were about 60% higher. LAR had relatively higher capital cost share compared to labor and this was one reason why it was profitable to use a high share of labor-hours in production. Another factor to explain the high number of employees at LAR was institutional rules. In Chapters 4 and 5 we analyzed the structure and content of knowledge transfers necessary to operate high-tech capital equipment. The differences suggested that LAR also must do a substantial knowledge upgrade to enter the level of Danpo's technology.

The total unit cost situation for Crysbro and KUPCO was about what we expected with lower costs through the vertical chain in Sri Lanka compared to Kuwait. Capital cost share was higher in Sri Lanka than in Kuwait. The situation in Kuwait and Sri Lanka showed that, from a labor cost perspective, their production had a very low labor cost share, far below the international average.

The wage level differences reflected the difference in cost structure between Brazil and Norway/Denmark. Ytterøy was labor cost intensive because of the position as a niche producer. Danpo labor cost shares were higher than expected, mainly because of what we can call a 'divisor effect'. When the total unit cost is low (and wage rates are high) then the necessary labor will get a relatively high cost share even if the production is technically capital intensive.

One key figure for competitiveness was the unit price of total production compared to the cost of live chicken and these numbers were used to calculate the Lerner Index. We found (in Chapter 6) that LAR was the only firm that was competitive on the international market without protective measures. They had a highly optimized vertical chain with a low wage level combined with low prices on important components of the feed like soya and corn. They also had good control of both animal health and stability of deliverance. We knew that Brazil was a world leader in white meat production and exports and this was confirmed by the numbers in Chapters 2 and 6. Danpo was competitive inside the EU with EU market rules and in the Danish national market. Throughout the book we witnessed Danpo as successful in utilization of high end technology, knowledge management and innovativeness. It is interesting to see how low Danpo can get the cost of live chicken with little direct control over the supply chain.

We presented a modified Lerner Index in Table 2.3 which suggests the relative market power of the firms. Competitiveness in Chapter 2 was assessed by how the firms were able to take advantage of cost-effectiveness and market power to operate successfully in the marketplace. The modified Lerner Index is a relative measure to express the distance (in this analysis) between the unit cost of the live chicken and total unit cost. The results from two firms, Danpo and LAR, showed the highest values relative to the other three firms but the differences were relatively small.

### 7.1.1 Conclusions

When we started the project, our perception was that white meat production was relatively labor-intensive so labor cost would play an important role. This is still true but the picture is a little more complex. We assess labor and labor cost from several aspects:

1. How is labor cost reflected through the total vertical chain and to what degree is the white meat production plant able to influence this?
2. We have national labor policies and institutional rules that influence labor cost in different directions.

3 We have local labor markets with large differences in qualifications.
4 We find differences in labor cost relative to capital cost.
5 We find differences in the knowledge and innovative potential for introduction of high-tech capital intensive technologies.

We found that the two firms that had the best competitive situation in international markets also had the best scores on the various indicators. However, this does not imply that the most competitive (in technical terms) and most labor-intensive firm, LAR, can implement radical changes overnight. An optimization of all cost elements will probably lead to the introduction of more capital intensive and technologically advanced equipment for LAR, but only incrementally, and coordinated with parallel developments of knowledge and skills. Through the project period Danpo had experienced a fast development in introducing high-tech labor saving equipment because labor cost was based on high wages.

The other three firms were more dependent on national markets and optimized cost accordingly, but in very different ways. The Norwegian firm did niche marketing and for this they needed a labor force with high knowledge and innovative capabilities. For the two other firms, the share of direct labor cost in production was low and we did not see any rapid change. New capital equipment seemed more important for securing production and improving quality than for just reducing labor cost.

## 7.2 Vertical integration and management of inputs to production

The main discussion in Chapter 3 was about vertical integration. This has been an important subject in business economics, management and organizational analysis for decades. We used the term vertical integration in an extended way where acquiring inputs is regulated by contractual arrangements from hierarchy to markets. We discussed vertical integration as a chain of processing operations where the different links can be separated from each other (like for white meat production). The main question dealt with in Chapter 3 was whether a theoretical optimal or best practice solution was most useful for comparisons among the researched firms. Vertical integration was of fundamental importance for the competitiveness for firms. In Chapter 2 we showed that the cost of buying the live chickens was a useful comparison to the total cost for the finished product.

Structural developments for firms buying inputs relate to at least two essential trends in recent decades. These include the more general reduction in transport costs and the use of advanced IT systems. The result of this for firms is a large efficiency gain in stock management but also more vulnerability for unforeseen events. In many countries, both in the developed and developing world, we see optimization within the separate links of the value chain and introduction of advanced IT systems.

The modern theory of vertical integration was established in the later part of the 1980's based on contributions of Williamson (1979; 1985) and Porter (1985).

Elements from the more general theory of cost procurement management merged with Williamson's analysis 'from hierarchy to markets' and with Porter's value chain. From the theory, we have seen the use of different instruments to coordinate production. In the market-based solution, we are expected to use economic incentives. In the hierarchical solution, we have access to institutional and hierarchical authority. The value chain of chicken production is generic and from theory this should indicate that best practice promotes vertical integration or at least strong vertical control but we did not find this as a general trend in the firms we studied.

We find the Kuwaiti case vertically integrated in such a way that they govern the value chain from a common manager. We experienced a strong administrative command and control based on respect for decisions made at a higher level in the firm. This can be explained by traditional hierarchical organizational behavior that in this case was enforced by the societal culture based on traditional Muslim values.

The Sri Lankan case was quite close to being vertically integrated, as 60% of the chicken breeding was done as a part of firm operations and 40% contracted. The contracts were organized so that the integrator had collateral in the farmers' land, and they withheld some of the payment to the farmers as security. Together, this was an expression of an extensive control regime with the farmers. The whole setup of the contracts indicated a system very close to hierarchy. The Sri Lankan regime was based on the likelihood of poor contractual farmers being tempted to sell feed or chickens on the free market to get quick money. Also in the Sri Lankan case, there was one common manager controlling all stages of the production.

In the Brazilian case, the integrator provided chickens, feed and medical input to the breeders and they had a system for measuring productivity based on feed conversion, weight, mortality, and days of breeding. They ranked breeders where the best breeders received higher payments than those who performed more poorly. They did not face any form of competition as described in US poultry production. Like the Sri Lankan case, the integrator had a structure where they closely followed up on the broiler breeders both with inspections and subsequent guidance on production. While not harsh, the regime (from the perspective of the US literature) can be described as necessary for contract follow-up on integrator assets (feed and chickens). The profit of the breeders was very much up to the breeders themselves and the effort they put into production. If they wanted better payment, they needed to put in some extra effort to improve the feed conversion rate and reduce mortality.

In the Nordic cases we did not find much that implied hierarchical vertical integration. Instead we found close to market-based solutions. In the Norwegian case we found ongoing contracts between integrators and the broiler breeding farmers. In the Danish case they operated with three- to five-year contracts. What we experienced in both Denmark and Norway was some sort of trust; much like a traditional cooperative within agricultural production. Our explanation for the stability of the organization of production throughout the value chain was the strong cooperative mindset among agribusiness firms in these countries.

In the Nordic cases, the farmers themselves provided chickens, feed and medical assistance, unlike the other cases. The production contracts were flat-fee contracts, where the total payment was based on how many kilos of chicken were delivered. The incentives could not be described as direct incentives as questions of efficiency were left with the breeders. The integrators were assured of the agreed size of broiler chickens, but how the weight measures were reached was not included in any incentive scheme.

### *7.2.1 Conclusions*

- We found significant variation in how vertical integration was accomplished among the different firms.
- We found the firm in Kuwait totally integrated and the one in Sri Lanka very close to being totally integrated.
- Every level of production was integrated in the Brazilian firm except broiler production.
- The two Nordic companies had a structure close to the market solution.
- We studied the firms with repeated visits for 5 years and we did not see a change in the direction towards the Nordic model in Brazil, Kuwait or Sri Lanka.
- Such a change would be impractical in Brazil because poultry production is a huge industry with many integrators. In Kuwait and Sri Lanka, change would be difficult because of elements in the institutional structure and societal culture.

The focus in the Nordic cases was on improving productivity at the slaughtering plant and 'streamlining' deliverance of chickens for optimal adaptation to the market projections, but further integration to do this was not on the agenda.

## 7.3 Knowledge and competitiveness

There have been many discussions and arguments on the question about a link between knowledge and competitiveness. This discussion received new attention about year 2000 with the MERITUM (2002) project which was inspired by the work of Edvinsson and Malone (1997) and others. The project addressed concepts of intangible assets and knowledge capital for firms and focused on three knowledge-based factors to determine the competitiveness of firms.

**Identification:** Here we need to look at knowledge in relation to the processes that are fundamental and decisive for value creation of the firm – often called core competencies.

**Measurement:** Here we need to find a useful set of indicators to measure the knowledge capital.

**Management:** Here we must develop a managerial system for the firm where we can consider the effects of knowledge capital to achieve corporate goals. In the normal case, these goals center on profit maximization.

Several organizations like The World Bank (2012) and the World Economic Forum (2015) have constructed indexes for individual countries to reflect their position in the knowledge economy with respect to competitiveness and innovation. These indexes are used to advise government policy formation and to analyze the situation for firms in markets. The KEI of the World Bank is divided into four sub-indexes: (1) Economic Incentive and Institutional Regime, (2) Innovation and Technological Adoption, (3) Education and Training and Information and (4) Information and Communication Technologies. These four sub-indexes cover the main factors we use in analyzing the knowledge economy. The interesting question addressed in this book relates to how relevant these indexes are when we look at the firm level. Here we will give a few highlights.

Like Stiglitz (1999), we emphasized how the functioning of institutions was vital for firms intent on taking advantage of the knowledge economy. The KEI index here suggests that Brazil is far down on the list; an indicator showing that institutions are not well-functioning. This was also the impression we got from our visits to LAR. The firm hired large numbers of employees to comply with governmental regulations; larger compared to what seemed necessary from a productivity point of view. We heard very few complaints from the Scandinavian firms about functioning of the public institutions. The Scandinavian countries also ranked at the top of the list for this sub-index.

A central theme addressed in this book reflects how knowledge transfers take place in firms. In this project we analyzed a large number of variables to measure knowledge and the competitive situation of the firms. This information was collected by interviewing group leaders (supervisors) three to four times between 2012 and 2016. Here we will comment on one outcome variable representing production and assess how it is related to communication and cultural variables.

The variable 'Speed of production ok' was measured on a five-level Lickert scale where group leaders were asked to evaluate the following question: '*To your knowledge was the speed of production satisfactory today?*'. The answers ranged from '1: A big problem' to '5: Going very well'. Results did not differ greatly. The highest values we found were for Danpo (4.36), then Ytterøy (4.03), LAR (3.97) and Crysbro (3.93). KUPCO was somewhat lower (3.52).

The structure and functioning of communication was vital for firms to take advantage knowledge to improve competitiveness. The number of communicative initiatives differed greatly between firms as shown in Table 7.1. The numbers were based on answers from the group leaders about how many times during an 'average' day they communicated to their manager or to their own

*Table 7.1* Number of communicative initiatives

| | *Communication number up to manager* | *Number speak to own group* | *Group member initiatives to you* |
|---|---|---|---|
| Danpo, N = 39 | 10.90 | 17.82 | 21.77 |
| LAR, N = 266 | 7.14 | 11.15 | 8.37 |
| Ytterøy, N = 30 | 9.67 | 10.93 | 10.63 |
| Crysbro, N = 40 | 5.60 | 5.48 | 5.21 |
| KUPCO, N = 33 | 3.58 | 3.21 | 2.70 |

Source: authors' data collection.

(N: number of observations)

*Table 7.2* Selected cultural construct

| | *Power unequal* |
|---|---|
| Danpo, N = 39 | 1.64 |
| LAR, N = 266 | 2.58 |
| Ytterøy, N = 30 | 1.67 |
| Crysbro, N = 40 | 3.19 |
| KUPCO, N = 33 | 4.24 |

Source: authors' data collection.

(N: number of observations)

group and how many initiatives members of the group took to communicate with them. We found many communicative initiatives in the Scandinavian firms, a medium level in the Brazilian firm, and a low level in both the Sri Lankan and Kuwaiti firm. One interesting difference was between the two most competitive firms in the study, Danpo and LAR. Danpo had a higher speed on the production line, front end technology and labor extensive production. But the communication pattern showed much more frequent contacts in Danpo compared to LAR.

Culture also played an important role as a 'filter' to determine the occurrence and structure of communication. We analyzed several cultural variables and the most interesting was related to what is often called power distance. This is based on a question that assessed if the group leader expected and agreed that power should be unequally shared (see Table 7.2). In combining information from Tables 7.1 and 7.2, we see that the situation for the day-to-day running of the firms is quite equal but the potential to take advantage of aspects from the knowledge economy to improve competitiveness varies greatly.

### 7.3.1 Conclusions

We found links between knowledge and competitiveness and institutions, culture and path dependency was of vital importance to understand how these links relate.

- Analyzing and identifying the links between knowledge and competitiveness on the firm level, we found the keywords Identification, Measurement and Management still relevant.
- The construction of knowledge indexes for countries can be useful at the firm level to provide useful directions for improvement. Our analysis suggests that to use these indexes for policy purposes requires caution.
- To manage knowledge transfers has been and will be essential for successful use of knowledge to improve competitiveness.
- We found that the communication structure varies greatly between countries and that cultural impacts are one explanation why communication contributes more to the success of firms some places compared to others.

## 7.4 Innovation, knowledge and competitiveness

Discussion and analysis of entrepreneurship and innovation concepts have been some of the most focused and fundamental themes in scientific research and economic policy in the last decades. It is interesting to observe the extensive attention these concepts have received from the public and media. Our ambition, from a scientific standpoint, is to dig deeper into these discussions about innovations with particular focus on links between innovation, knowledge and competitiveness

Among the various ways to do this, we have chosen three specific approaches. The first is to look at innovations from the more generic point of view. Here we assess how the concept emerged and how it can be operationalized. Then we used a case study of firms to see how we can link theory to practice.

The next approach addresses innovative initiatives. Here we explain how creativity leads to innovation. We collected data from white meat producers about innovative initiatives. The data reflects how employees contribute with innovative suggestions for improvement. This was then assessed with respect to possible links between knowledge generation and utilization and how this can lead to innovative initiatives.

The third approach was related to innovation management. Innovations are essential for firms but they must have a system for management of the innovation process to improve competitiveness.

The innovation concept has always been problematic because it has been linked to words like 'change' and 'something new'. Schumpeter started at the macro level and wanted to explain how the capitalist economy developed. His fundamental belief was based on disequilibrium of economic development.

To explain this, he introduced the entrepreneur that seeks new combinations via creative destruction. This remains fundamental to how we look at innovation using categories such as products, processes, markets and organizations.

Our case study from the firm Danpo assessed how they changed from quality control by inspection from employees using their eyes looking at the chicken to digital scanning taking two pictures of every bird. This fits into Schumpeter's perception of what an innovation is and according to the Oslo Manual (OECD, 2005) is called a process innovation. This new way of doing product quality control by using IT technology adds a new aspect to the production process. The production was accomplished in a technically new way which required changes in routines, knowledge level and transfer. It also allowed an increase in the speed of production. The new technology was acquired from other types of meat production but two novel features include the speed of taking pictures and the size of the birds compared to other animals. The innovation, from a technical point of view, lies in the software which operates the system.

During the 1990's we saw an emerging number of studies trying to explain what they called innovative behavior in organizations. Innovative behavior is often looked at as an employee's intentional introduction or application of new ideas, products, processes, and procedures at work. This raises questions of how we analyze innovative behavior and how we explain why some employees are more innovative than others.

When we analyze innovative behavior, it is important to be aware of which level in the organization we put focus. Normally, these include the individual, work group or team, and organizational levels. Of course, there is interaction among levels, but our data collection and analytical results suggests that production takes place in teams consisting of multiple individuals. Results are important for all levels including the organizational. Most studies consider that firms as organizations are divided into groups (or departments). In each group there is typically one person that has managerial responsibility. Individual attributes of both the leader and the participants in the group are of fundamental importance.

In the empirical part we analyzed the innovative behavior process. We looked at suggested changes in routines as the indicator for innovative routines. We found large differences between the firms. Firms where the communication process was well-functioning with frequent communicative contacts had higher numbers of innovative initiatives. We also found support for the view that higher skills lead to higher levels of overall innovative behavior. Higher skills also contribute to more suggestions for formalized changes to routines. We also looked at cultural variables and found that trust was important in the innovation process.

Without successful innovation, management firms were not able to take advantage of innovations to enhance competitiveness. There are numerous models and suggestions about how to manage innovations. In the empirical part, we looked at the new quality control technology employed at Danpo and how LAR utilized the vertical chain in an innovative way as an organizational innovation. We used several keywords to analyze innovation management.

Knowledge management was essential for the success of innovating activities at both Danpo and LAR. At Danpo, the new technology was essential not only in the production line making quality control more efficient but in all important aspects of production. Central to the organizational success of production, new technology must match knowledge flows. By match we mean that knowledge has the appropriate level and focus.

LAR also took knowledge management seriously because departments were interconnected and had frequent meetings to coordinate knowledge dissemination. We found two areas of special importance. The first was a linkage between the sales department and production planning and control. The second was the general management of knowledge through the vertical chain.

The main innovating activity at LAR was supply chain management. The innovation strategy must be a central part of firm strategy. The firm has control of different stages of production. For LAR, a little less than 50% of the total cost was made up of live chickens. A favorable cost situation for production was based on high efficiency in feed production (the main ingredient in the feed is soya and corn). This was accomplished by the way the firm managed vertical deliveries. For Danpo, the situation and challenges were different. Danpo had to successfully integrate technology into their firm strategy. The focus at Danpo was how much the innovation contributed to profits and to a strengthened competitive situation. The integration to a large degree was about optimization of production and quality control.

### 7.4.1 *Conclusions*

- The innovation concept is increasing in importance in scientific research as an analytic tool and in policy formulations. It is still a problematic concept because of difficulties to give an operational definition and conceptual clarity. An understanding of Schumpeter's discussion and use is still highly relevant.
- Firms must face the knowledge economy and we found that innovations change the knowledge structure through the production process for firms. It is not enough for a firm to introduce new knowledge for innovative change of one function of the firm. New knowledge demands must be followed and managed throughout the total production process.
- Innovations must start somewhere. We found increased innovative initiatives are linked to a successful and frequent communication process. Improved skill development also positively stimulates innovative initiatives.
- Innovation management must be an integrated part of overall firm strategy. We found that when firms did this efficiently it contributed to improved competitiveness.

## 7.5 Competitiveness in the global chicken market

In our discussion of competitiveness in the global chicken market (Chapter 6), we first assessed more general developments and then applied them to the countries of special interest in this book (Denmark, Brazil, Norway, Sri Lanka and

Kuwait). We analyzed the situation for competitiveness of countries according to traditional theories of international trade using different measures.

When a firm decides to internationalize it faces unrecoverable costs in activities such as transportation, marketing, distribution and adaptation of the product to the requirements of the new market. The firms must also allocate resources to enhance qualifications of personnel for external links like external sales and others, this we see for the two firms in our study (LAR and Danpo) that are active in the international market.

The total worldwide 2014 production of chicken meat was close to double what it was in 2000. The annual growth rate for production per capita was 3.5% for the same period. The main reason for this is that chicken meat is looked at as a healthy and inexpensive source of protein compared to other types of meat. Cultural and religious barriers to the consumption of pork and beef also contribute to the expansion of poultry consumption.

Over the period 2000 to 2014, the poultry market has been very dynamic. In 2000, Brazil was the fourth largest exporter of poultry in the world with exports of US$879 million (10.6% of the total). The evolution of Brazilian poultry exports showed exceptional growth reaching US$7.1 billion in 2014, an increase of 702% in current prices. This performance gave Brazil the position of the world's largest poultry exporter in 2014, outperforming the United States and the Netherlands. Overall, the largest poultry exporter countries are Brazil, the United States, the European Union, China, Hong Kong, Turkey and Argentina.

Brazil, the United States, Poland, Turkey and Argentina are highly specialized countries in the production of chicken meat. Several EU countries are among the world's leading exporters, but are not among the largest per capita producers in this market, except for the Netherlands and Poland. France, Belgium, Hong Kong, China and Denmark lost competitiveness and market share between 2000 and 2014.

The five largest importers in the world during the period 2000–2014 were Germany, United Kingdom, Saudi Arabia, Hong Kong and Japan. Imports overall became less concentrated during the period. Imports to the five countries of interest (Brazil, Denmark, Kuwait, Norway and Sri Lanka) accounted for about 2% of total imports in 2014.

The poultry market can be subdivided into categories. The markets for frozen poultry not cut in pieces was of special interest to our study. Here Brazil was the absolute leader with a total export of US$2.44 billion in 2014. (52.17% of market share). In 2014 Brazil exported to 104 countries. Of the total value of Brazilian exports in this sector, US$1.76 billion (or 72.33% of the total) were exported to countries in the Arab world. Other important importers of frozen whole birds from Brazil include the USA, China and Russia. Brazil is also the leader in the international market for frozen poultry cut in pieces. The exports here were larger (4.6 billion US dollars) than in the other frozen category but the market dominance of Brazil was less. Results for other countries of interest in this research (Denmark, Kuwait, Norway and Sri Lanka) suggested that none of these actors had a comparative advantage in the export market of fresh or chilled meat. Denmark was competitive in the subgroup of frozen poultry meat not cut in pieces.

In Sri Lanka, chicken meat is preferred over pork and beef for cultural and religious reasons. Our analysis showed that Sri Lanka was not competitive in the international chicken meat market. The Sri Lankan government regulates the import of chicken meat to protect local producers and foster the domestic industry. In addition to the import control, the Sri Lankan government has adopted a controlled pricing system so that local companies take the price set by the government as given. In this case, to compete in the domestic market and to make a profit, Crysbro had to minimize production costs. Kuwait needed to import chicken to meet domestic demand and KUPCO's production was geared to the local market with negligible exports.

The domestic market for chicken is extremely competitive in Brazil. LAR's production represented only 1.7% of the total production in Brazil. For LAR, approximately 60% of production was focused on the domestic market, while exports represented 40% of total production. LAR's production line was intensive in less-skilled labors, whose salary was higher than those observed in Kuwait and Sri Lanka, but lower when compared to those observed in Nordic companies. Throughout this book we have shown that the comparative advantages of LAR in international markets were associated with the purchase of inputs, identifying target markets and the management of the production chain and costs.

Danpo (Denmark) had a combined sale of about 50% of production for the domestic market and 50% for export. Danpo's export goes to European Union countries (mainly Germany). This means that Danpo's export was protected by EU rules and that the export ended up relatively close to the firm's production base. From Chapter 2 we saw that Danpo was competitive on the domestic market. In the international context, Danpo was competitive inside the EU. This also corresponds with the impression that Danpo made a substantial part of its profit from the domestic market. Danpo appears to be well-prepared for international trends when it comes to traceability of products and an IT system functioning throughout the vertical chain which allows it to respond to rapid market changes.

Ytterøy is a small niche oriented producer that rationalized production and market management processes to remain competitive in the domestic market. Ytterøy used the international market only to a very limited degree to export low value-added by-products that did not meet demand in the domestic market (such as feet, carcass and viscera).

Finally, it is important to note that firms entering the international market remain attentive to exchange rate fluctuations. Unexpected currency depreciation can corrode the profit obtained from exports, making it an additional challenge for firms. This is particularly true for firms in developing economies.

## 7.6 Final reflections

In Chapter 1, we ask how do local firms compete using knowledge in domestic and international markets in an increasingly globalized world. The prevailing cost structure will always be the fundament for a start of this discussion and was the source of some surprises. We have looked at firms in the food processing industries, often labelled as traditional firms, with labor-intensive production. We saw that the notion of labor-intensive had to be dealt with from at least two angles: how many employees (person-hours) are needed to produce one ton of meat, and what are the labor cost as a percentage of total cost. The key factor here is the wage rate. The Scandinavian firms have a high wage rate and it is important for them to implement high-tech capital equipment to save wage cost. The high wage also means that the education level and competence in general is high, allowing communication and innovative activities to contribute more efficiently to competitiveness.

LAR is internationally competitive because of low wages throughout the vertical chain combined with a natural environment where feed can be produced with low costs. LAR encouraged knowledge to flow efficiently through the vertical chain and inside the firm, but because the knowledge level was lower and institutions partly counterproductive, LAR did not have the same potential to take advantage of the knowledge economy as the Scandinavians. For the firms in Sri Lanka and Kuwait, the wage cost as part of total cost was so low that the firms cannot be characterized as labor cost intensive. Here also, the link between wage level and competence was an obstacle for the firms to enter the knowledge economy, and this was reinforced, especially in the Kuwait case, by cultural aspects.

When we go more closely into the analysis of the vertical chain we assumed from the start that since the value chain of chicken production is generic this should from theory indicate that best practice promotes vertical integration or at least strong vertical control. But we did not find this as a general trend in the firms we studied. In the Nordic cases we did not find much that implied hierarchical vertical integration, instead we found close to market-based solutions. The other three firms had different variations of integrated solutions. Cost-effectiveness was the common point of departure for the firm and the success of LAR in the international market was dependent of this through the vertical chain. Danpo also took advantage of a cost-effective value chain but mainly based on market solutions. To fully understand this, we must look more detailed what characterized these markets and one important element here was some sort of trust; much like a traditional cooperative within agricultural production.

Innovations have been and will be a keyword for firms to enter the knowledge economy. We find that innovations change the knowledge structure through the whole production process for firms. But to do this successfully we are back to the keywords about competence, communication and the ICT structure of the firm.

LAR was the only competitive firm on the international market while Danpo was competitive inside the EU. The other firms operated inside different types of trade regulated systems in their home markets. LAR's competitiveness in the international market is linked to the customization of products geared to rapidly growing market niches. It was a combination of a very competitive home market and exports that was decisive for their strong market position.

## References

Edvinsson, L., & Malone, M. S. (1997). *Intellectual capital: Realizing your company's true value by finding its hidden brainpower.* London: HarperCollins.

MERITUM Project. (2002). *Guidelines for managing and reporting on intangibles.* Madrid: Fundacion Airtel Movil.

OECD. (2005). *Proposed guidelines for collecting and interpreting technological innovation data: Oslo manual* (3rd revised ed.). Paris: OECD.

Porter, M. E. (1985). *Competitive advantage: Creating and sustaining superior performance.* New York: Free Press.

Stiglitz, J. (1999). *Public policy for a knowledge economy.* Remarks at the Department for Trade and Industry and Center for Economic Policy Research London, U.K. January 27, 1999.

Williamson, O. E. (1979). Transaction-cost economics: The governance of contractual relations. *Journal of Law and Economics, 22*(2), 233–261.

Williamson, O. E. (1985). *The economic institutions of capitalism.* New York: The Free Press.

World Bank. (2012). *Knowledge Economy Index (KEI) 2012 Rankings.* Retrieved from http://siteresources.worldbank.org/INTUNIKAM/Resources/2012.pdf.

World Economic Forum (Mercer). (2015). *The human capital report 2015.* Geneva, Switzerland: World Economic Forum.

# Index